SiMPSONS™

COMICS

CHAOS

TITAN BOOKS

SIMPSONS COMICS CHAOS

Simpsons Comics #112, 113, 114, 115,
and Simpsons Summer Shindig #6

Published in the UK by Titan Books, a division of Titan Publishing Group Ltd.,
144 Southwark St., London SE1 0UP, under licence from Bongo Entertainment, Inc.

FIRST EDITION: MARCH 2016

ISBN 9781785652059

2 4 6 8 10 9 7 5 3 1

Publisher: Matt Groening
Creative Director: Nathan Kane
Managing Editor: Terry Delegeane
Director of Operations: Robert Zaugh
Art Director: Jason Ho
Art Director Special Projects: Serban Cristescu
Assistant Art Director: Mike Rote
Production Manager: Christopher Ungar
Assistant Editor: Karen Bates
Production: Art Villanueva
Administration: Ruth Waytz
Legal Guardian: Susan A. Grode

Printed by TC Transcontinental, Beauceville, QC, Canada. 11/23/2015

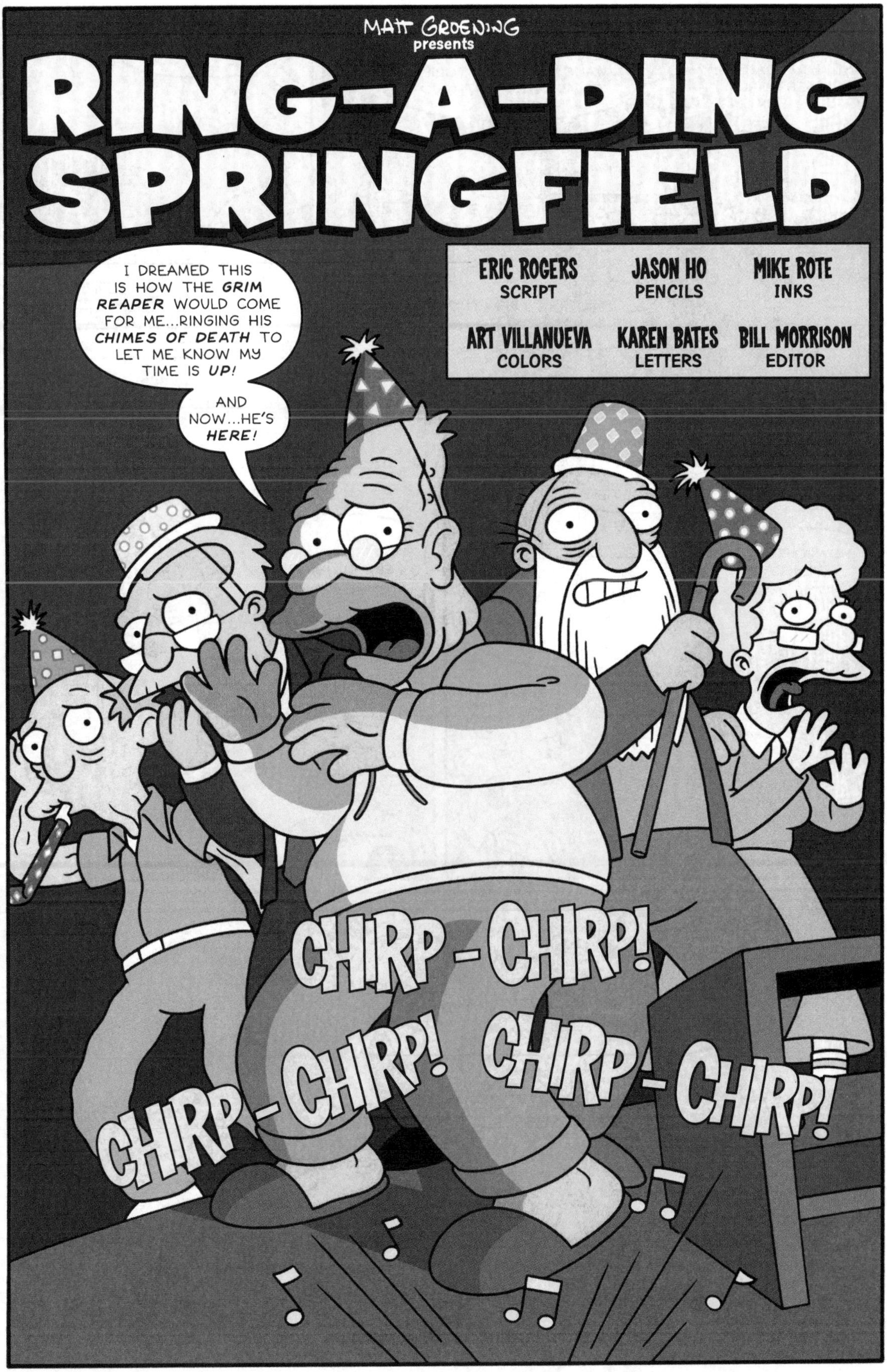
MATT GROENING
presents
RING-A-DING SPRINGFIELD
ERIC ROGERS SCRIPT
JASON HO PENCILS
MIKE ROTE INKS
ART VILLANUEVA COLORS
KAREN BATES LETTERS
BILL MORRISON EDITOR
I DREAMED THIS IS HOW THE GRIM REAPER WOULD COME FOR ME...RINGING HIS CHIMES OF DEATH TO LET ME KNOW MY TIME IS UP!
AND NOW...HE'S HERE!
CHIRP-CHIRP!
CHIRP-CHIRP!
CHIRP-CHIRP!
CHIRP-CHIRP!

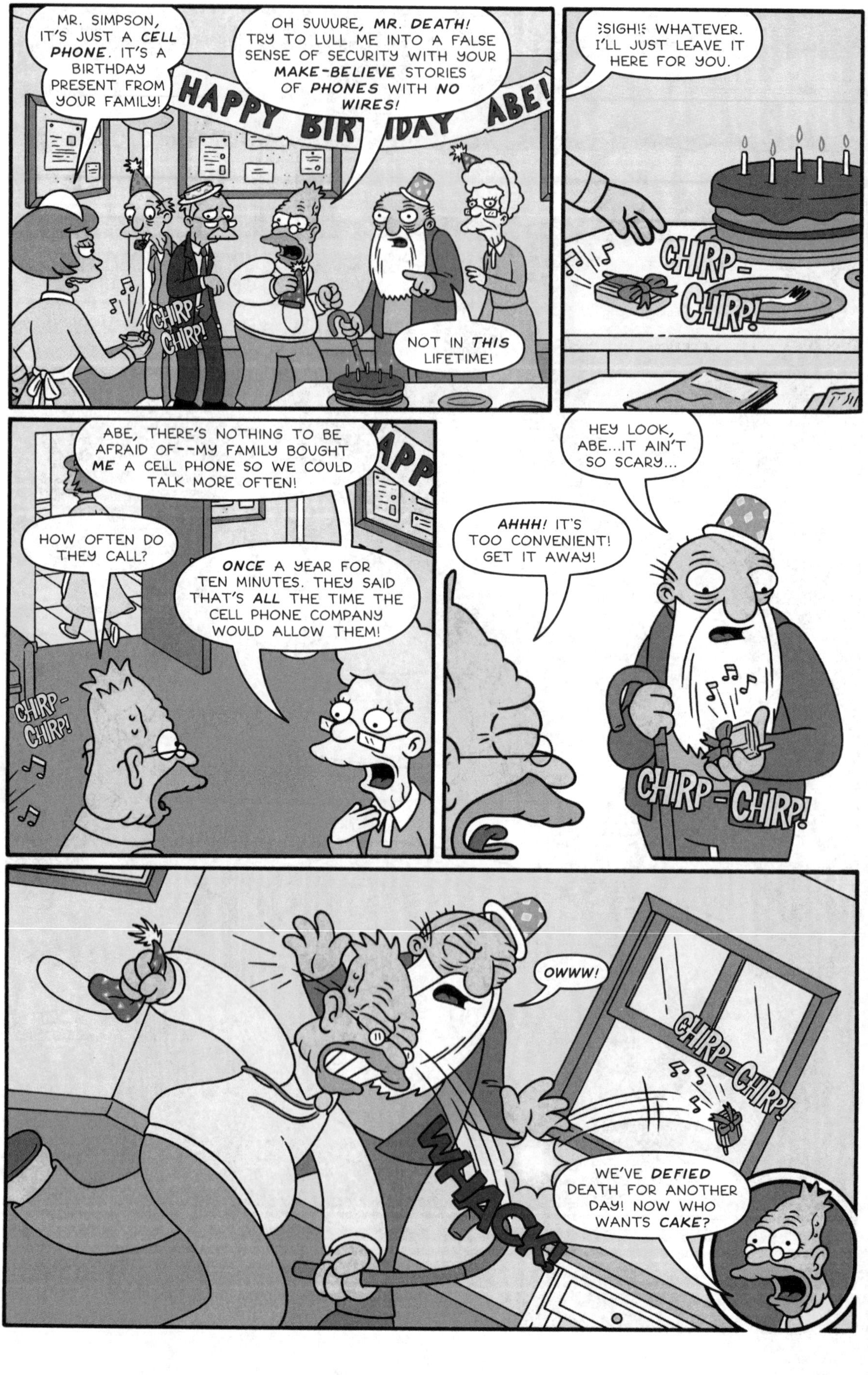
MR. SIMPSON, IT'S JUST A CELL PHONE. IT'S A BIRTHDAY PRESENT FROM YOUR FAMILY!
OH SUUURE, MR. DEATH! TRY TO LULL ME INTO A FALSE SENSE OF SECURITY WITH YOUR MAKE-BELIEVE STORIES OF PHONES WITH NO WIRES!
HAPPY BIRTHDAY ABE!
CHIRP-CHIRP!
NOT IN THIS LIFETIME!
SIGH! WHATEVER. I'LL JUST LEAVE IT HERE FOR YOU.
CHIRP-CHIRP!
ABE, THERE'S NOTHING TO BE AFRAID OF--MY FAMILY BOUGHT ME A CELL PHONE SO WE COULD TALK MORE OFTEN!
HOW OFTEN DO THEY CALL?
ONCE A YEAR FOR TEN MINUTES. THEY SAID THAT'S ALL THE TIME THE CELL PHONE COMPANY WOULD ALLOW THEM!
CHIRP-CHIRP!
HEY LOOK, ABE...IT AIN'T SO SCARY...
AHHH! IT'S TOO CONVENIENT! GET IT AWAY!
CHIRP-CHIRP!
OWWW!
CHIRP-CHIRP!
WHACK!
WE'VE DEFIED DEATH FOR ANOTHER DAY! NOW WHO WANTS CAKE?

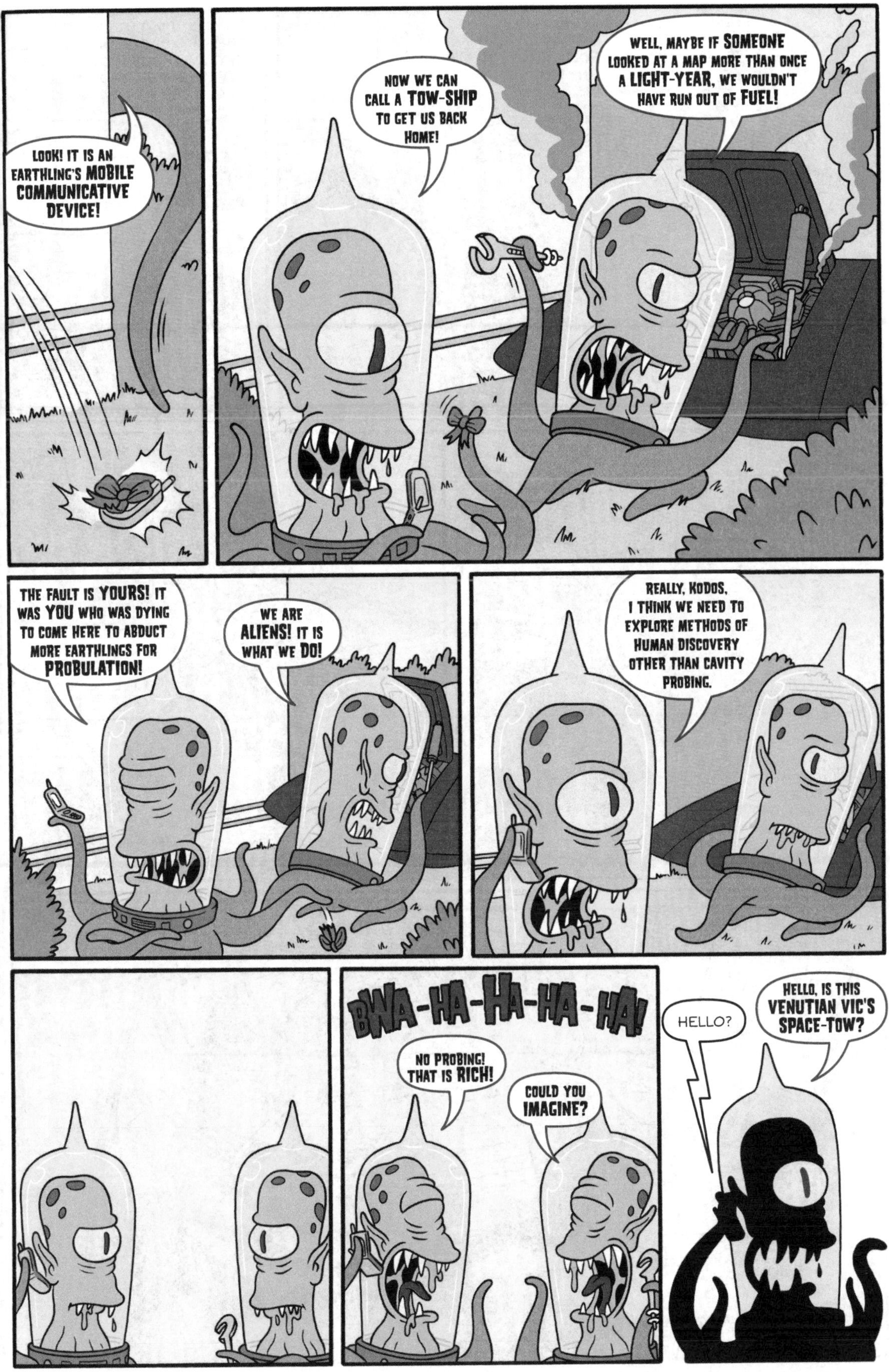
LOOK! IT IS AN EARTHLING'S MOBILE COMMUNICATIVE DEVICE!
NOW WE CAN CALL A TOW-SHIP TO GET US BACK HOME!
WELL, MAYBE IF SOMEONE LOOKED AT A MAP MORE THAN ONCE A LIGHT-YEAR, WE WOULDN'T HAVE RUN OUT OF FUEL!
THE FAULT IS YOURS! IT WAS YOU WHO WAS DYING TO COME HERE TO ABDUCT MORE EARTHLINGS FOR PROBULATION!
WE ARE ALIENS! IT IS WHAT WE DO!
REALLY, KODOS, I THINK WE NEED TO EXPLORE METHODS OF HUMAN DISCOVERY OTHER THAN CAVITY PROBING.
BWA-HA-HA-HA-HA!
NO PROBING! THAT IS RICH!
COULD YOU IMAGINE?
HELLO?
HELLO, IS THIS VENUTIAN VIC'S SPACE-TOW?

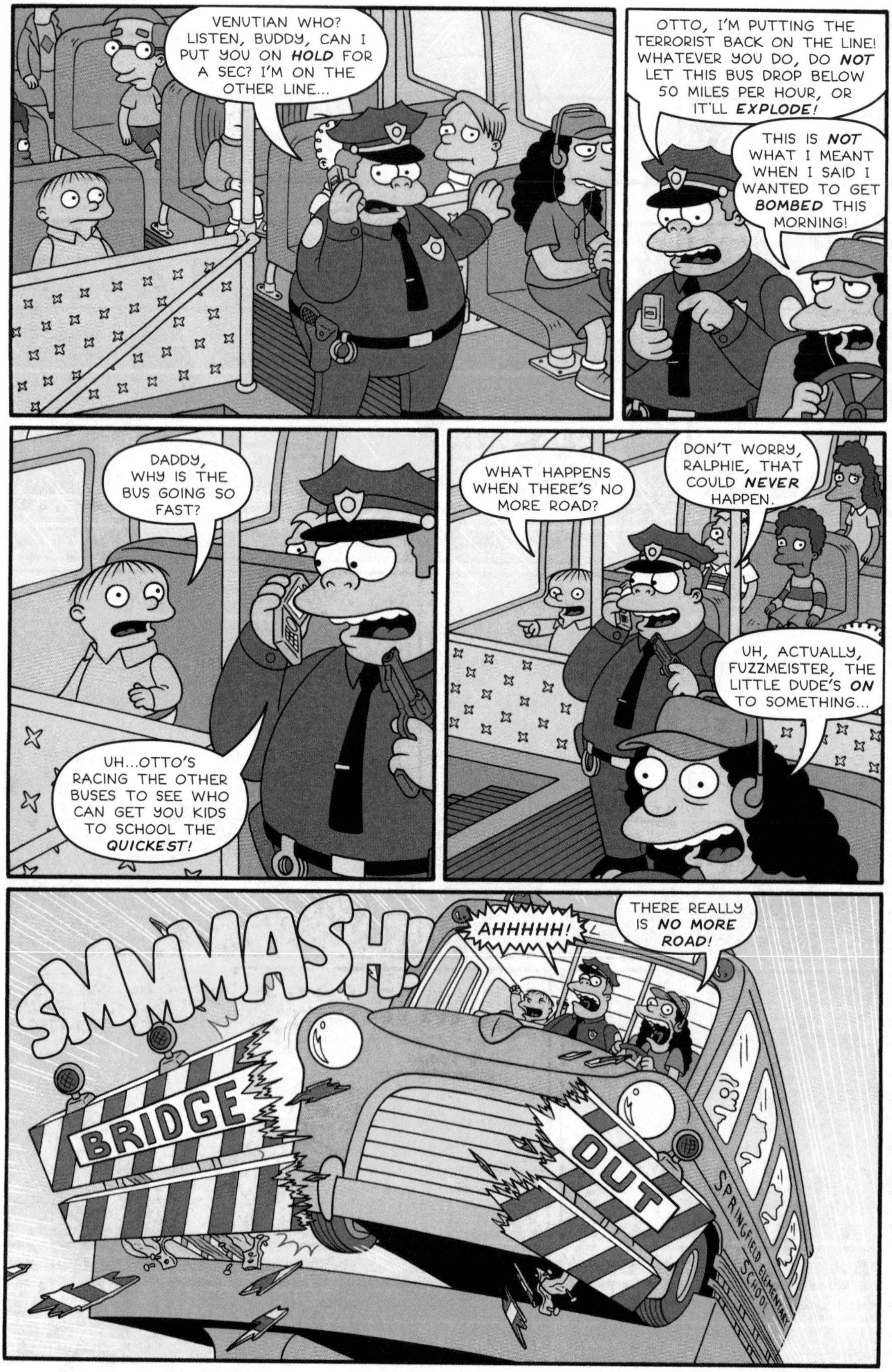
VENUTIAN WHO? LISTEN, BUDDY, CAN I PUT YOU ON HOLD FOR A SEC? I'M ON THE OTHER LINE...
OTTO, I'M PUTTING THE TERRORIST BACK ON THE LINE! WHATEVER YOU DO, DO NOT LET THIS BUS DROP BELOW 50 MILES PER HOUR, OR IT'LL EXPLODE!
THIS IS NOT WHAT I MEANT WHEN I SAID I WANTED TO GET BOMBED THIS MORNING!
DADDY, WHY IS THE BUS GOING SO FAST?
UH...OTTO'S RACING THE OTHER BUSES TO SEE WHO CAN GET YOU KIDS TO SCHOOL THE QUICKEST!
WHAT HAPPENS WHEN THERE'S NO MORE ROAD?
DON'T WORRY, RALPHIE, THAT COULD NEVER HAPPEN.
UH, ACTUALLY, FUZZMEISTER, THE LITTLE DUDE'S ON TO SOMETHING...
SMMMASH!
AHHHHH!
THERE REALLY IS NO MORE ROAD!
BRIDGE
OUT
SPRINGFIELD ELEMENTARY SCHOOL

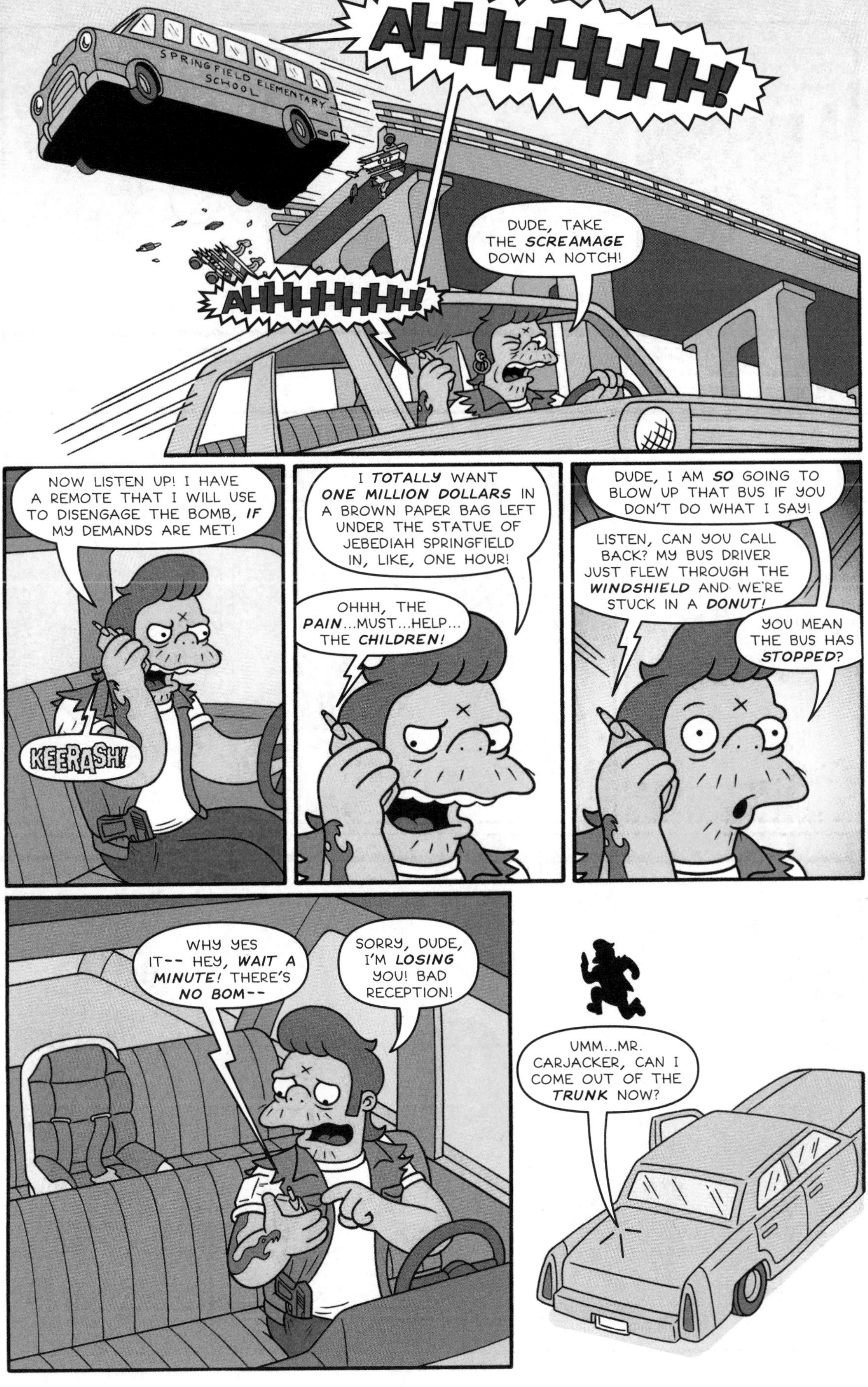
SPRINGFIELD ELEMENTARY SCHOOL
AHHHHHHHH!
AHHHHHHHH!
DUDE, TAKE THE *SCREAMAGE* DOWN A NOTCH!
NOW LISTEN UP! I HAVE A REMOTE THAT I WILL USE TO DISENGAGE THE BOMB, *IF* MY DEMANDS ARE MET!
KEERASH!
I *TOTALLY* WANT *ONE MILLION DOLLARS* IN A BROWN PAPER BAG LEFT UNDER THE STATUE OF JEBEDIAH SPRINGFIELD IN, LIKE, ONE HOUR!
OHHH, THE *PAIN*...MUST...HELP... THE *CHILDREN*!
DUDE, I AM *SO* GOING TO BLOW UP THAT BUS IF YOU DON'T DO WHAT I SAY!
LISTEN, CAN YOU CALL BACK? MY BUS DRIVER JUST FLEW THROUGH THE *WINDSHIELD* AND WE'RE STUCK IN A *DONUT*!
YOU MEAN THE BUS HAS *STOPPED*?
WHY YES IT-- HEY, *WAIT A MINUTE*! THERE'S *NO BOM*--
SORRY, DUDE, I'M *LOSING* YOU! BAD RECEPTION!
UMM...MR. CARJACKER, CAN I COME OUT OF THE *TRUNK* NOW?

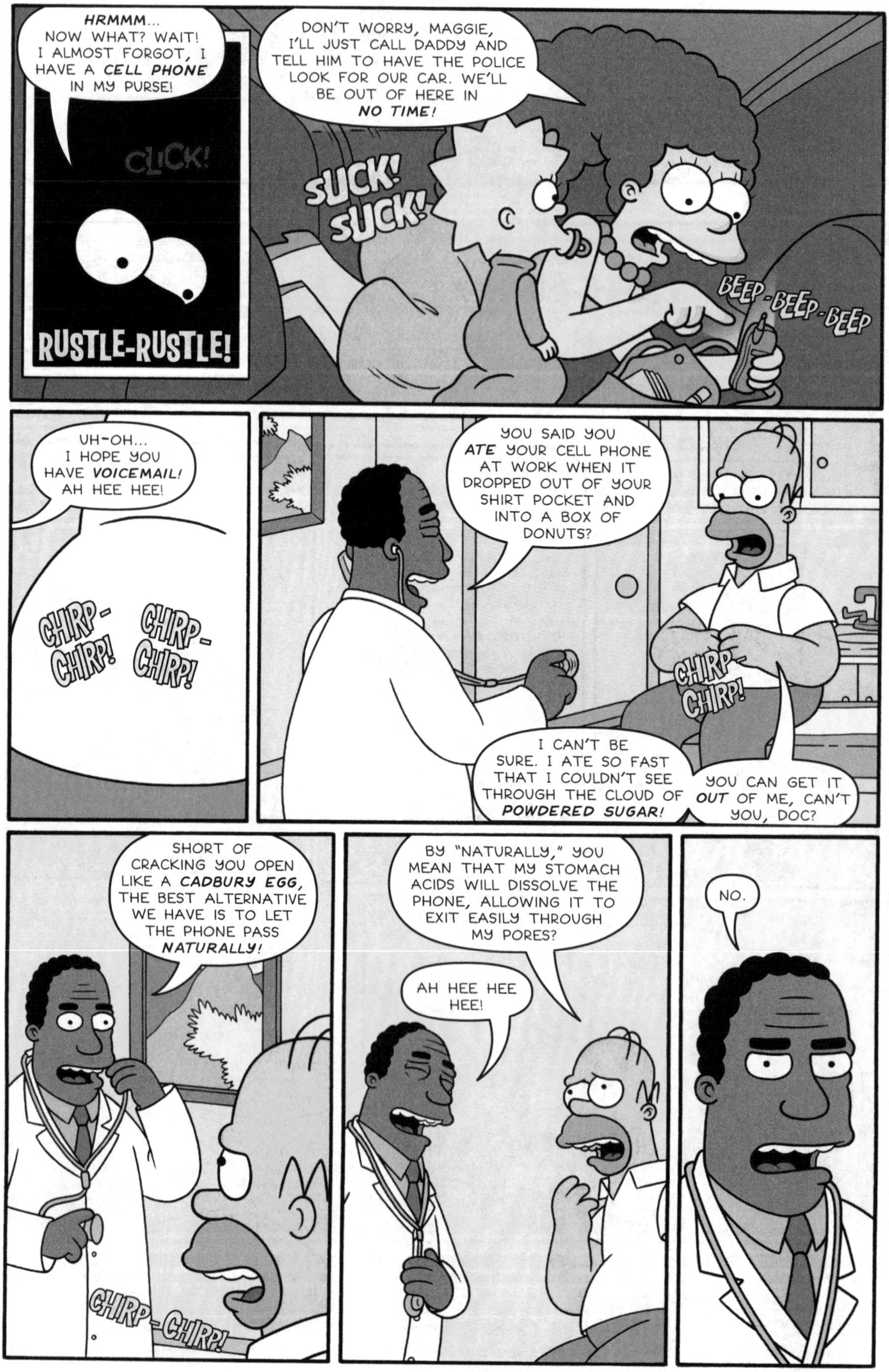
HRMMM... NOW WHAT? WAIT! I ALMOST FORGOT, I HAVE A CELL PHONE IN MY PURSE!
CLICK!
RUSTLE-RUSTLE!
DON'T WORRY, MAGGIE, I'LL JUST CALL DADDY AND TELL HIM TO HAVE THE POLICE LOOK FOR OUR CAR. WE'LL BE OUT OF HERE IN NO TIME!
SUCK! SUCK!
BEEP-BEEP-BEEP
UH-OH... I HOPE YOU HAVE VOICEMAIL! AH HEE HEE!
CHIRP-CHIRP! CHIRP-CHIRP!
YOU SAID YOU ATE YOUR CELL PHONE AT WORK WHEN IT DROPPED OUT OF YOUR SHIRT POCKET AND INTO A BOX OF DONUTS?
CHIRP-CHIRP!
I CAN'T BE SURE. I ATE SO FAST THAT I COULDN'T SEE THROUGH THE CLOUD OF POWDERED SUGAR!
YOU CAN GET IT OUT OF ME, CAN'T YOU, DOC?
SHORT OF CRACKING YOU OPEN LIKE A CADBURY EGG, THE BEST ALTERNATIVE WE HAVE IS TO LET THE PHONE PASS NATURALLY!
CHIRP-CHIRP!
BY "NATURALLY," YOU MEAN THAT MY STOMACH ACIDS WILL DISSOLVE THE PHONE, ALLOWING IT TO EXIT EASILY THROUGH MY PORES?
AH HEE HEE HEE!
NO.

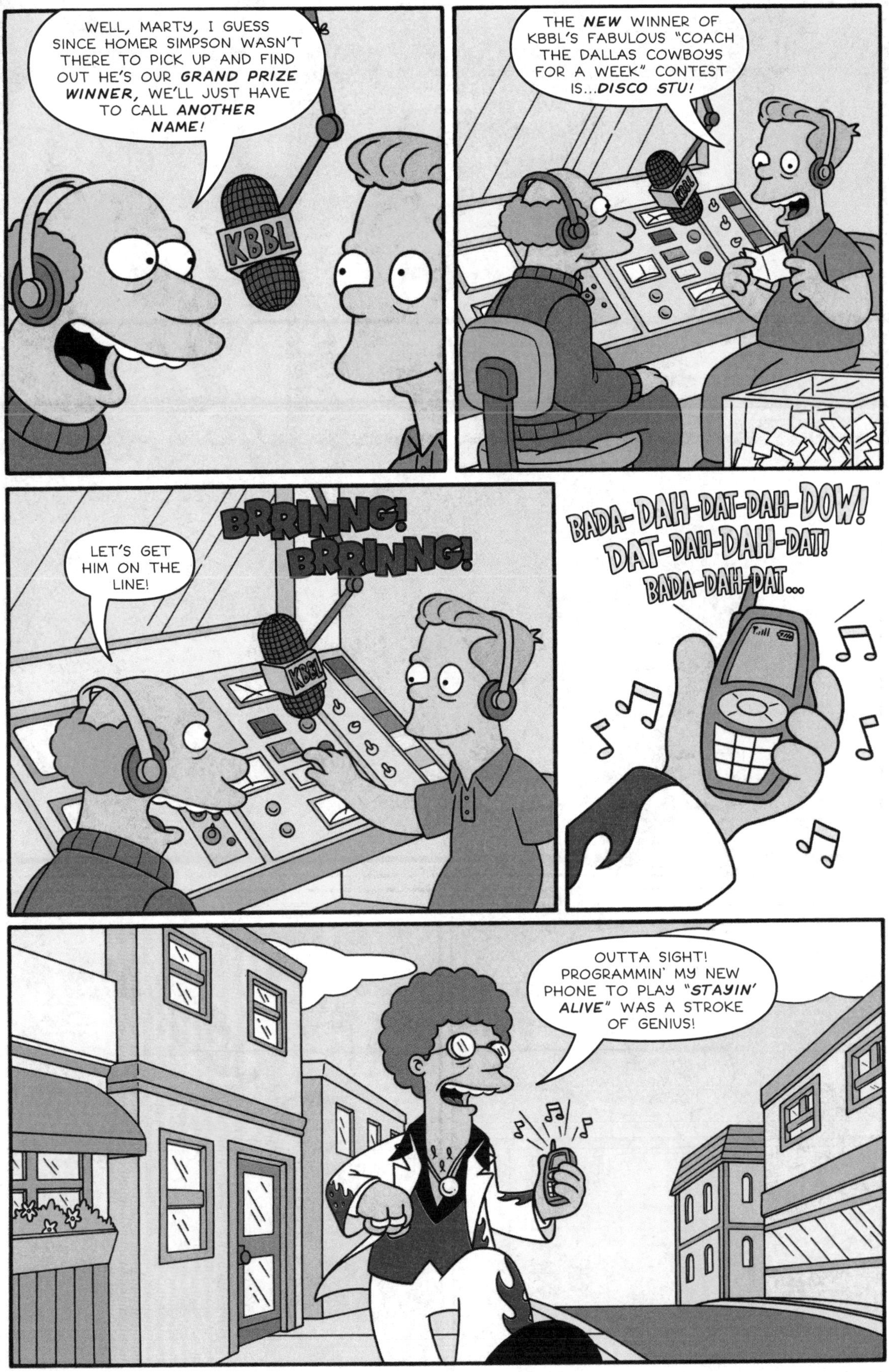
WELL, MARTY, I GUESS SINCE HOMER SIMPSON WASN'T THERE TO PICK UP AND FIND OUT HE'S OUR GRAND PRIZE WINNER, WE'LL JUST HAVE TO CALL ANOTHER NAME!
KBBL
THE NEW WINNER OF KBBL'S FABULOUS "COACH THE DALLAS COWBOYS FOR A WEEK" CONTEST IS...DISCO STU!
BRRINNG! BRRINNG!
LET'S GET HIM ON THE LINE!
KBBL
BADA-DAH-DAT-DAH-DOW! DAT-DAH-DAH-DAT! BADA-DAH-DAT...
OUTTA SIGHT! PROGRAMMIN' MY NEW PHONE TO PLAY "STAYIN' ALIVE" WAS A STROKE OF GENIUS!

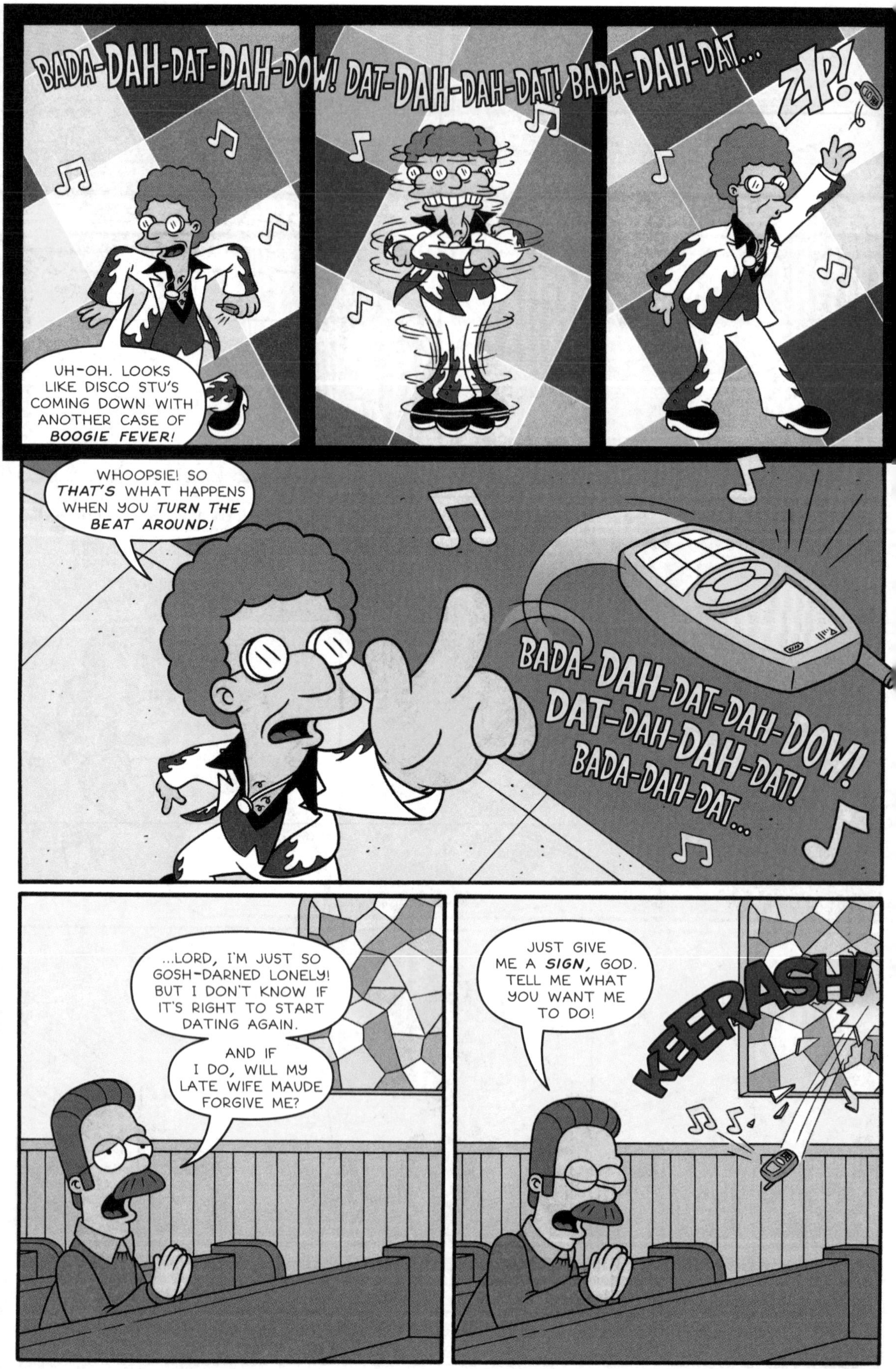

BADA-DAH-DAT-DAH-DOW! DAT-DAH-DAH-DAT! BADA-DAH-DAT...
UH-OH. LOOKS LIKE DISCO STU'S COMING DOWN WITH ANOTHER CASE OF BOOGIE FEVER!
ZIP!
WHOOPSIE! SO THAT'S WHAT HAPPENS WHEN YOU TURN THE BEAT AROUND!
BADA-DAH-DAT-DAH-DOW! DAT-DAH-DAH-DAT! BADA-DAH-DAT...
...LORD, I'M JUST SO GOSH-DARNED LONELY! BUT I DON'T KNOW IF IT'S RIGHT TO START DATING AGAIN.
AND IF I DO, WILL MY LATE WIFE MAUDE FORGIVE ME?
JUST GIVE ME A SIGN, GOD. TELL ME WHAT YOU WANT ME TO DO!
KEERASH!

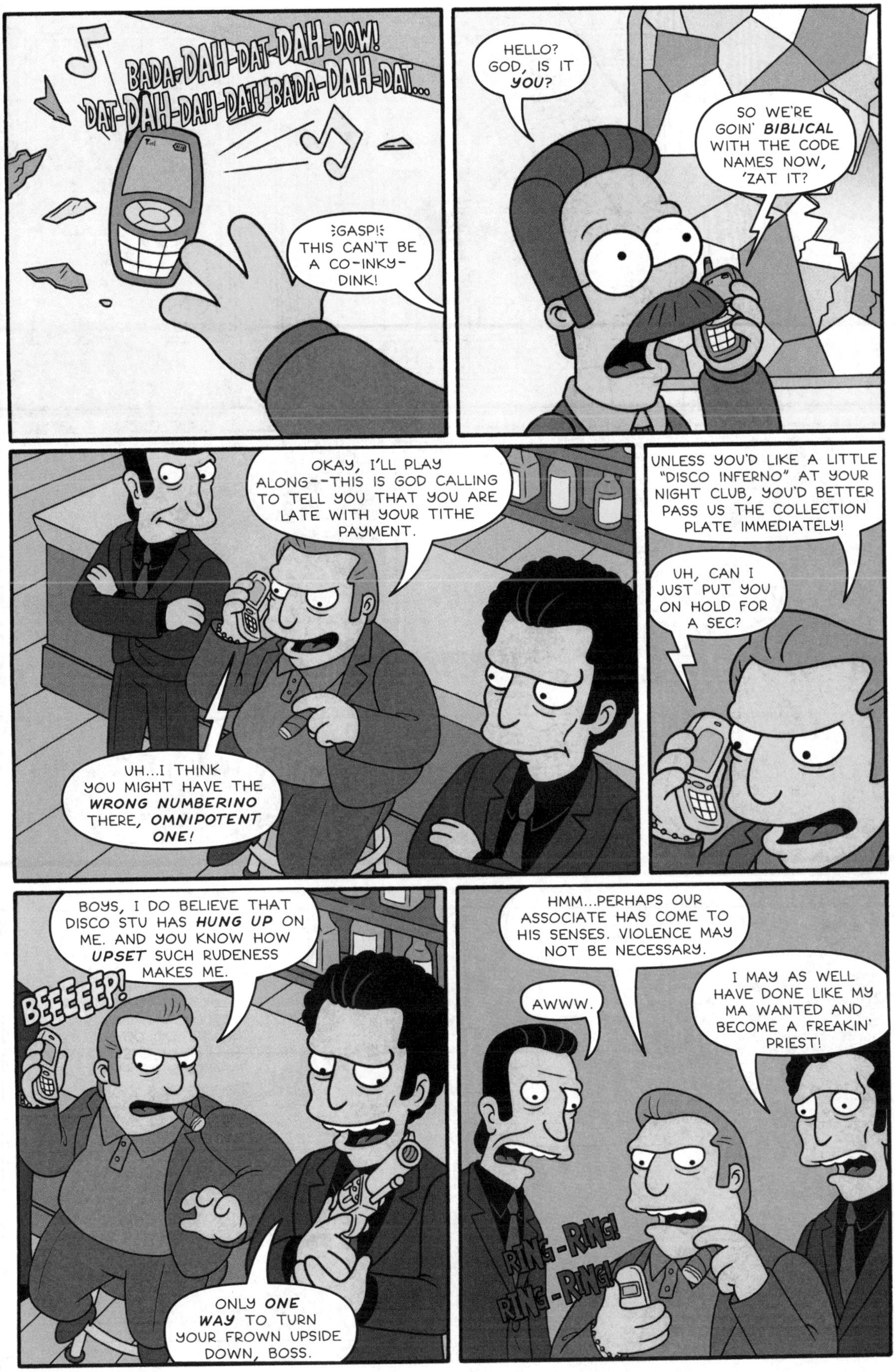
BADA-DAH-DAT-DAH-DOW! DAT-DAH-DAH-DAT! BADA-DAH-DAT...
:GASP!: THIS CAN'T BE A CO-INKY-DINK!
HELLO? GOD, IS IT ***YOU***?
SO WE'RE GOIN' ***BIBLICAL*** WITH THE CODE NAMES NOW, 'ZAT IT?
OKAY, I'LL PLAY ALONG--THIS IS GOD CALLING TO TELL YOU THAT YOU ARE LATE WITH YOUR TITHE PAYMENT.
UH...I THINK YOU MIGHT HAVE THE ***WRONG NUMBERINO*** THERE, ***OMNIPOTENT ONE***!
UNLESS YOU'D LIKE A LITTLE "DISCO INFERNO" AT YOUR NIGHT CLUB, YOU'D BETTER PASS US THE COLLECTION PLATE IMMEDIATELY!
UH, CAN I JUST PUT YOU ON HOLD FOR A SEC?
BOYS, I DO BELIEVE THAT DISCO STU HAS ***HUNG UP*** ON ME. AND YOU KNOW HOW ***UPSET*** SUCH RUDENESS MAKES ME.
BEEEEEP!
ONLY ***ONE WAY*** TO TURN YOUR FROWN UPSIDE DOWN, BOSS.
HMM...PERHAPS OUR ASSOCIATE HAS COME TO HIS SENSES. VIOLENCE MAY NOT BE NECESSARY.
AWWW.
I MAY AS WELL HAVE DONE LIKE MY MA WANTED AND BECOME A FREAKIN' PRIEST!
RING-RING! RING-RING!

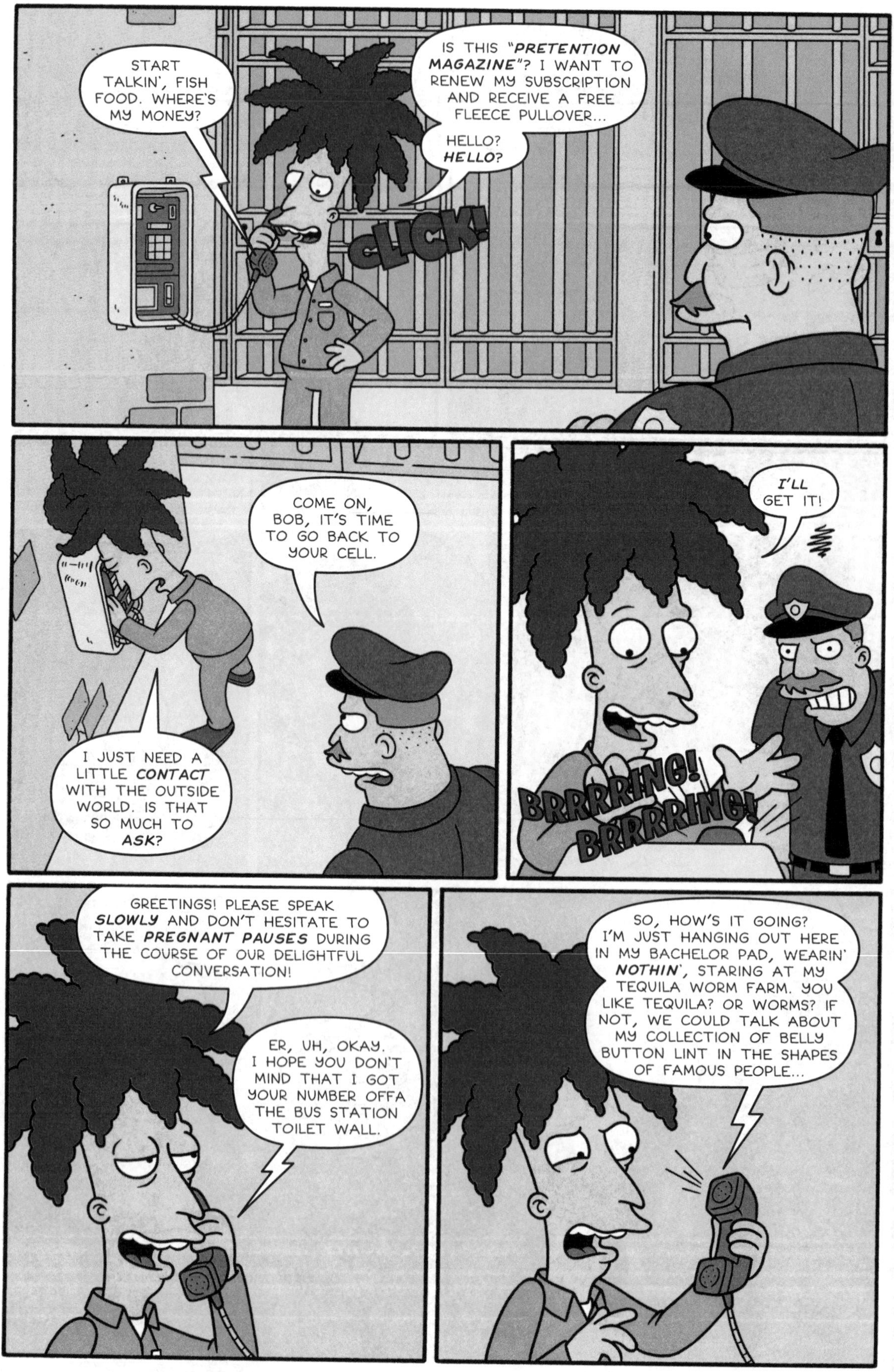
START TALKIN', FISH FOOD. WHERE'S MY MONEY?
IS THIS "PRETENTION MAGAZINE"? I WANT TO RENEW MY SUBSCRIPTION AND RECEIVE A FREE FLEECE PULLOVER...
HELLO? HELLO?
CLICK!
COME ON, BOB, IT'S TIME TO GO BACK TO YOUR CELL.
I JUST NEED A LITTLE CONTACT WITH THE OUTSIDE WORLD. IS THAT SO MUCH TO ASK?
I'LL GET IT!
BRRRRING! BRRRRING!
GREETINGS! PLEASE SPEAK SLOWLY AND DON'T HESITATE TO TAKE PREGNANT PAUSES DURING THE COURSE OF OUR DELIGHTFUL CONVERSATION!
ER, UH, OKAY. I HOPE YOU DON'T MIND THAT I GOT YOUR NUMBER OFFA THE BUS STATION TOILET WALL.
SO, HOW'S IT GOING? I'M JUST HANGING OUT HERE IN MY BACHELOR PAD, WEARIN' NOTHIN', STARING AT MY TEQUILA WORM FARM. YOU LIKE TEQUILA? OR WORMS? IF NOT, WE COULD TALK ABOUT MY COLLECTION OF BELLY BUTTON LINT IN THE SHAPES OF FAMOUS PEOPLE...

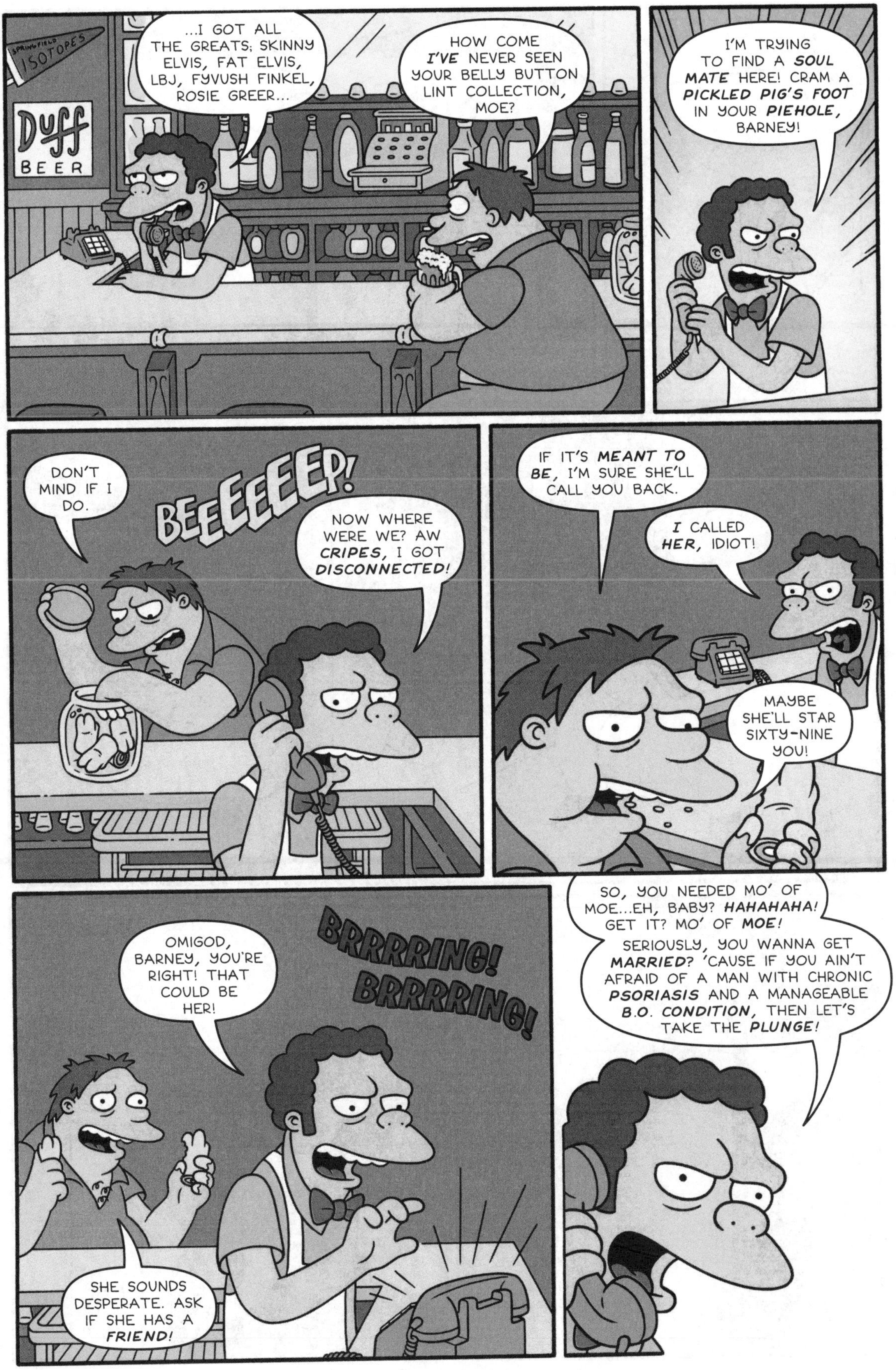
SPRINGFIELD ISOTOPES
Duff BEER
...I GOT ALL THE GREATS; SKINNY ELVIS, FAT ELVIS, LBJ, FYVUSH FINKEL, ROSIE GREER...
HOW COME I'VE NEVER SEEN YOUR BELLY BUTTON LINT COLLECTION, MOE?
I'M TRYING TO FIND A SOUL MATE HERE! CRAM A PICKLED PIG'S FOOT IN YOUR PIEHOLE, BARNEY!
DON'T MIND IF I DO.
BEEEEEEP!
NOW WHERE WERE WE? AW CRIPES, I GOT DISCONNECTED!
IF IT'S MEANT TO BE, I'M SURE SHE'LL CALL YOU BACK.
I CALLED HER, IDIOT!
MAYBE SHE'LL STAR SIXTY-NINE YOU!
OMIGOD, BARNEY, YOU'RE RIGHT! THAT COULD BE HER!
BRRRRING! BRRRRING!
SHE SOUNDS DESPERATE. ASK IF SHE HAS A FRIEND!
SO, YOU NEEDED MO' OF MOE...EH, BABY? HAHAHAHA! GET IT? MO' OF MOE!
SERIOUSLY, YOU WANNA GET MARRIED? 'CAUSE IF YOU AIN'T AFRAID OF A MAN WITH CHRONIC PSORIASIS AND A MANAGEABLE B.O. CONDITION, THEN LET'S TAKE THE PLUNGE!

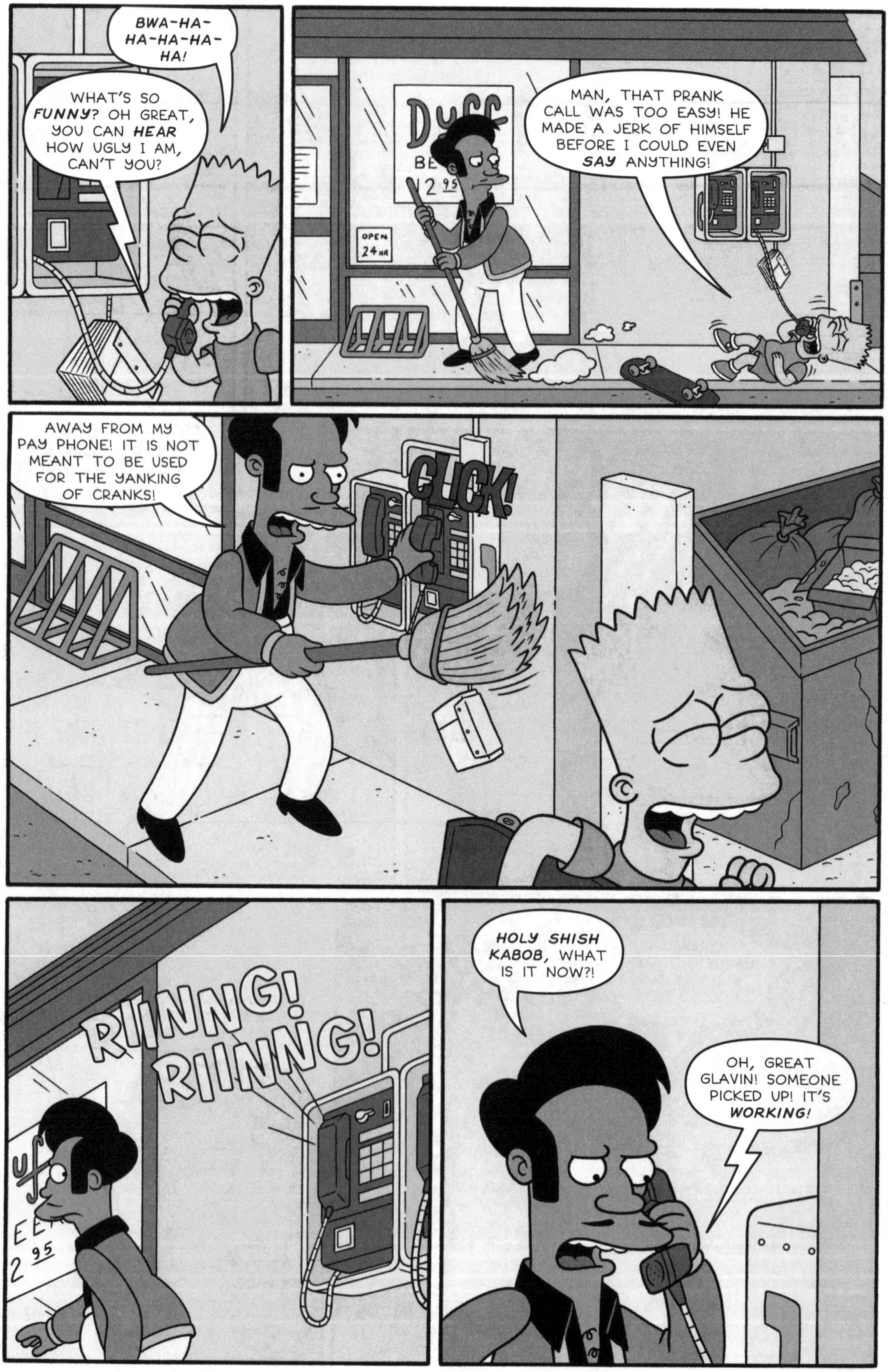
BWA-HA-HA-HA-HA-HA!
WHAT'S SO FUNNY? OH GREAT, YOU CAN HEAR HOW UGLY I AM, CAN'T YOU?
Duff BE 12 95
OPEN 24 HR
MAN, THAT PRANK CALL WAS TOO EASY! HE MADE A JERK OF HIMSELF BEFORE I COULD EVEN SAY ANYTHING!
AWAY FROM MY PAY PHONE! IT IS NOT MEANT TO BE USED FOR THE YANKING OF CRANKS!
CLICK!
RIINNG! RIINNG!
HOLY SHISH KABOB, WHAT IS IT NOW?!
OH, GREAT GLAVIN! SOMEONE PICKED UP! IT'S WORKING!

I'VE FINALLY INVENTED A PHONE THAT CAN CALL *ALTERNATE UNIVERSES!*

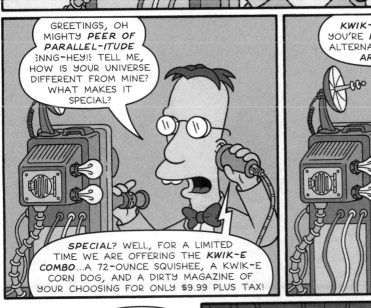

GREETINGS, OH MIGHTY *PEER OF PARALLEL-ITUDE* ⟨NNG-HEY!⟩ TELL ME, HOW IS YOUR UNIVERSE DIFFERENT FROM MINE? WHAT MAKES IT SPECIAL?

SPECIAL? WELL, FOR A LIMITED TIME WE ARE OFFERING THE *KWIK-E COMBO*...A 72-OUNCE SQUISHEE, A KWIK-E CORN DOG, AND A DIRTY MAGAZINE OF YOUR CHOOSING FOR ONLY $9.99 PLUS TAX!

KWIK-E COMBO?! YOU'RE *NOT* FROM AN ALTERNATE UNIVERSE, *ARE* YOU?

SIR, YOU HAVE OBVIOUSLY NOT BEEN TO CALCUTTA.

WHAT'S THE USE? MY PHONE IS A FLOP!

BUT I WON'T GIVE UP! DID *POPEIL* QUIT AFTER HIS FIRST FORTY-SEVEN ATTEMPTS TO INVENT *THE VEGEMATIC? NO!* AND NOW THE WORLD ENJOYS THE CONVENIENCE OF CRINKLE-CUT CARROTS AT HOME WITH THE SLICING AND THE DICING AND THE JULIENNE FRIES ⟨GLAVIN!⟩

I'VE GOT TO TRY *ONE MORE TIME!*

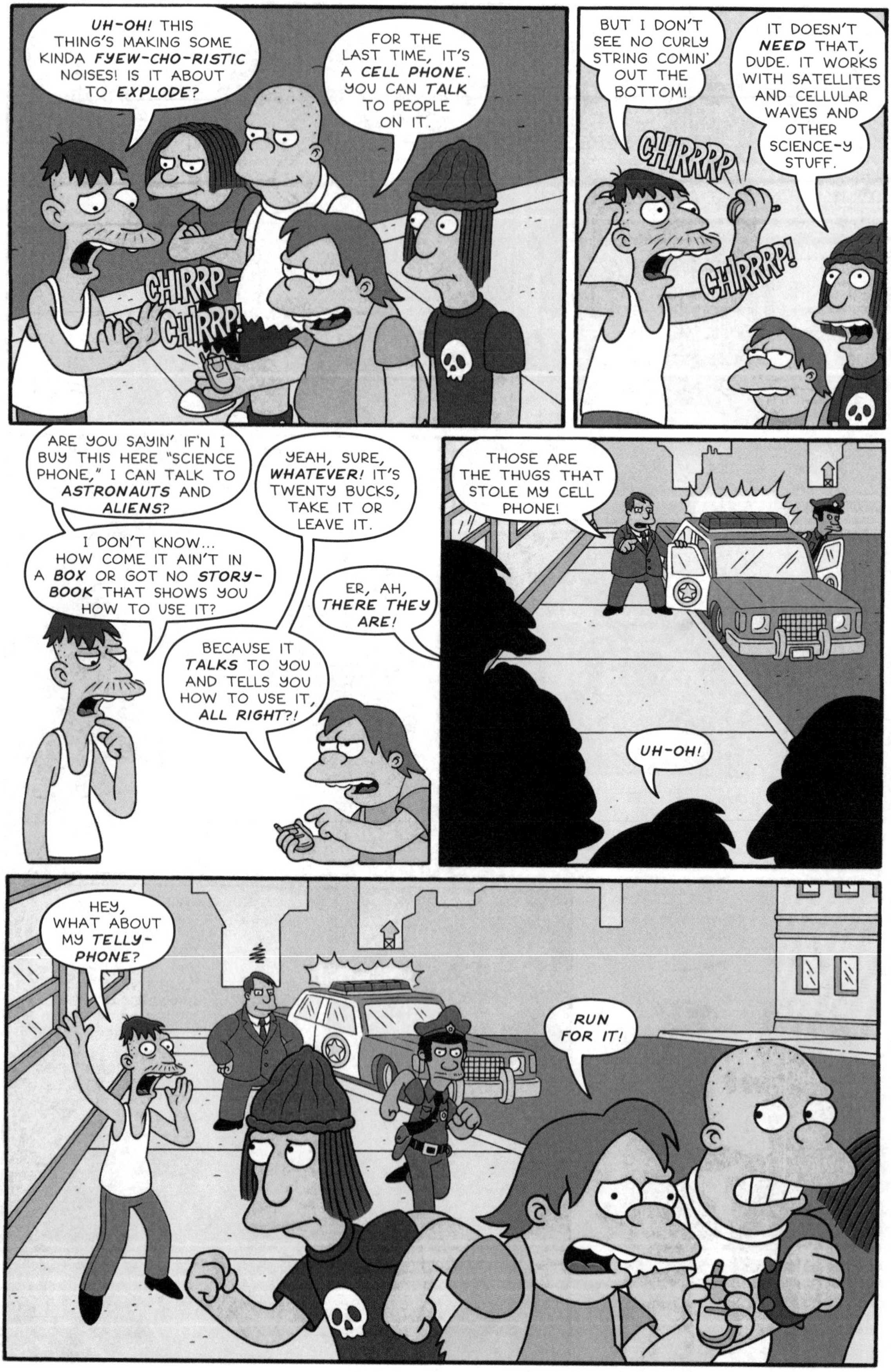
UH-OH! THIS THING'S MAKING SOME KINDA FYEW-CHO-RISTIC NOISES! IS IT ABOUT TO EXPLODE?
FOR THE LAST TIME, IT'S A CELL PHONE. YOU CAN TALK TO PEOPLE ON IT.
CHIRRP-CHIRRP!
BUT I DON'T SEE NO CURLY STRING COMIN' OUT THE BOTTOM!
IT DOESN'T NEED THAT, DUDE. IT WORKS WITH SATELLITES AND CELLULAR WAVES AND OTHER SCIENCE-Y STUFF.
CHIRRRP!
CHIRRRP!
ARE YOU SAYIN' IF'N I BUY THIS HERE "SCIENCE PHONE," I CAN TALK TO ASTRONAUTS AND ALIENS?
YEAH, SURE, WHATEVER! IT'S TWENTY BUCKS, TAKE IT OR LEAVE IT.
I DON'T KNOW... HOW COME IT AIN'T IN A BOX OR GOT NO STORY-BOOK THAT SHOWS YOU HOW TO USE IT?
ER, AH, THERE THEY ARE!
BECAUSE IT TALKS TO YOU AND TELLS YOU HOW TO USE IT, ALL RIGHT?!
THOSE ARE THE THUGS THAT STOLE MY CELL PHONE!
UH-OH!
HEY, WHAT ABOUT MY TELLY-PHONE?
RUN FOR IT!

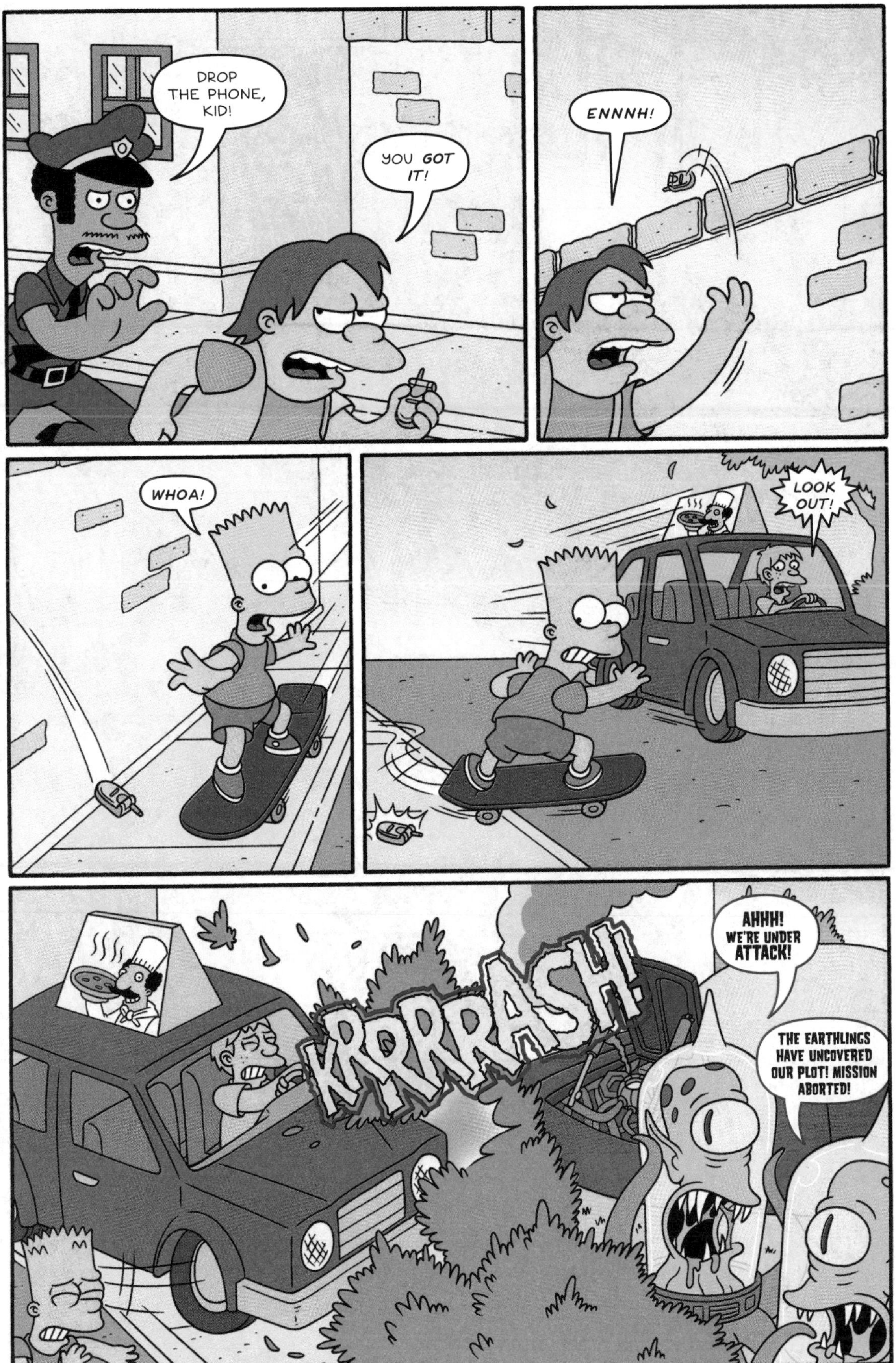
DROP THE PHONE, KID!
YOU GOT IT!
ENNNH!
WHOA!
LOOK OUT!
AHHH! WE'RE UNDER ATTACK!
KRRRRASH!
THE EARTHLINGS HAVE UNCOVERED OUR PLOT! MISSION ABORTED!

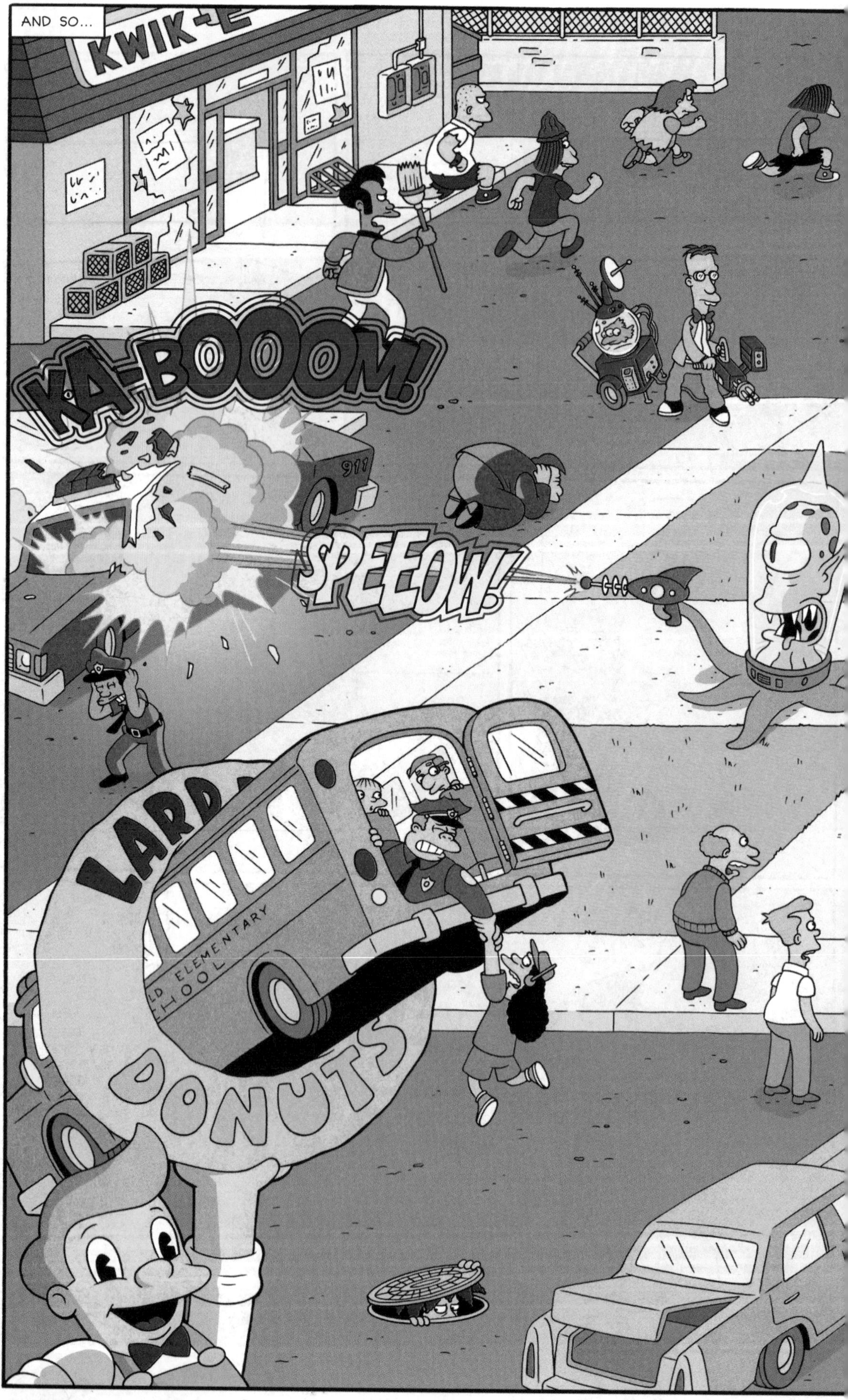
AND SO...
KWIK-E
KA-BOOOOM!
911
SPEEOW!
LARD
DONUTS
ELEMENTARY
SCHOOL

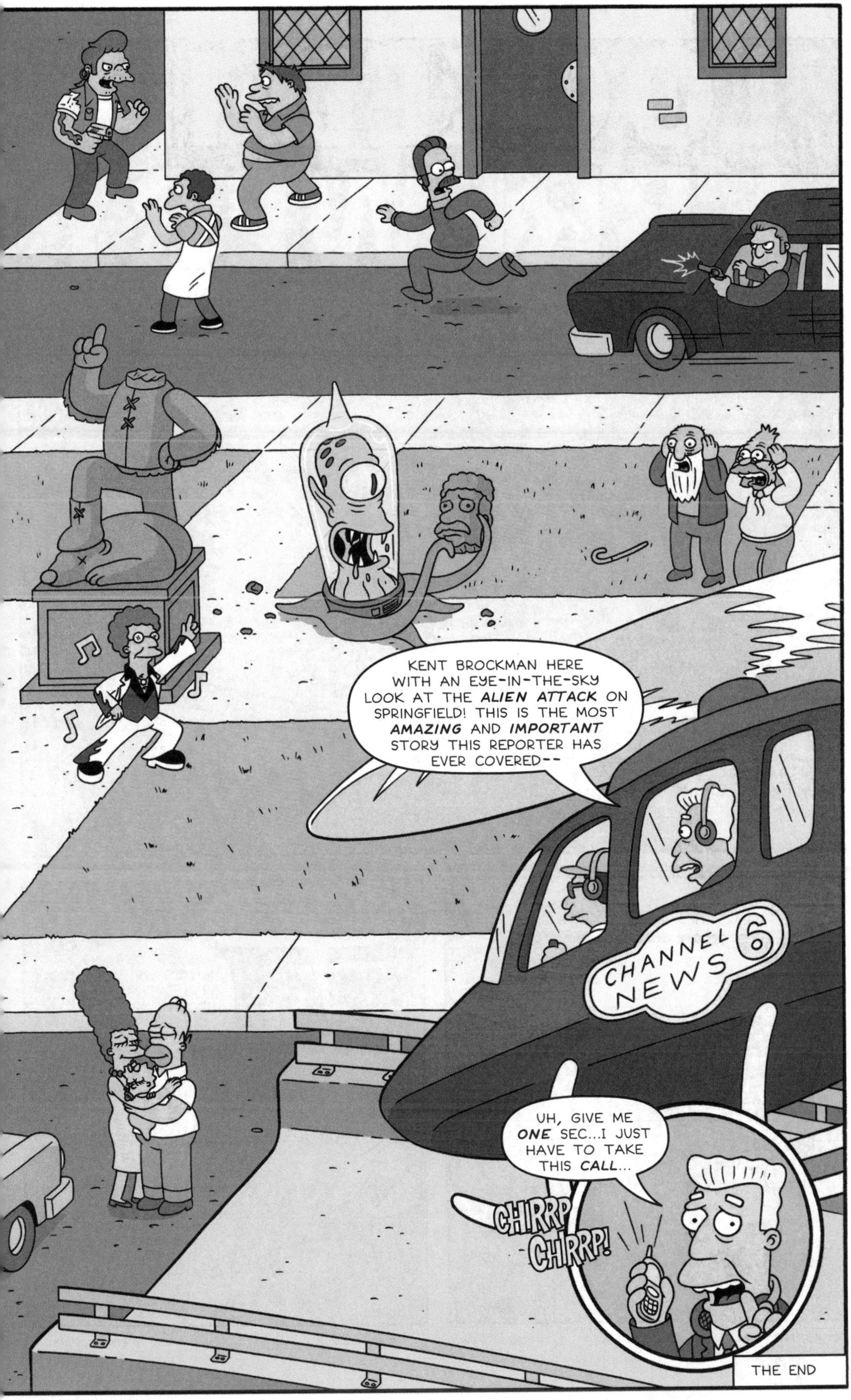
KENT BROCKMAN HERE WITH AN EYE-IN-THE-SKY LOOK AT THE ALIEN ATTACK ON SPRINGFIELD! THIS IS THE MOST AMAZING AND IMPORTANT STORY THIS REPORTER HAS EVER COVERED--
CHANNEL NEWS 6
UH, GIVE ME ONE SEC...I JUST HAVE TO TAKE THIS CALL...
CHIRRP CHIRRP!
THE END

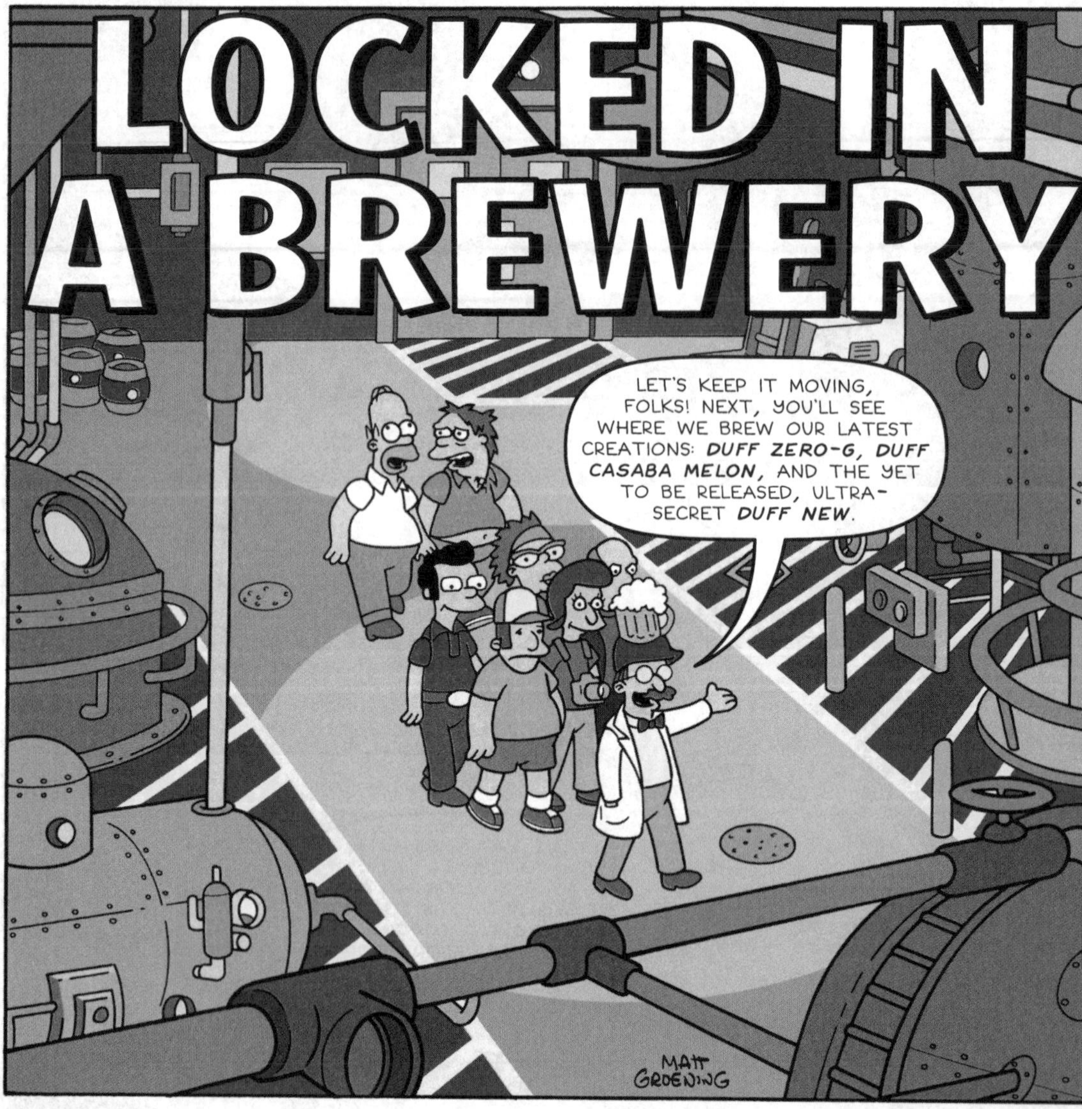
LOCKED IN A BREWERY
LET'S KEEP IT MOVING, FOLKS! NEXT, YOU'LL SEE WHERE WE BREW OUR LATEST CREATIONS: DUFF ZERO-G, DUFF CASABA MELON, AND THE YET TO BE RELEASED, ULTRA-SECRET DUFF NEW.
MATT GROENING

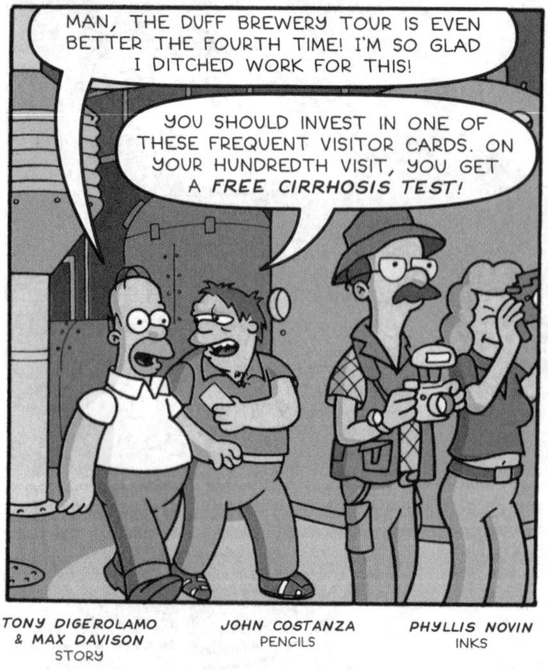
MAN, THE DUFF BREWERY TOUR IS EVEN BETTER THE FOURTH TIME! I'M SO GLAD I DITCHED WORK FOR THIS!
YOU SHOULD INVEST IN ONE OF THESE FREQUENT VISITOR CARDS. ON YOUR HUNDREDTH VISIT, YOU GET A FREE CIRRHOSIS TEST!

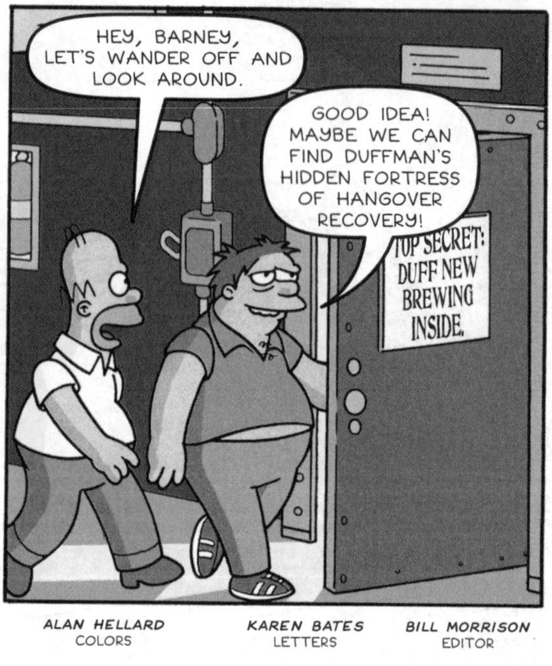
HEY, BARNEY, LET'S WANDER OFF AND LOOK AROUND.
GOOD IDEA! MAYBE WE CAN FIND DUFFMAN'S HIDDEN FORTRESS OF HANGOVER RECOVERY!
TOP SECRET: DUFF NEW BREWING INSIDE.

TONY DIGEROLAMO & MAX DAVISON STORY · *JOHN COSTANZA* PENCILS · *PHYLLIS NOVIN* INKS · *ALAN HELLARD* COLORS · *KAREN BATES* LETTERS · *BILL MORRISON* EDITOR

BARNEY, DUFFMAN ISN'T REAL.

OF COURSE HE'S REAL! YOU JUST HAVE TO *BELIEVE*. :BRRAAAP!:

TOP SECRET: DUFF NEW BREWING INSIDE.

I'LL TELL YOU WHAT'S WRONG WITH THIS COMPANY: OUR CUSTOMERS! I MEAN, LOOK AT THE PEOPLE ON THESE TOURS. IT'S LIKE THEY LOST 25% OF THEIR BRAIN CAPACITY *BEFORE* THEY STARTED DRINKING DUFF.

THE LATEST FIGURES PUT IT AT 28%, SIR.

DON'T CORRECT ME, BARRY.

AFTER WE ROLL OUT *DUFF NEW*, WE CAN DRUM UP NEW BUSINESS! MEANING SMARTER, *BETTER* CUSTOMERS!

WHY IS THIS DOOR OPEN? DON'T WE HAVE RULES ABOUT SECURITY AROUND HERE?

DUFFMAN DOESN'T PLAY BY ANYONE'S RULES. NOT EVEN HIS OWN!

SLAM!

TOP SEC DUFF N BREW INSID

HOW ABOUT YOU DITCH THE COSTUME, AND WE'LL CATCH THE TAIL END OF HAPPY HOUR?

DUFFMAN IS A DEDICATED METHOD ACTOR AND MUST STAY IN CHARACTER AT ALL TIMES! OH, YEAH!

OKAY, WHATEVER, BARRY.

MMM... CONFIDENTIAL BEER.

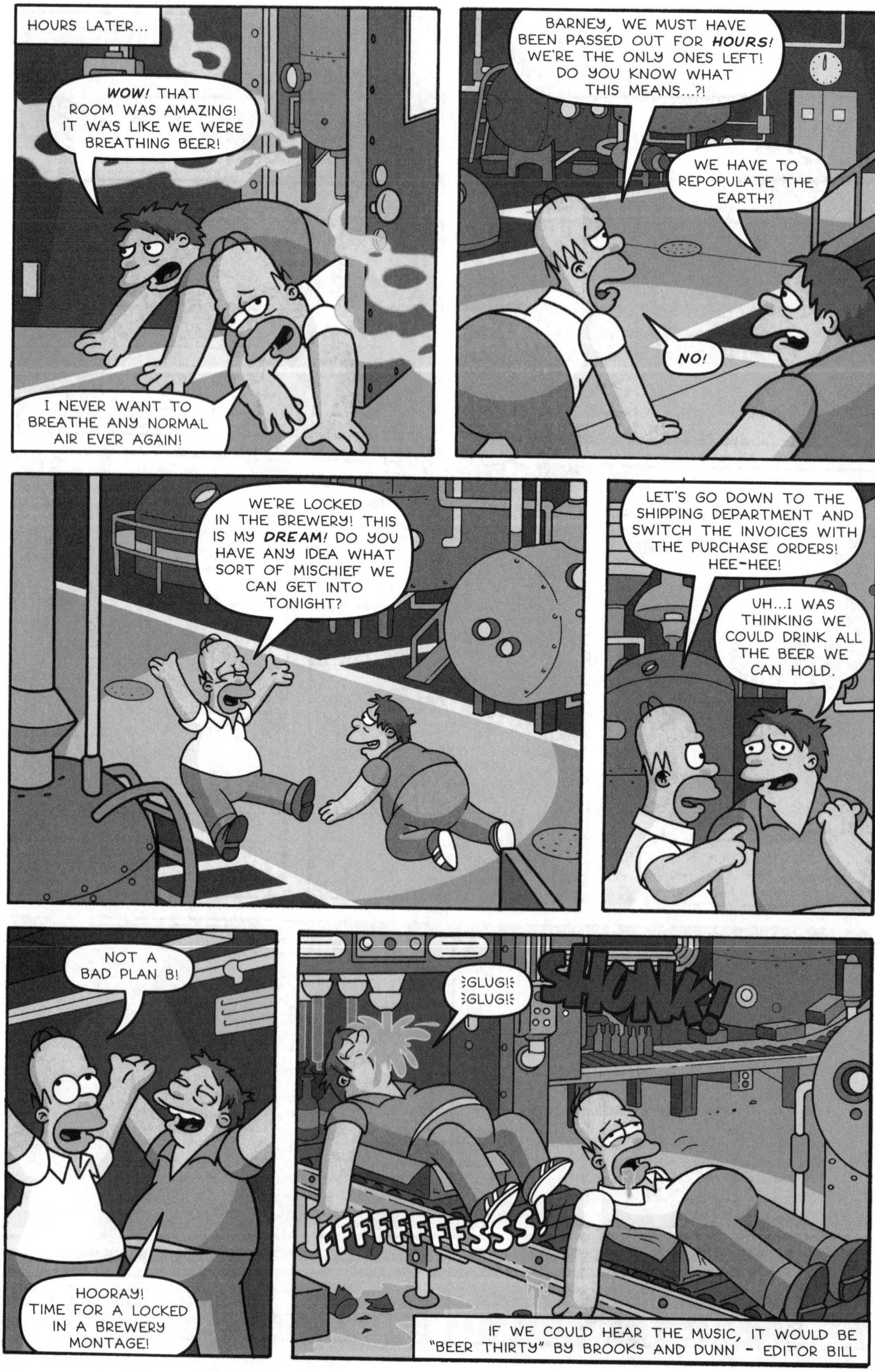
HOURS LATER...
WOW! THAT ROOM WAS AMAZING! IT WAS LIKE WE WERE BREATHING BEER!
I NEVER WANT TO BREATHE ANY NORMAL AIR EVER AGAIN!
BARNEY, WE MUST HAVE BEEN PASSED OUT FOR HOURS! WE'RE THE ONLY ONES LEFT! DO YOU KNOW WHAT THIS MEANS...?!
WE HAVE TO REPOPULATE THE EARTH?
NO!
WE'RE LOCKED IN THE BREWERY! THIS IS MY DREAM! DO YOU HAVE ANY IDEA WHAT SORT OF MISCHIEF WE CAN GET INTO TONIGHT?
LET'S GO DOWN TO THE SHIPPING DEPARTMENT AND SWITCH THE INVOICES WITH THE PURCHASE ORDERS! HEE-HEE!
UH...I WAS THINKING WE COULD DRINK ALL THE BEER WE CAN HOLD.
NOT A BAD PLAN B!
HOORAY! TIME FOR A LOCKED IN A BREWERY MONTAGE!
GLUG! GLUG!
SHUNK!
FFFFFFFFSSS!
IF WE COULD HEAR THE MUSIC, IT WOULD BE "BEER THIRTY" BY BROOKS AND DUNN - EDITOR BILL

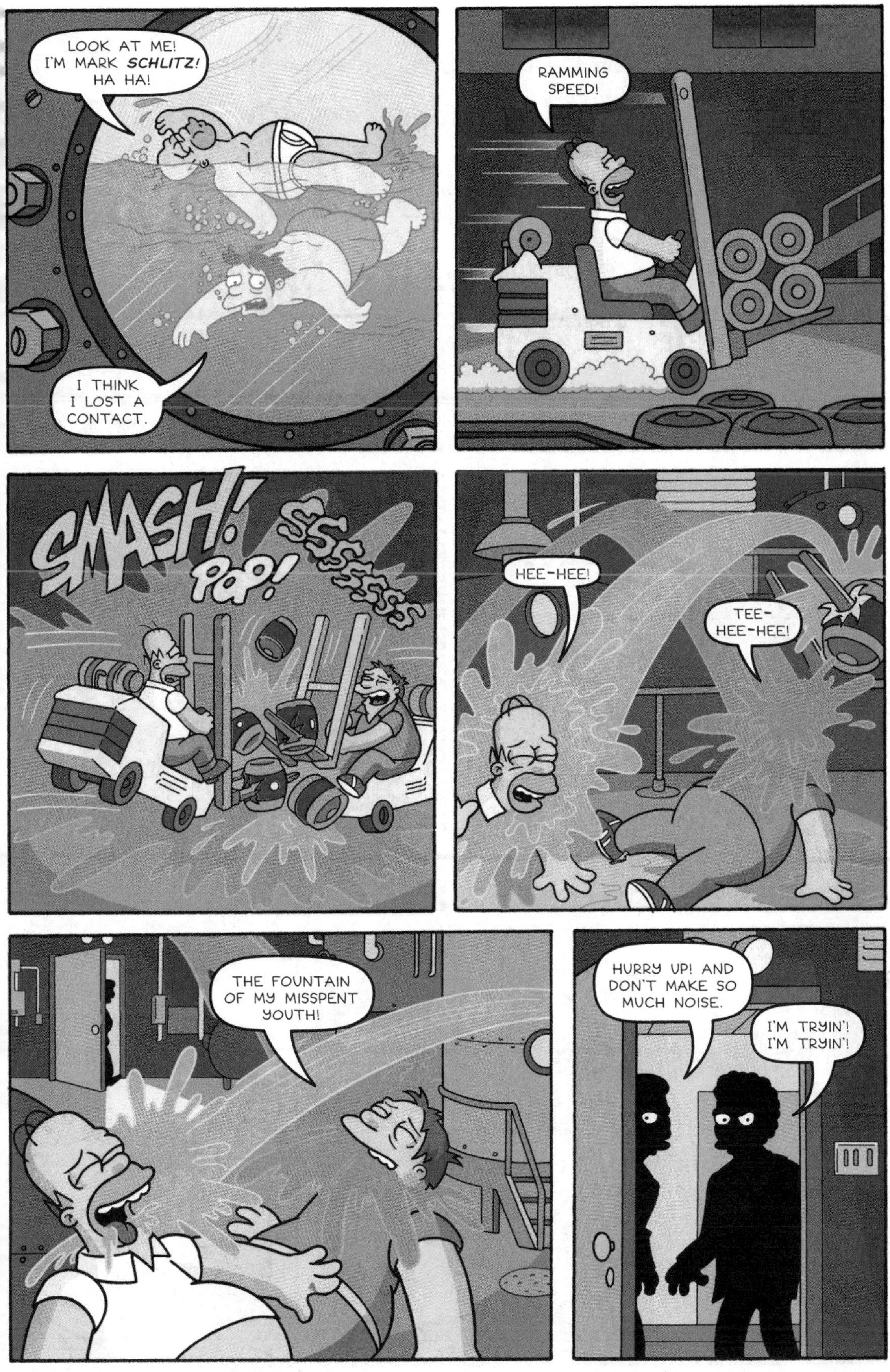
LOOK AT ME! I'M MARK SCHLITZ! HA HA!
I THINK I LOST A CONTACT.
RAMMING SPEED!
SMASH!
POP!
SSSSSSS
HEE-HEE!
TEE-HEE-HEE!
THE FOUNTAIN OF MY MISSPENT YOUTH!
HURRY UP! AND DON'T MAKE SO MUCH NOISE.
I'M TRYIN'! I'M TRYIN'!

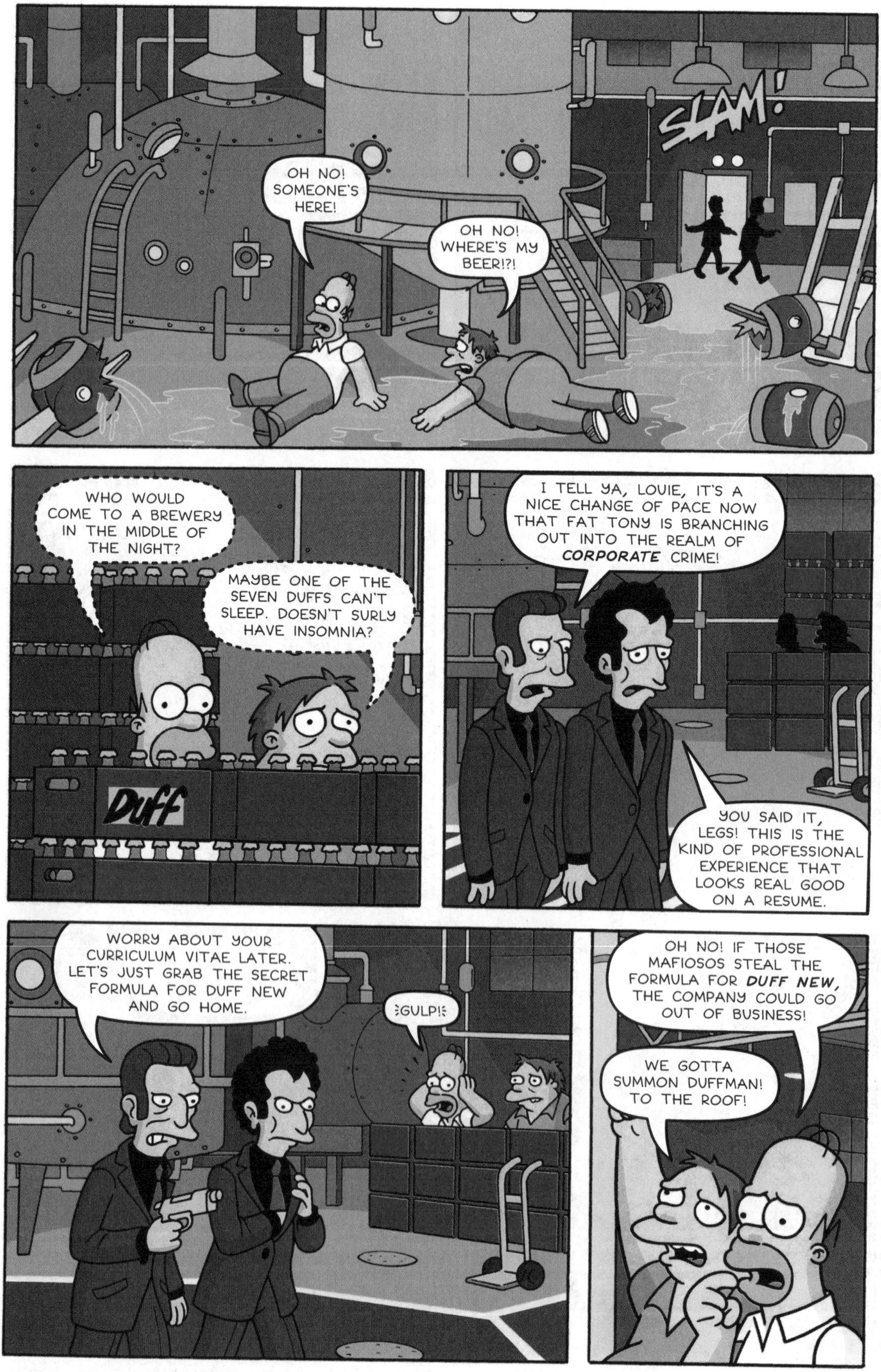
SLAM!
OH NO! SOMEONE'S HERE!
OH NO! WHERE'S MY BEER!?!
WHO WOULD COME TO A BREWERY IN THE MIDDLE OF THE NIGHT?
MAYBE ONE OF THE SEVEN DUFFS CAN'T SLEEP. DOESN'T SURLY HAVE INSOMNIA?
Duff
I TELL YA, LOUIE, IT'S A NICE CHANGE OF PACE NOW THAT FAT TONY IS BRANCHING OUT INTO THE REALM OF CORPORATE CRIME!
YOU SAID IT, LEGS! THIS IS THE KIND OF PROFESSIONAL EXPERIENCE THAT LOOKS REAL GOOD ON A RESUME.
WORRY ABOUT YOUR CURRICULUM VITAE LATER. LET'S JUST GRAB THE SECRET FORMULA FOR DUFF NEW AND GO HOME.
GULP!
OH NO! IF THOSE MAFIOSOS STEAL THE FORMULA FOR DUFF NEW, THE COMPANY COULD GO OUT OF BUSINESS!
WE GOTTA SUMMON DUFFMAN! TO THE ROOF!

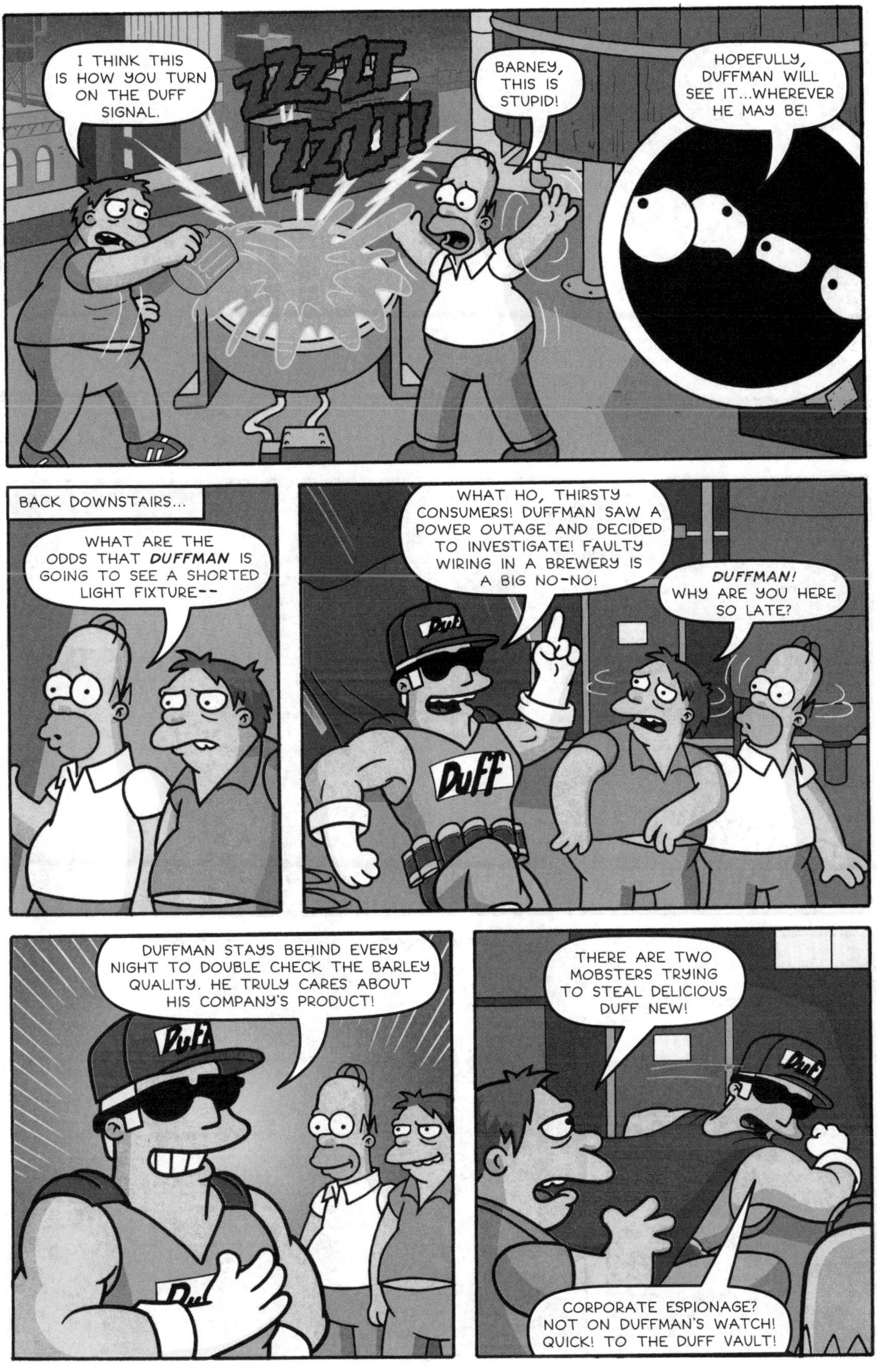
I THINK THIS IS HOW YOU TURN ON THE DUFF SIGNAL.
ZZZZLT ZZZZLT!
BARNEY, THIS IS STUPID!
HOPEFULLY, DUFFMAN WILL SEE IT...WHEREVER HE MAY BE!
BACK DOWNSTAIRS...
WHAT ARE THE ODDS THAT DUFFMAN IS GOING TO SEE A SHORTED LIGHT FIXTURE--
WHAT HO, THIRSTY CONSUMERS! DUFFMAN SAW A POWER OUTAGE AND DECIDED TO INVESTIGATE! FAULTY WIRING IN A BREWERY IS A BIG NO-NO!
DUFFMAN! WHY ARE YOU HERE SO LATE?
DUFFMAN STAYS BEHIND EVERY NIGHT TO DOUBLE CHECK THE BARLEY QUALITY. HE TRULY CARES ABOUT HIS COMPANY'S PRODUCT!
THERE ARE TWO MOBSTERS TRYING TO STEAL DELICIOUS DUFF NEW!
CORPORATE ESPIONAGE? NOT ON DUFFMAN'S WATCH! QUICK! TO THE DUFF VAULT!

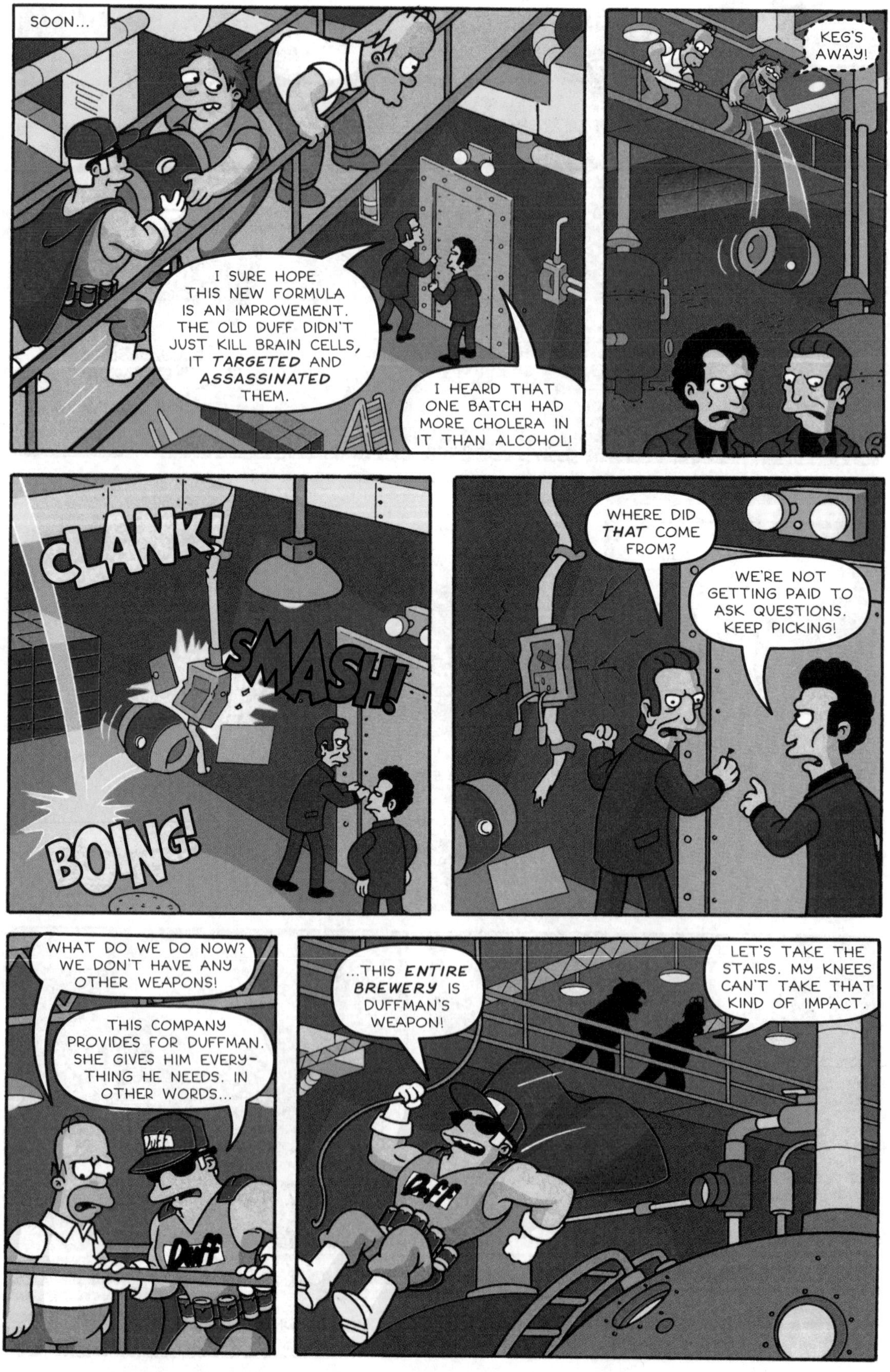
SOON...
I SURE HOPE THIS NEW FORMULA IS AN IMPROVEMENT. THE OLD DUFF DIDN'T JUST KILL BRAIN CELLS, IT TARGETED AND ASSASSINATED THEM.
I HEARD THAT ONE BATCH HAD MORE CHOLERA IN IT THAN ALCOHOL!
KEG'S AWAY!
CLANK!
SMASH!
BOING!
WHERE DID THAT COME FROM?
WE'RE NOT GETTING PAID TO ASK QUESTIONS. KEEP PICKING!
WHAT DO WE DO NOW? WE DON'T HAVE ANY OTHER WEAPONS!
THIS COMPANY PROVIDES FOR DUFFMAN. SHE GIVES HIM EVERY-THING HE NEEDS. IN OTHER WORDS...
...THIS ENTIRE BREWERY IS DUFFMAN'S WEAPON!
LET'S TAKE THE STAIRS. MY KNEES CAN'T TAKE THAT KIND OF IMPACT.

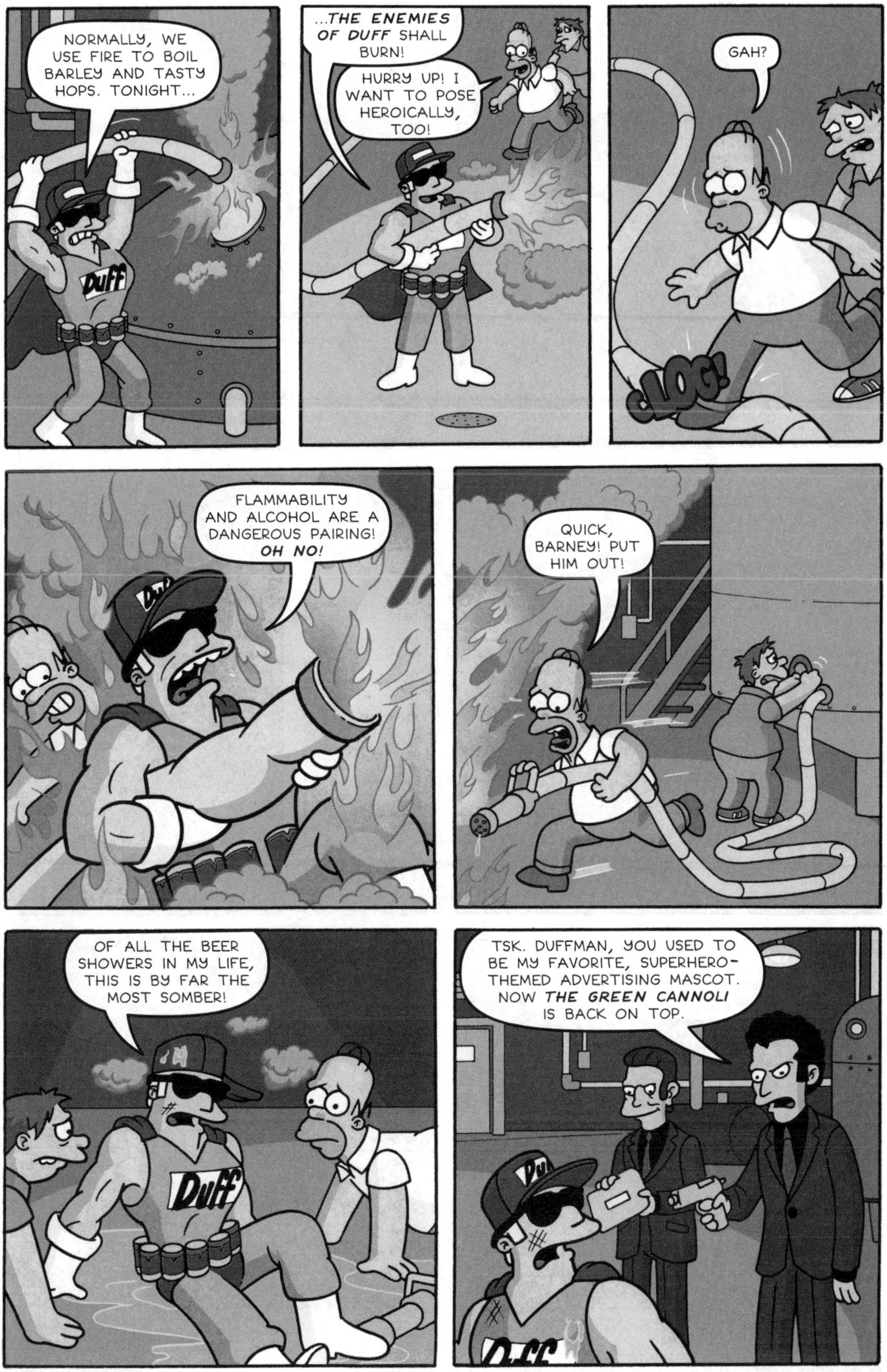
NORMALLY, WE USE FIRE TO BOIL BARLEY AND TASTY HOPS. TONIGHT...
...THE ENEMIES OF DUFF SHALL BURN!
HURRY UP! I WANT TO POSE HEROICALLY, TOO!
GAH?
CLOG!
FLAMMABILITY AND ALCOHOL ARE A DANGEROUS PAIRING! OH NO!
QUICK, BARNEY! PUT HIM OUT!
OF ALL THE BEER SHOWERS IN MY LIFE, THIS IS BY FAR THE MOST SOMBER!
TSK. DUFFMAN, YOU USED TO BE MY FAVORITE, SUPERHERO-THEMED ADVERTISING MASCOT. NOW THE GREEN CANNOLI IS BACK ON TOP.

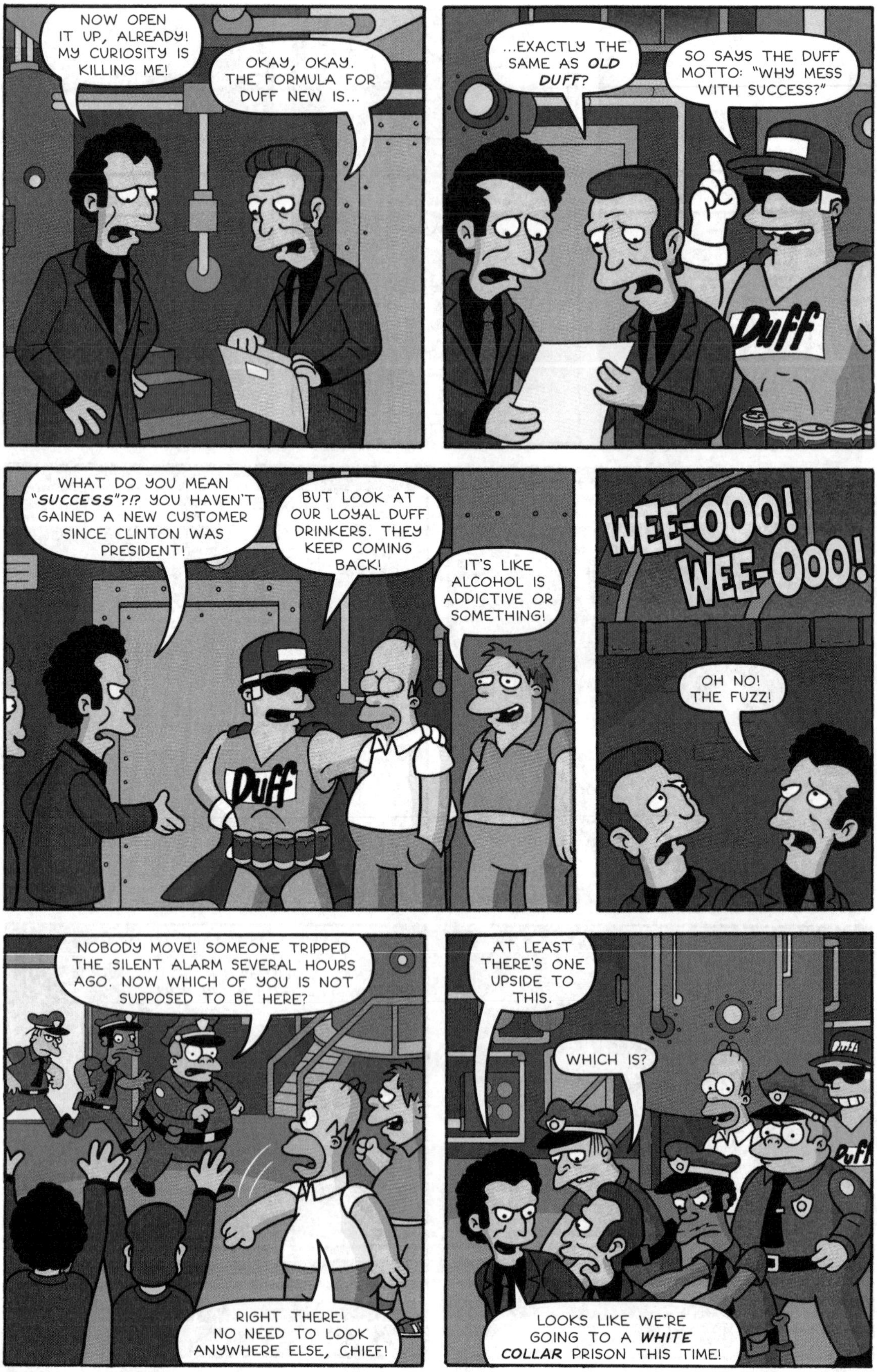

NOW OPEN IT UP, ALREADY! MY CURIOSITY IS KILLING ME!
OKAY, OKAY. THE FORMULA FOR DUFF NEW IS...
...EXACTLY THE SAME AS *OLD DUFF*?
SO SAYS THE DUFF MOTTO: "WHY MESS WITH SUCCESS?"
Duff
WHAT DO YOU MEAN "*SUCCESS*"?!? YOU HAVEN'T GAINED A NEW CUSTOMER SINCE CLINTON WAS PRESIDENT!
BUT LOOK AT OUR LOYAL DUFF DRINKERS. THEY KEEP COMING BACK!
IT'S LIKE ALCOHOL IS ADDICTIVE OR SOMETHING!
Duff
WEE-OOO! WEE-OOO!
OH NO! THE FUZZ!
NOBODY MOVE! SOMEONE TRIPPED THE SILENT ALARM SEVERAL HOURS AGO. NOW WHICH OF YOU IS NOT SUPPOSED TO BE HERE?
RIGHT THERE! NO NEED TO LOOK ANYWHERE ELSE, CHIEF!
AT LEAST THERE'S ONE UPSIDE TO THIS.
WHICH IS?
LOOKS LIKE WE'RE GOING TO A *WHITE COLLAR* PRISON THIS TIME!

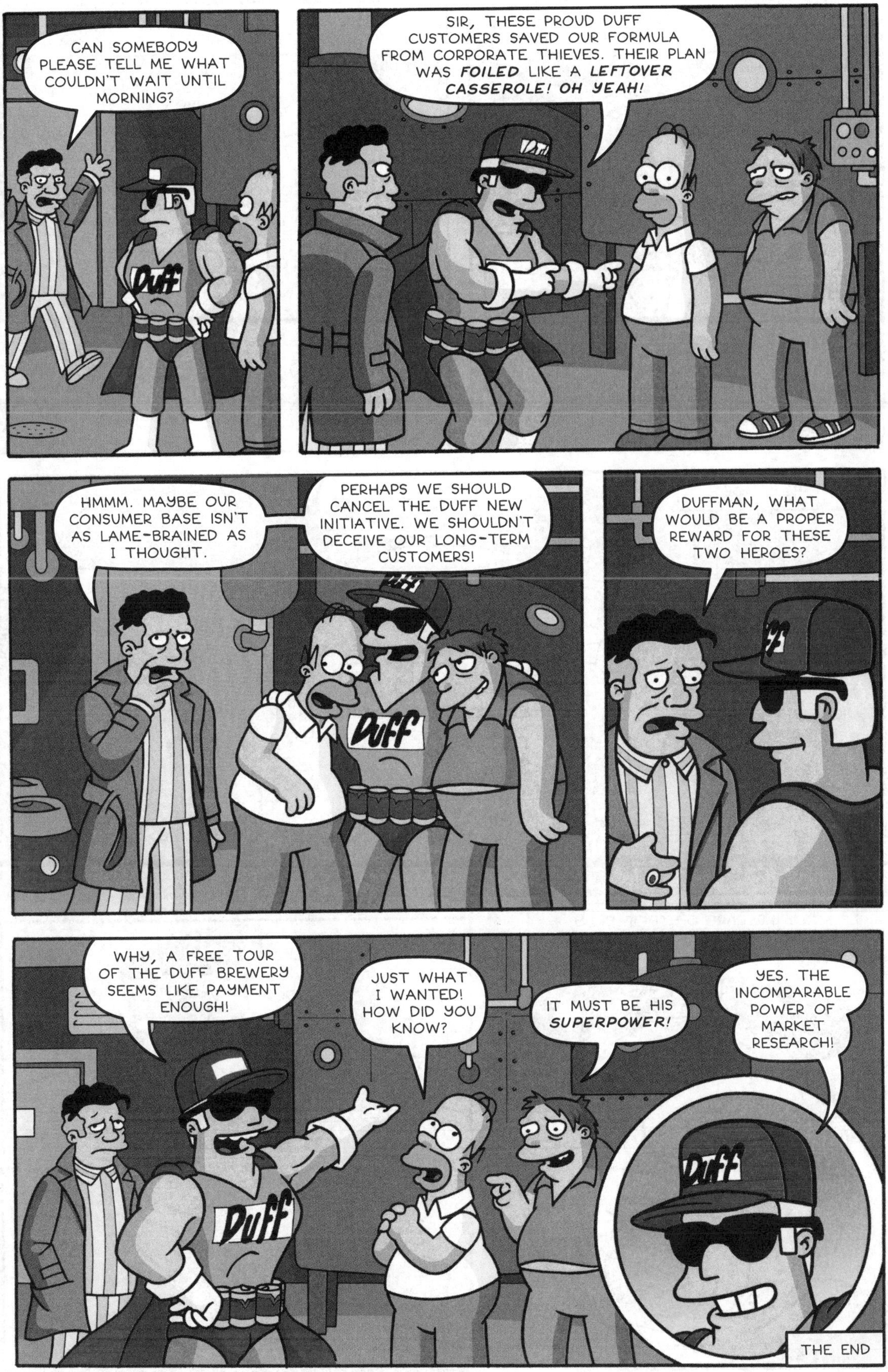
CAN SOMEBODY PLEASE TELL ME WHAT COULDN'T WAIT UNTIL MORNING?
SIR, THESE PROUD DUFF CUSTOMERS SAVED OUR FORMULA FROM CORPORATE THIEVES. THEIR PLAN WAS FOILED LIKE A LEFTOVER CASSEROLE! OH YEAH!
HMMM. MAYBE OUR CONSUMER BASE ISN'T AS LAME-BRAINED AS I THOUGHT.
PERHAPS WE SHOULD CANCEL THE DUFF NEW INITIATIVE. WE SHOULDN'T DECEIVE OUR LONG-TERM CUSTOMERS!
DUFFMAN, WHAT WOULD BE A PROPER REWARD FOR THESE TWO HEROES?
WHY, A FREE TOUR OF THE DUFF BREWERY SEEMS LIKE PAYMENT ENOUGH!
JUST WHAT I WANTED! HOW DID YOU KNOW?
IT MUST BE HIS SUPERPOWER!
YES. THE INCOMPARABLE POWER OF MARKET RESEARCH!
THE END

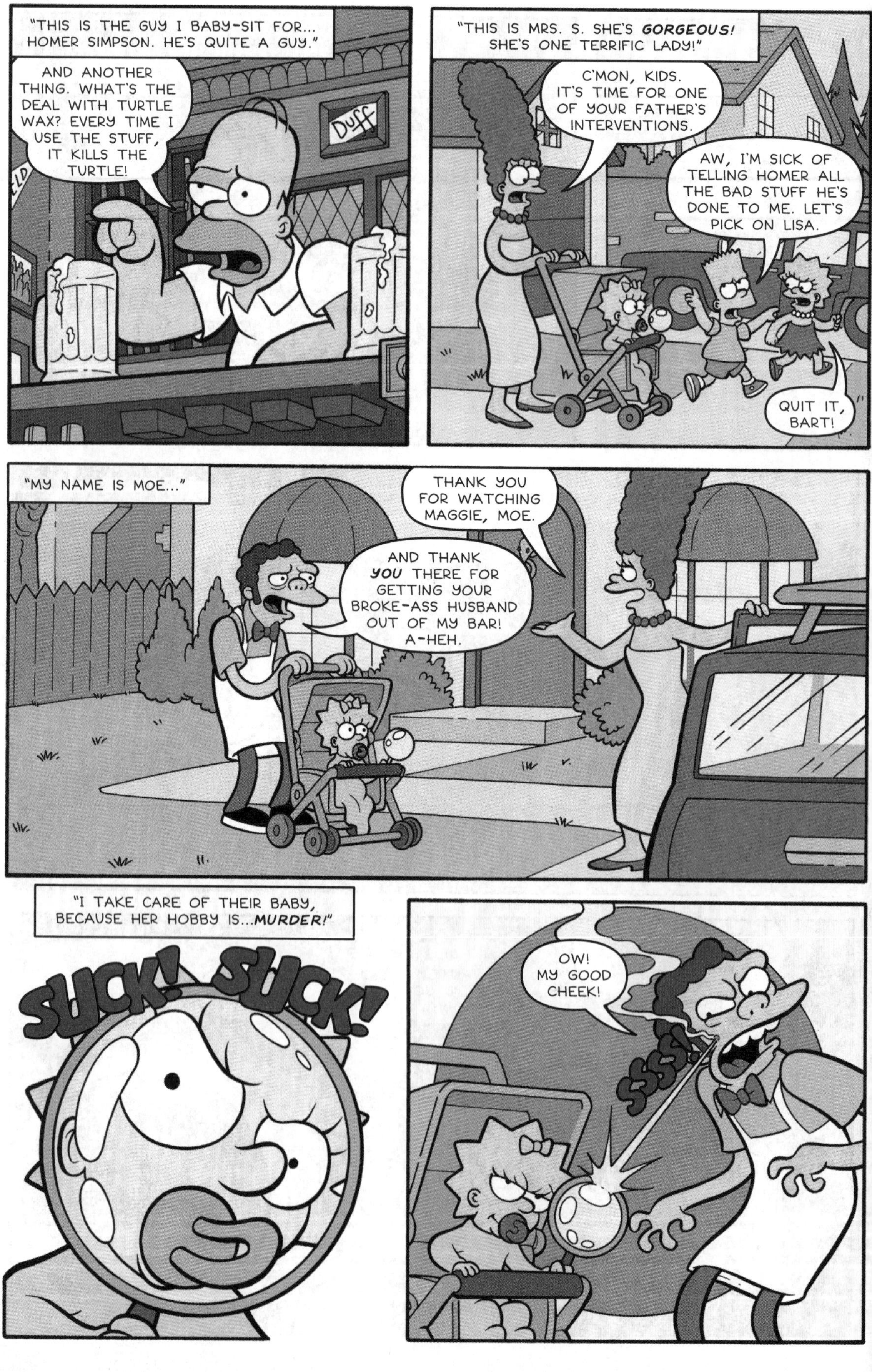
"THIS IS THE GUY I BABY-SIT FOR... HOMER SIMPSON. HE'S QUITE A GUY."
AND ANOTHER THING. WHAT'S THE DEAL WITH TURTLE WAX? EVERY TIME I USE THE STUFF, IT KILLS THE TURTLE!
Duff
"THIS IS MRS. S. SHE'S **GORGEOUS!** SHE'S ONE TERRIFIC LADY!"
C'MON, KIDS. IT'S TIME FOR ONE OF YOUR FATHER'S INTERVENTIONS.
AW, I'M SICK OF TELLING HOMER ALL THE BAD STUFF HE'S DONE TO ME. LET'S PICK ON LISA.
QUIT IT, BART!
"MY NAME IS MOE..."
THANK YOU FOR WATCHING MAGGIE, MOE.
AND THANK ***YOU*** THERE FOR GETTING YOUR BROKE-ASS HUSBAND OUT OF MY BAR! A-HEH.
"I TAKE CARE OF THEIR BABY, BECAUSE HER HOBBY IS...***MURDER!***"
SUCK! SUCK!
OW! MY GOOD CHEEK!

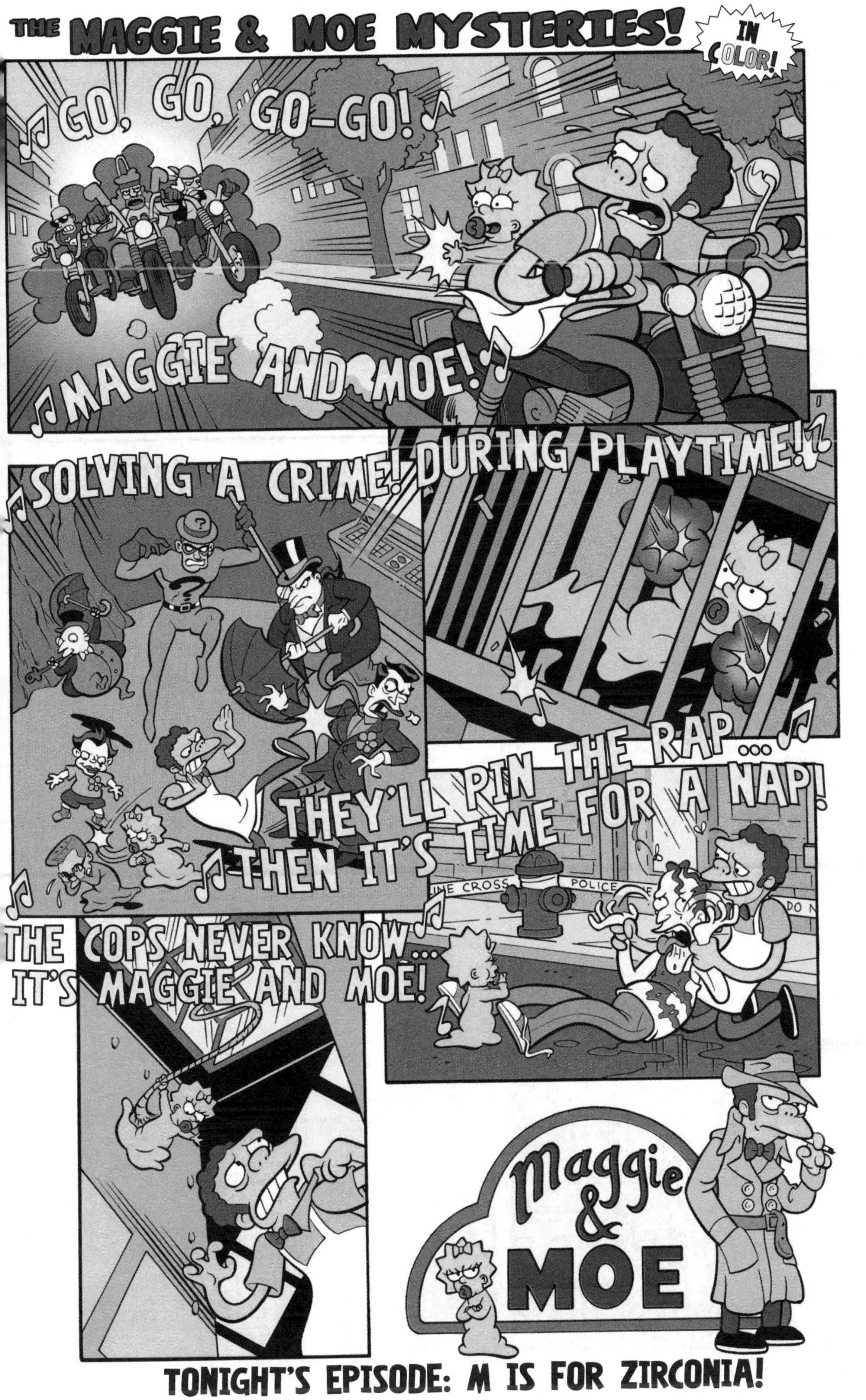

THE MAGGIE & MOE MYSTERIES!
IN COLOR!
GO, GO, GO-GO!
MAGGIE AND MOE!
SOLVING A CRIME! DURING PLAYTIME!
THEY'LL PIN THE RAP...
THEN IT'S TIME FOR A NAP!
POLICE
THE COPS NEVER KNOW...
IT'S MAGGIE AND MOE!
Maggie & MOE
TONIGHT'S EPISODE: M IS FOR ZIRCONIA!

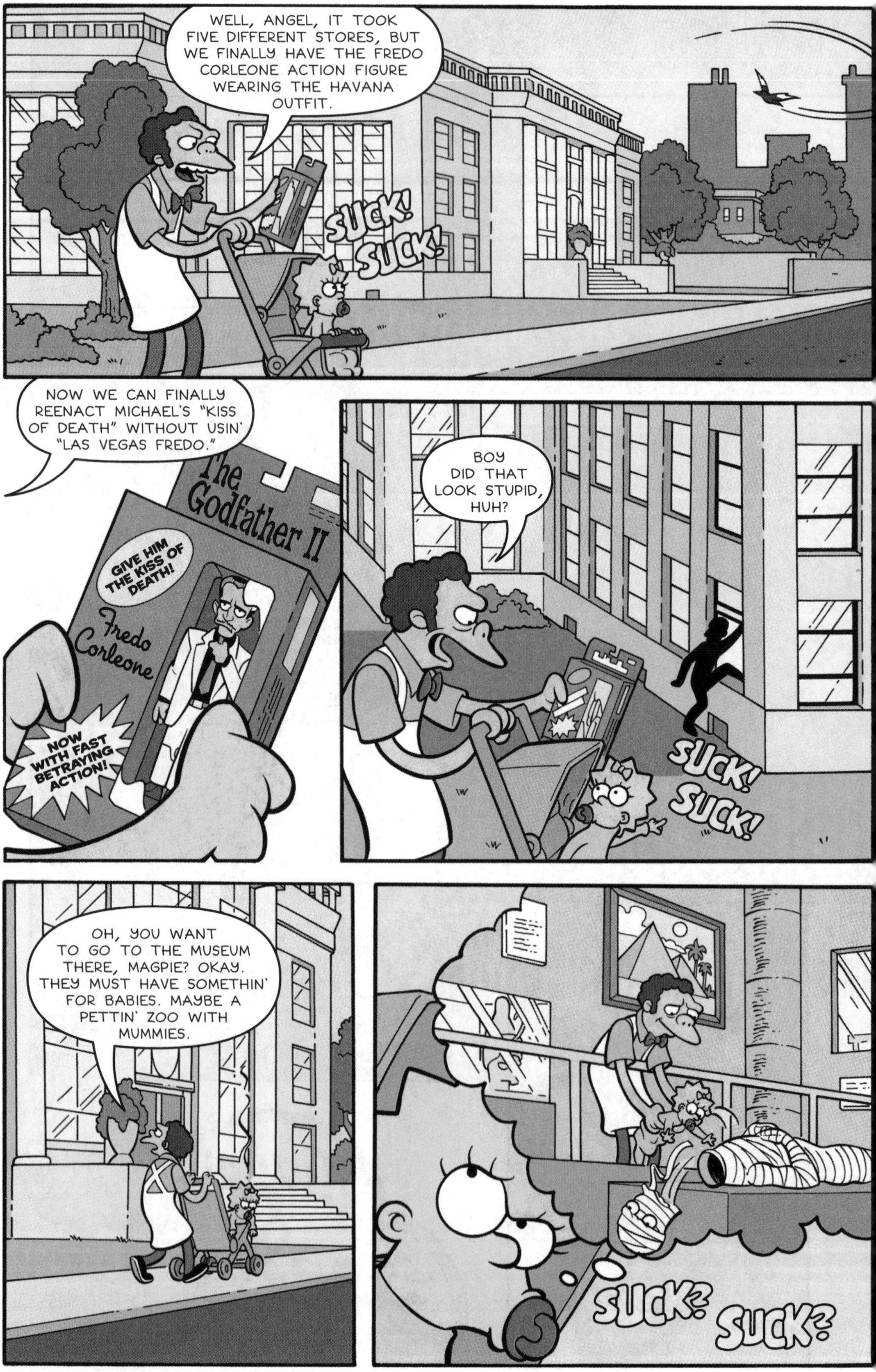

WELL, ANGEL, IT TOOK FIVE DIFFERENT STORES, BUT WE FINALLY HAVE THE FREDO CORLEONE ACTION FIGURE WEARING THE HAVANA OUTFIT.
SUCK! SUCK!
NOW WE CAN FINALLY REENACT MICHAEL'S "KISS OF DEATH" WITHOUT USIN' "LAS VEGAS FREDO."
The Godfather II
GIVE HIM THE KISS OF DEATH!
Fredo Corleone
NOW WITH FAST BETRAYING ACTION!
BOY DID THAT LOOK STUPID, HUH?
SUCK! SUCK!
OH, YOU WANT TO GO TO THE MUSEUM THERE, MAGPIE? OKAY. THEY MUST HAVE SOMETHIN' FOR BABIES. MAYBE A PETTIN' ZOO WITH MUMMIES.
SUCK? SUCK?

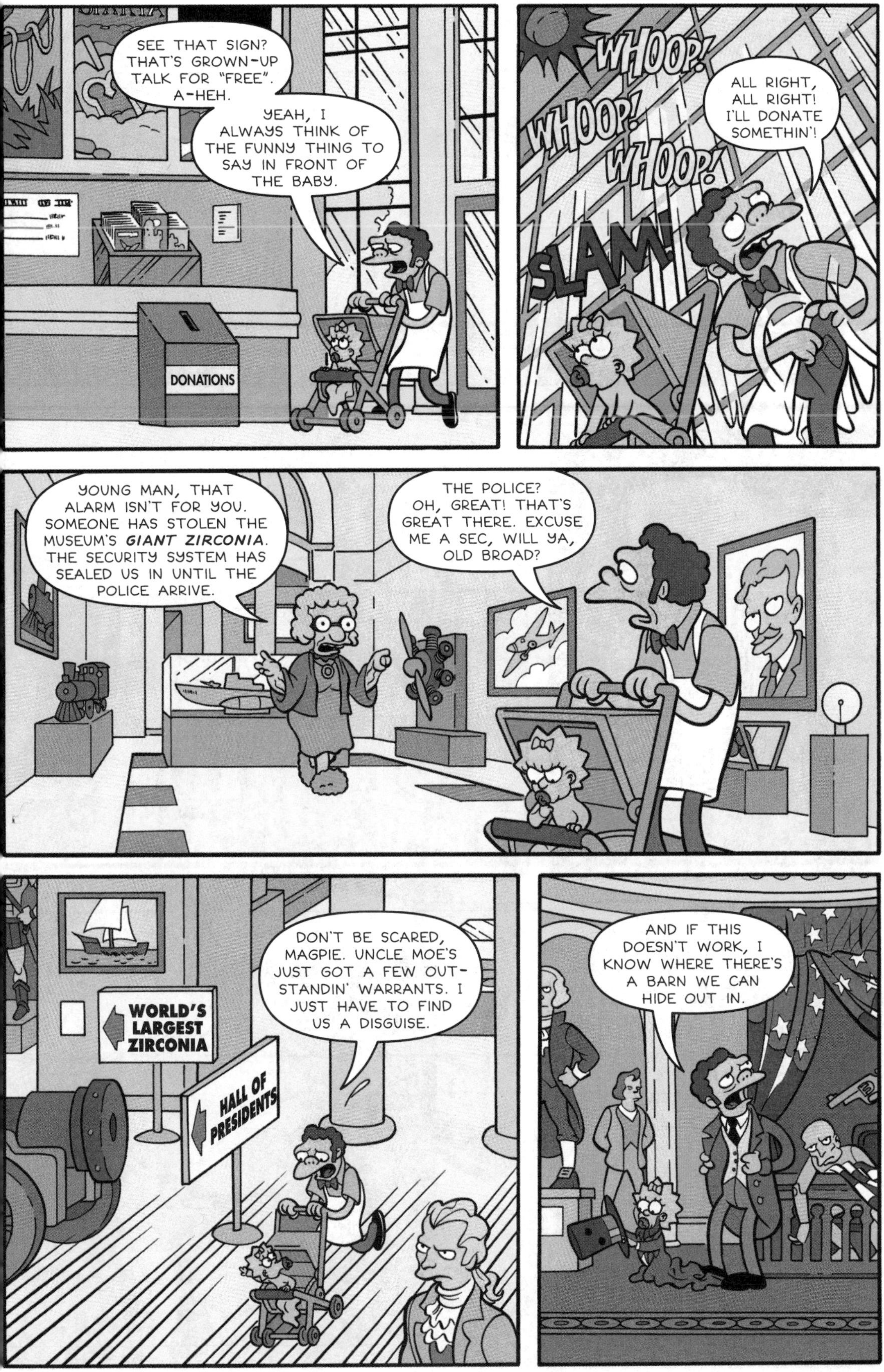
SEE THAT SIGN? THAT'S GROWN-UP TALK FOR "FREE". A-HEH.
YEAH, I ALWAYS THINK OF THE FUNNY THING TO SAY IN FRONT OF THE BABY.
DONATIONS
WHOOP! WHOOP! WHOOP!
ALL RIGHT, ALL RIGHT! I'LL DONATE SOMETHIN'!
SLAM!
YOUNG MAN, THAT ALARM ISN'T FOR YOU. SOMEONE HAS STOLEN THE MUSEUM'S *GIANT ZIRCONIA*. THE SECURITY SYSTEM HAS SEALED US IN UNTIL THE POLICE ARRIVE.
THE POLICE? OH, GREAT! THAT'S GREAT THERE. EXCUSE ME A SEC, WILL YA, OLD BROAD?
WORLD'S LARGEST ZIRCONIA
HALL OF PRESIDENTS
DON'T BE SCARED, MAGPIE. UNCLE MOE'S JUST GOT A FEW OUT-STANDIN' WARRANTS. I JUST HAVE TO FIND US A DISGUISE.
AND IF THIS DOESN'T WORK, I KNOW WHERE THERE'S A BARN WE CAN HIDE OUT IN.

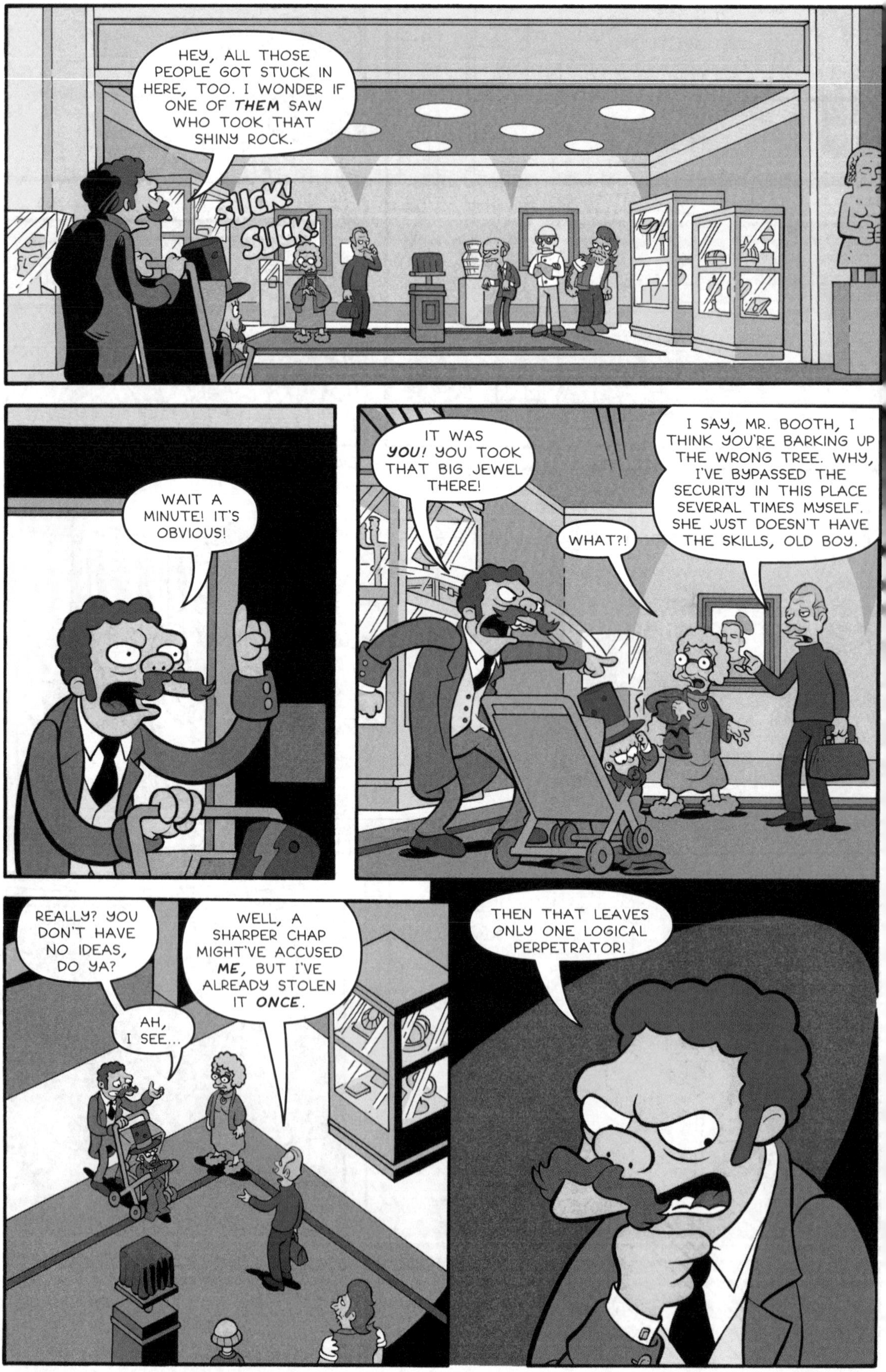

HEY, ALL THOSE PEOPLE GOT STUCK IN HERE, TOO. I WONDER IF ONE OF **THEM** SAW WHO TOOK THAT SHINY ROCK.
SUCK!
SUCK!
WAIT A MINUTE! IT'S OBVIOUS!
IT WAS ***YOU!*** YOU TOOK THAT BIG JEWEL THERE!
WHAT?!
I SAY, MR. BOOTH, I THINK YOU'RE BARKING UP THE WRONG TREE. WHY, I'VE BYPASSED THE SECURITY IN THIS PLACE SEVERAL TIMES MYSELF. SHE JUST DOESN'T HAVE THE SKILLS, OLD BOY.
REALLY? YOU DON'T HAVE NO IDEAS, DO YA?
AH, I SEE...
WELL, A SHARPER CHAP MIGHT'VE ACCUSED **ME**, BUT I'VE ALREADY STOLEN IT ***ONCE***.
THEN THAT LEAVES ONLY ONE LOGICAL PERPETRATOR!

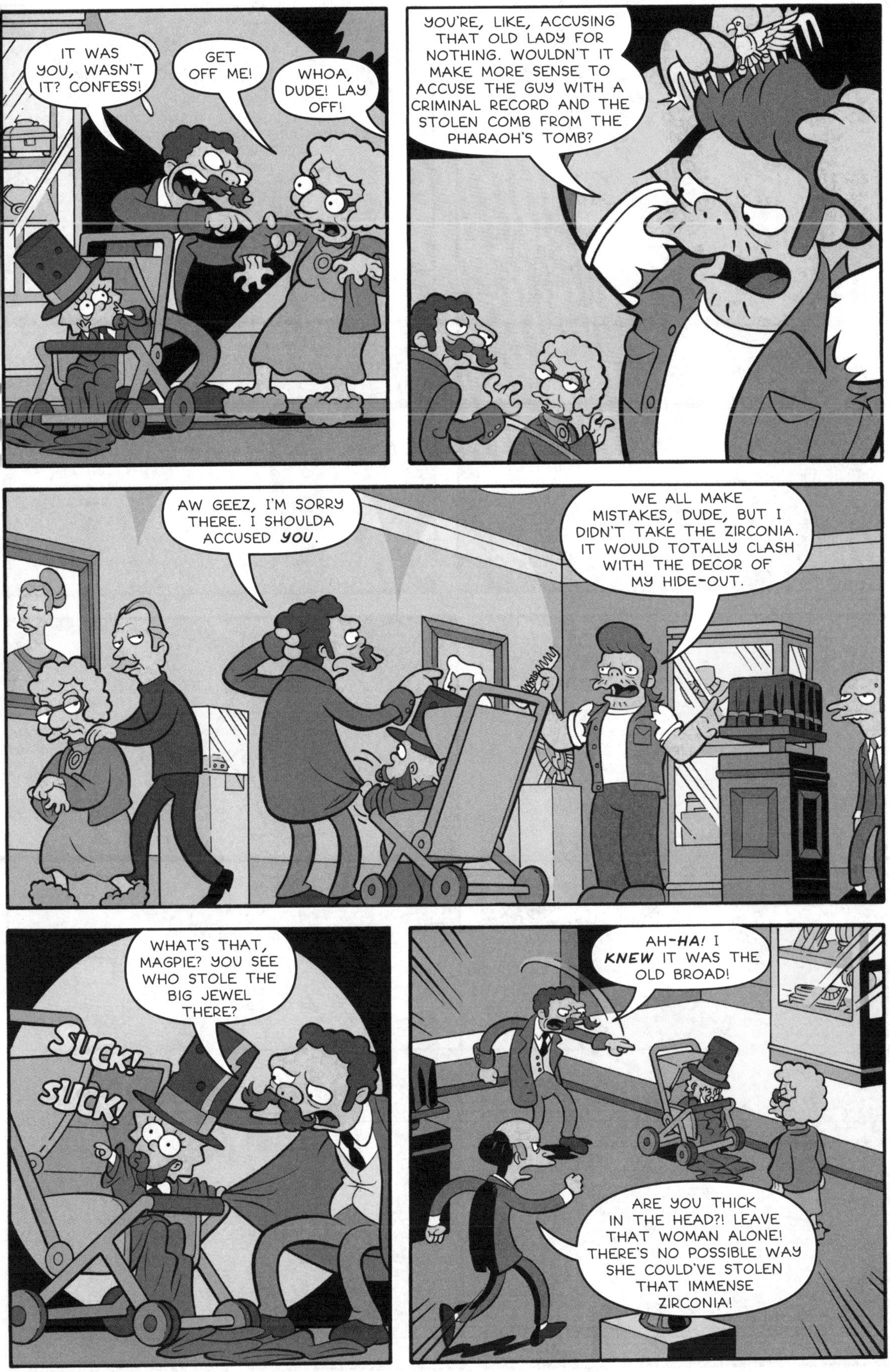
IT WAS YOU, WASN'T IT? CONFESS!
GET OFF ME!
WHOA, DUDE! LAY OFF!
YOU'RE, LIKE, ACCUSING THAT OLD LADY FOR NOTHING. WOULDN'T IT MAKE MORE SENSE TO ACCUSE THE GUY WITH A CRIMINAL RECORD AND THE STOLEN COMB FROM THE PHARAOH'S TOMB?
AW GEEZ, I'M SORRY THERE. I SHOULDA ACCUSED **YOU**.
WE ALL MAKE MISTAKES, DUDE, BUT I DIDN'T TAKE THE ZIRCONIA. IT WOULD TOTALLY CLASH WITH THE DECOR OF MY HIDE-OUT.
WHAT'S THAT, MAGPIE? YOU SEE WHO STOLE THE BIG JEWEL THERE?
SUCK!
SUCK!
AH-**HA**! I **KNEW** IT WAS THE OLD BROAD!
ARE YOU THICK IN THE HEAD?! LEAVE THAT WOMAN ALONE! THERE'S NO POSSIBLE WAY SHE COULD'VE STOLEN THAT IMMENSE ZIRCONIA!

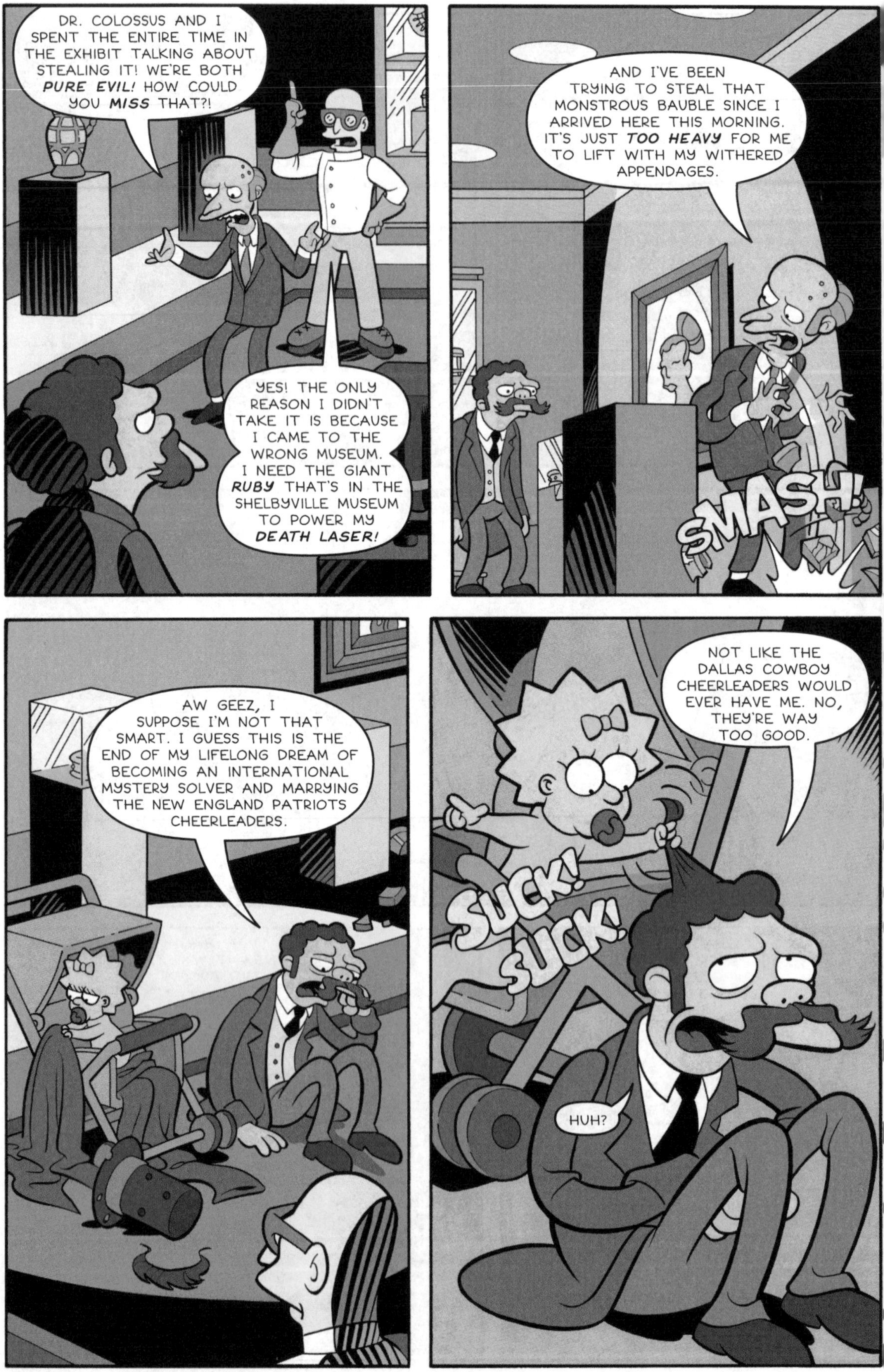
DR. COLOSSUS AND I SPENT THE ENTIRE TIME IN THE EXHIBIT TALKING ABOUT STEALING IT! WE'RE BOTH ***PURE EVIL!*** HOW COULD YOU ***MISS*** THAT?!
YES! THE ONLY REASON I DIDN'T TAKE IT IS BECAUSE I CAME TO THE WRONG MUSEUM. I NEED THE GIANT ***RUBY*** THAT'S IN THE SHELBYVILLE MUSEUM TO POWER MY ***DEATH LASER!***
AND I'VE BEEN TRYING TO STEAL THAT MONSTROUS BAUBLE SINCE I ARRIVED HERE THIS MORNING. IT'S JUST ***TOO HEAVY*** FOR ME TO LIFT WITH MY WITHERED APPENDAGES.
SMASH!
AW GEEZ, I SUPPOSE I'M NOT THAT SMART. I GUESS THIS IS THE END OF MY LIFELONG DREAM OF BECOMING AN INTERNATIONAL MYSTERY SOLVER AND MARRYING THE NEW ENGLAND PATRIOTS CHEERLEADERS.
NOT LIKE THE DALLAS COWBOY CHEERLEADERS WOULD EVER HAVE ME. NO, THEY'RE WAY TOO GOOD.
SUCK! SUCK!
HUH?

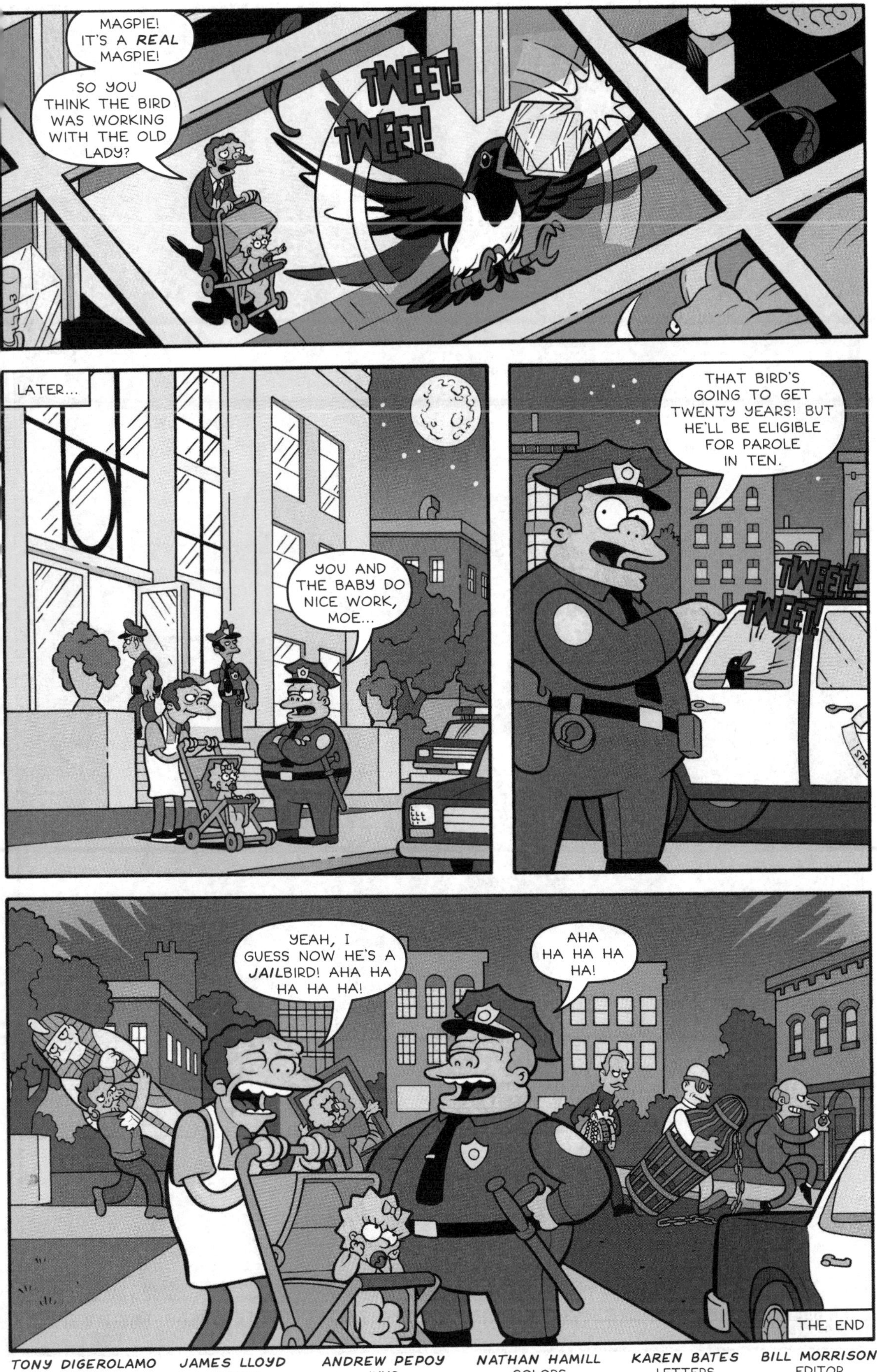
MAGPIE! IT'S A REAL MAGPIE!
SO YOU THINK THE BIRD WAS WORKING WITH THE OLD LADY?
TWEET! TWEET!
LATER...
YOU AND THE BABY DO NICE WORK, MOE...
THAT BIRD'S GOING TO GET TWENTY YEARS! BUT HE'LL BE ELIGIBLE FOR PAROLE IN TEN.
TWEET! TWEET!
YEAH, I GUESS NOW HE'S A JAILBIRD! AHA HA HA HA HA!
AHA HA HA HA HA!
THE END

TONY DIGEROLAMO SCRIPT · **JAMES LLOYD** PENCILS · **ANDREW PEPOY** INKS · **NATHAN HAMILL** COLORS · **KAREN BATES** LETTERS · **BILL MORRISON** EDITOR

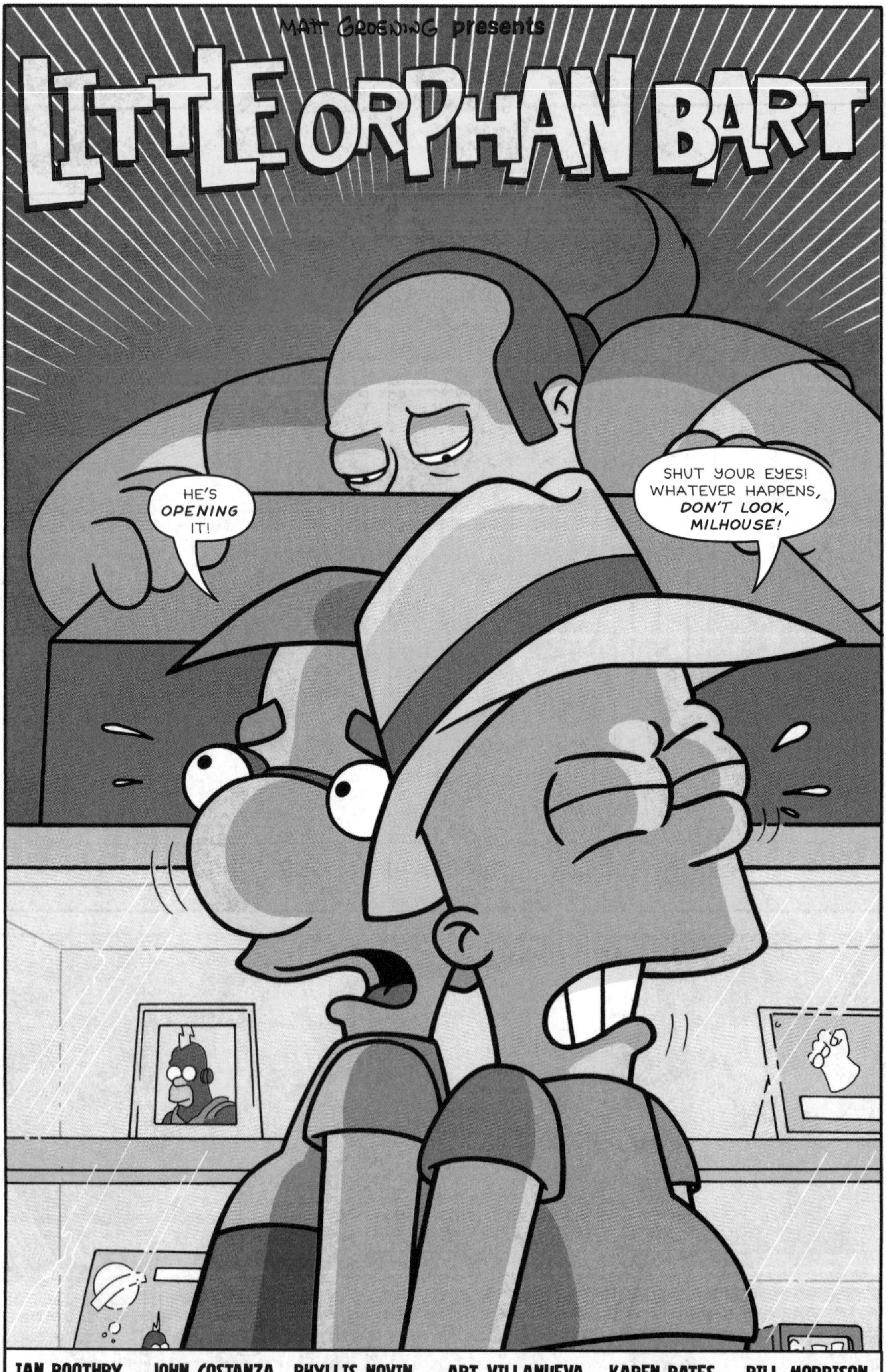
MATT GROENING presents
LITTLE ORPHAN BART
HE'S OPENING IT!
SHUT YOUR EYES! WHATEVER HAPPENS, DON'T LOOK, MILHOUSE!

IAN BOOTHBY SCRIPT | JOHN COSTANZA PENCILS | PHYLLIS NOVIN INKS | ART VILLANUEVA COLORS | KAREN BATES LETTERS | BILL MORRISON EDITOR

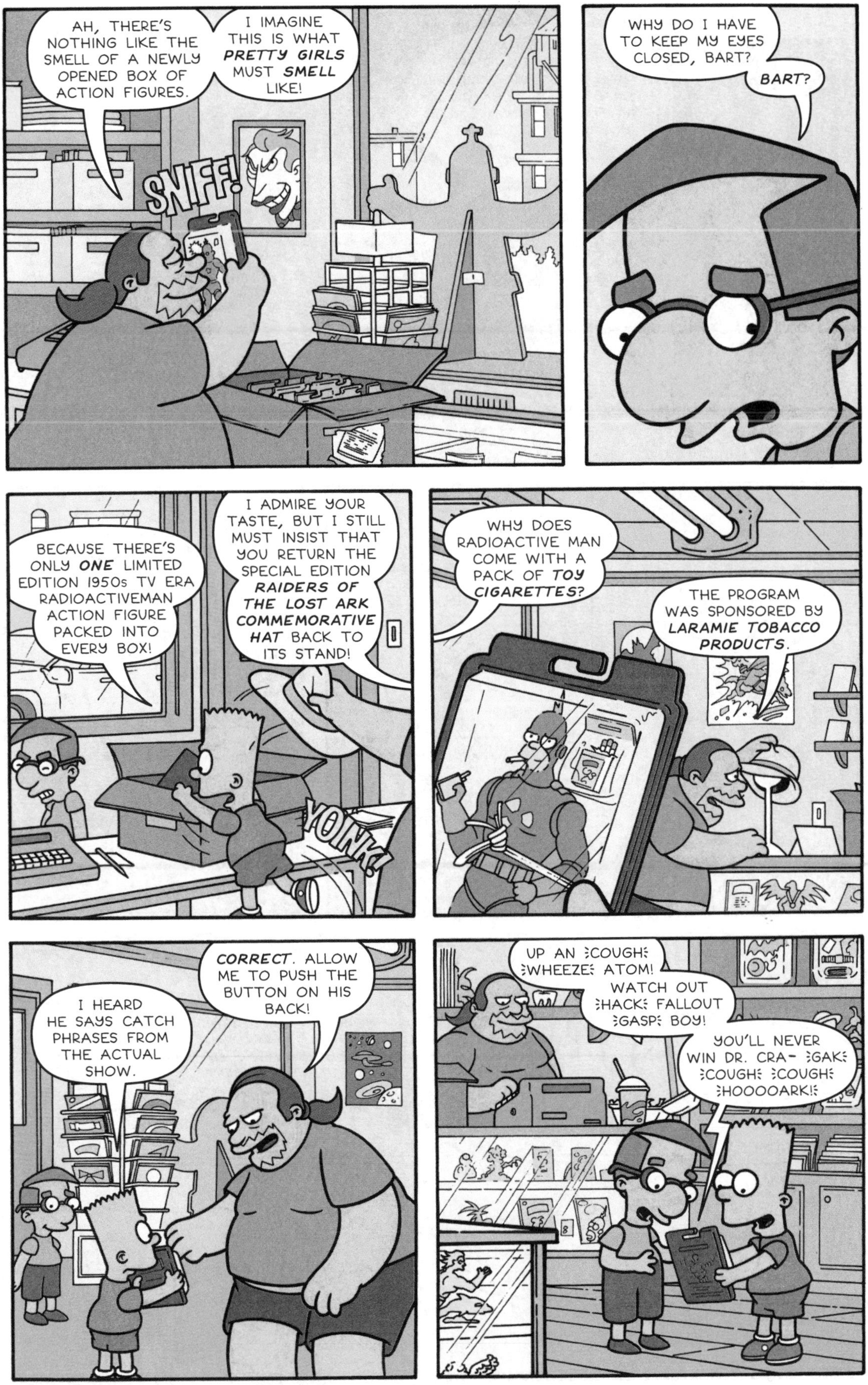
AH, THERE'S NOTHING LIKE THE SMELL OF A NEWLY OPENED BOX OF ACTION FIGURES.
I IMAGINE THIS IS WHAT PRETTY GIRLS MUST SMELL LIKE!
SNIFF!
WHY DO I HAVE TO KEEP MY EYES CLOSED, BART?
BART?
BECAUSE THERE'S ONLY ONE LIMITED EDITION 1950s TV ERA RADIOACTIVEMAN ACTION FIGURE PACKED INTO EVERY BOX!
I ADMIRE YOUR TASTE, BUT I STILL MUST INSIST THAT YOU RETURN THE SPECIAL EDITION RAIDERS OF THE LOST ARK COMMEMORATIVE HAT BACK TO ITS STAND!
YOINK!
WHY DOES RADIOACTIVE MAN COME WITH A PACK OF TOY CIGARETTES?
THE PROGRAM WAS SPONSORED BY LARAMIE TOBACCO PRODUCTS.
I HEARD HE SAYS CATCH PHRASES FROM THE ACTUAL SHOW.
CORRECT. ALLOW ME TO PUSH THE BUTTON ON HIS BACK!
UP AN ⁑COUGH⁑ ⁑WHEEZE⁑ ATOM!
WATCH OUT ⁑HACK⁑ FALLOUT ⁑GASP⁑ BOY!
YOU'LL NEVER WIN DR. CRA- ⁑GAK⁑ ⁑COUGH⁑ ⁑COUGH⁑ ⁑HOOOOARK!⁑

LATER...

YOU MAY HAVE KILLED OPTIMUS PRIME, HE-MAN, AND THAT GENERIC G.I.-JOE KNOCK-OFF DOLL FROM THE TRY-N-SAVE, BUT YOU'LL NEVER DEFEAT RADIOACTIVE MAN, *DR. CAT!*

CAN MAGGIE AND I PLAY DOLLS WITH YOU, BART?

I'M NOT PLAYING WITH *DOLLS*, THESE ARE *ACTION FIGURES!* THEY'RE *TOTALLY* DIFFERENT!

SUCK! SUCK!

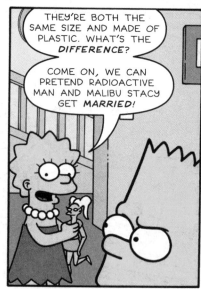

THEY'RE BOTH THE SAME SIZE AND MADE OF PLASTIC. WHAT'S THE *DIFFERENCE*?

COME ON, WE CAN PRETEND RADIOACTIVE MAN AND MALIBU STACY GET *MARRIED!*

C'MON, *RADIOACTIVE MAN!* THE *MAYOR'S* BEEN *KIDNAPPED!*

SORRY, OLD CHUM, I'M TOO *BUSY!* I HAD TO GET A *REAL JOB.* STACY'S *DREAM HOME* AND *DREAM CAR* DON'T PAY FOR THEMSELVES.

STILL, I CAN'T COMPLAIN. STACY'S WORKING THREE JOBS AS A *TEACHER, ASTRONAUT,* AND THE *PRESIDENT OF THE UNITED STATES!*

BYE, HON! IF THE PRIME MINISTER CALLS, I'M TEACHING A *KINDERGARTEN CLASS* ON MARS!

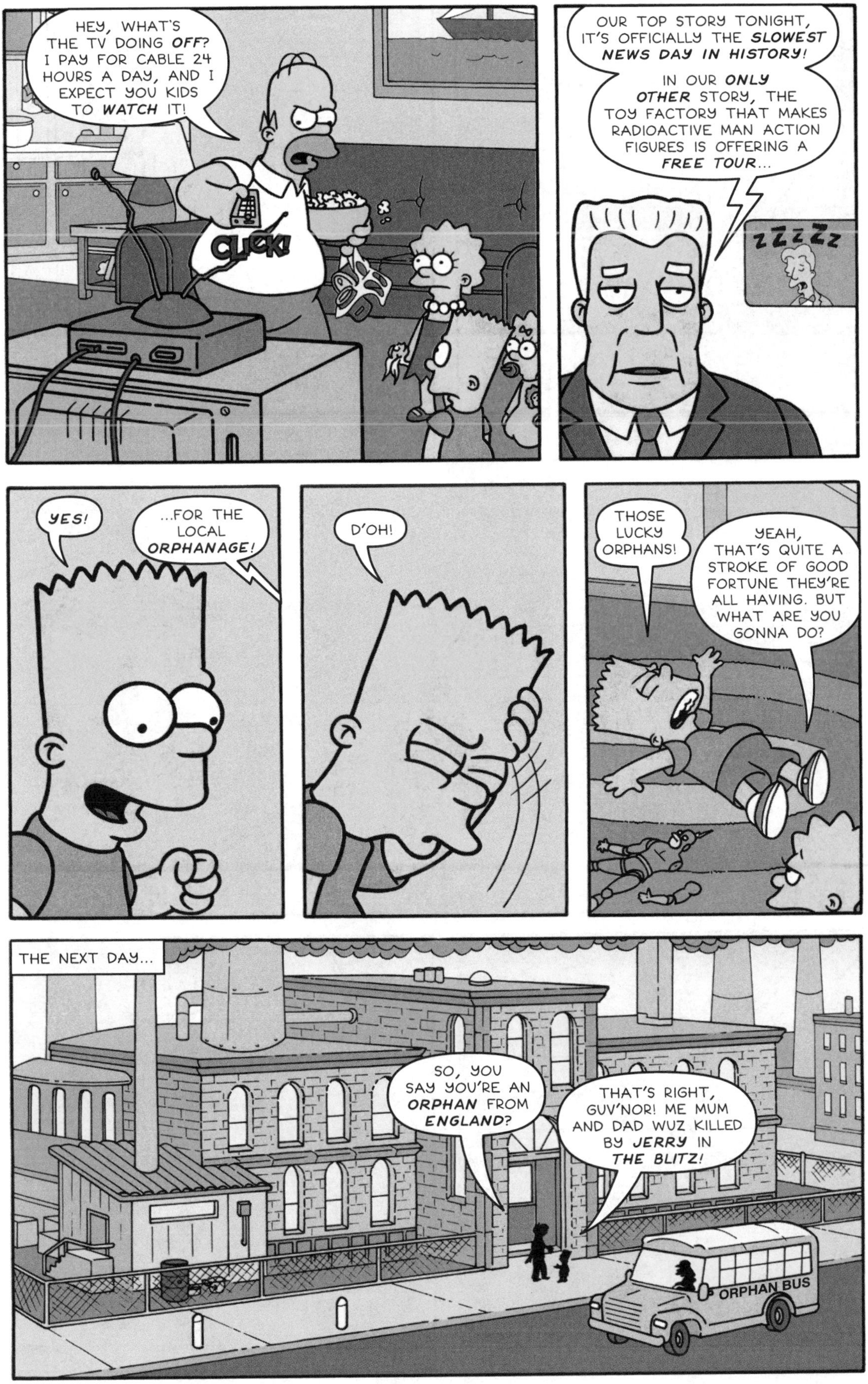
HEY, WHAT'S THE TV DOING OFF? I PAY FOR CABLE 24 HOURS A DAY, AND I EXPECT YOU KIDS TO WATCH IT!
CLICK!
OUR TOP STORY TONIGHT, IT'S OFFICIALLY THE SLOWEST NEWS DAY IN HISTORY!
IN OUR ONLY OTHER STORY, THE TOY FACTORY THAT MAKES RADIOACTIVE MAN ACTION FIGURES IS OFFERING A FREE TOUR...
ZZZZZ
YES!
...FOR THE LOCAL ORPHANAGE!
D'OH!
THOSE LUCKY ORPHANS!
YEAH, THAT'S QUITE A STROKE OF GOOD FORTUNE THEY'RE ALL HAVING. BUT WHAT ARE YOU GONNA DO?
THE NEXT DAY...
SO, YOU SAY YOU'RE AN ORPHAN FROM ENGLAND?
THAT'S RIGHT, GUV'NOR! ME MUM AND DAD WUZ KILLED BY JERRY IN THE BLITZ!
ORPHAN BUS

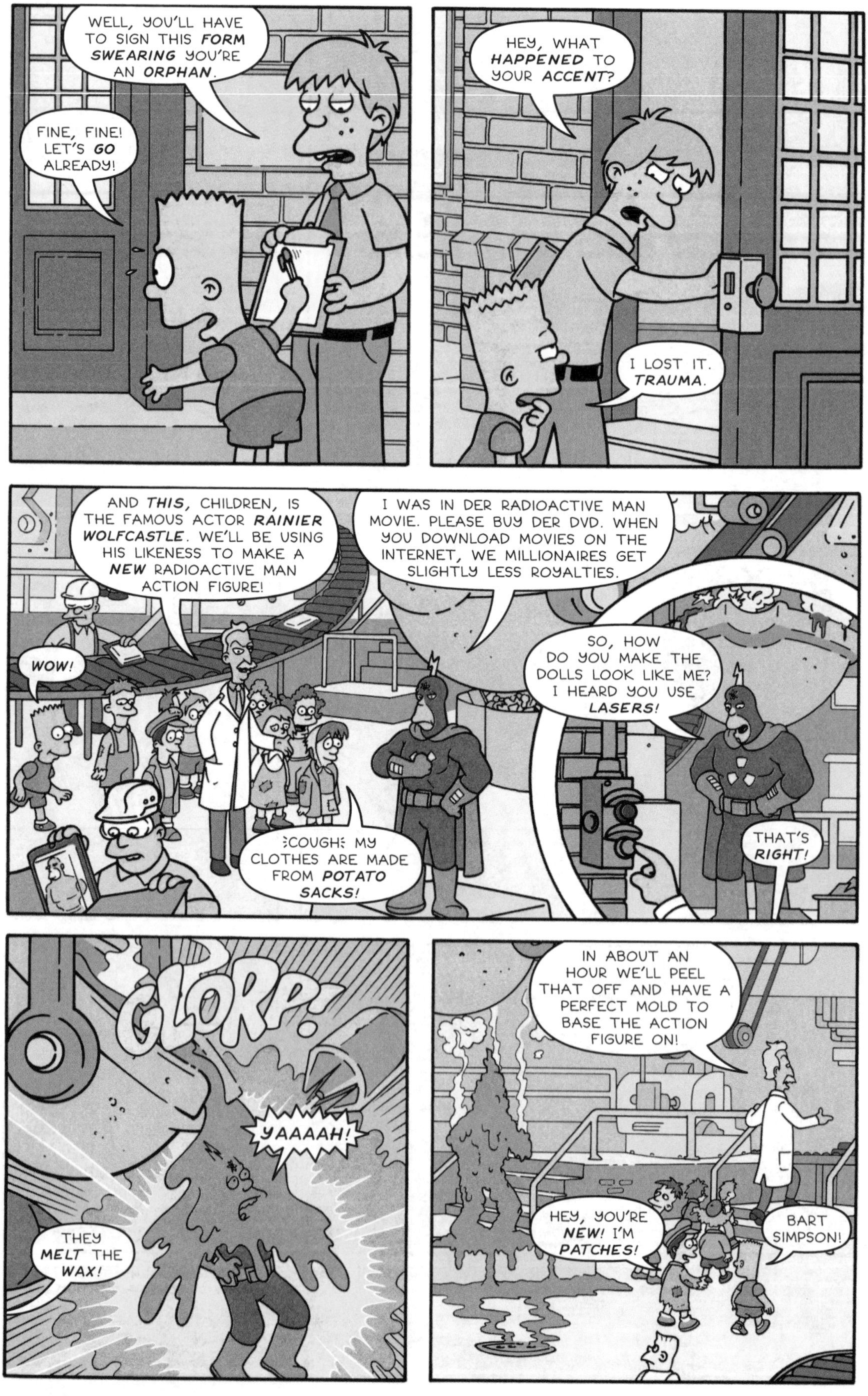
WELL, YOU'LL HAVE TO SIGN THIS FORM SWEARING YOU'RE AN ORPHAN.
FINE, FINE! LET'S GO ALREADY!
HEY, WHAT HAPPENED TO YOUR ACCENT?
I LOST IT. TRAUMA.
AND THIS, CHILDREN, IS THE FAMOUS ACTOR RAINIER WOLFCASTLE. WE'LL BE USING HIS LIKENESS TO MAKE A NEW RADIOACTIVE MAN ACTION FIGURE!
I WAS IN DER RADIOACTIVE MAN MOVIE. PLEASE BUY DER DVD. WHEN YOU DOWNLOAD MOVIES ON THE INTERNET, WE MILLIONAIRES GET SLIGHTLY LESS ROYALTIES.
WOW!
:COUGH: MY CLOTHES ARE MADE FROM POTATO SACKS!
SO, HOW DO YOU MAKE THE DOLLS LOOK LIKE ME? I HEARD YOU USE LASERS!
THAT'S RIGHT!
GLORP!
YAAAAH!
THEY MELT THE WAX!
IN ABOUT AN HOUR WE'LL PEEL THAT OFF AND HAVE A PERFECT MOLD TO BASE THE ACTION FIGURE ON!
HEY, YOU'RE NEW! I'M PATCHES!
BART SIMPSON!

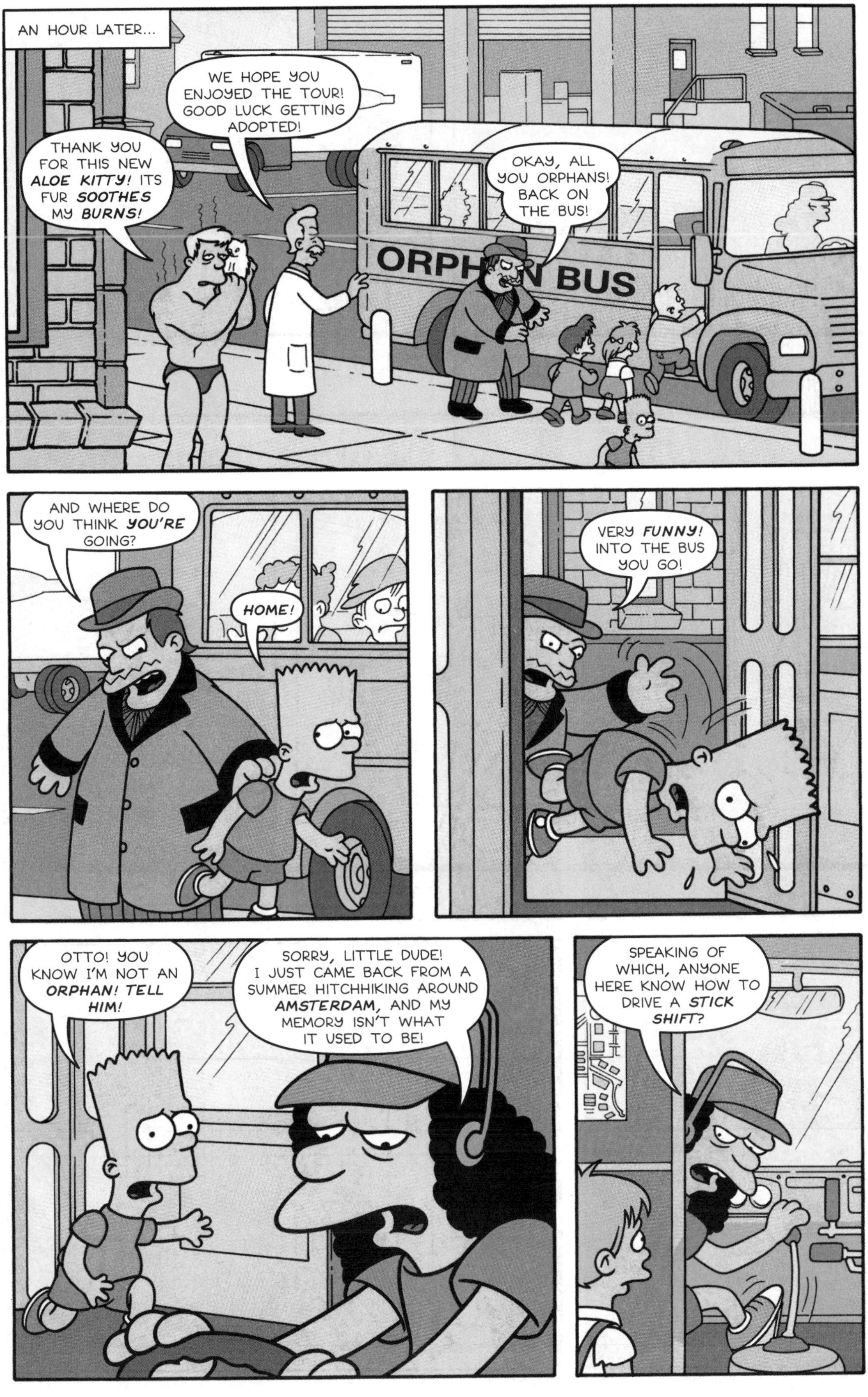
AN HOUR LATER...
THANK YOU FOR THIS NEW ALOE KITTY! ITS FUR SOOTHES MY BURNS!
WE HOPE YOU ENJOYED THE TOUR! GOOD LUCK GETTING ADOPTED!
OKAY, ALL YOU ORPHANS! BACK ON THE BUS!
ORPH N BUS
AND WHERE DO YOU THINK YOU'RE GOING?
HOME!
VERY FUNNY! INTO THE BUS YOU GO!
OTTO! YOU KNOW I'M NOT AN ORPHAN! TELL HIM!
SORRY, LITTLE DUDE! I JUST CAME BACK FROM A SUMMER HITCHHIKING AROUND AMSTERDAM, AND MY MEMORY ISN'T WHAT IT USED TO BE!
SPEAKING OF WHICH, ANYONE HERE KNOW HOW TO DRIVE A STICK SHIFT?

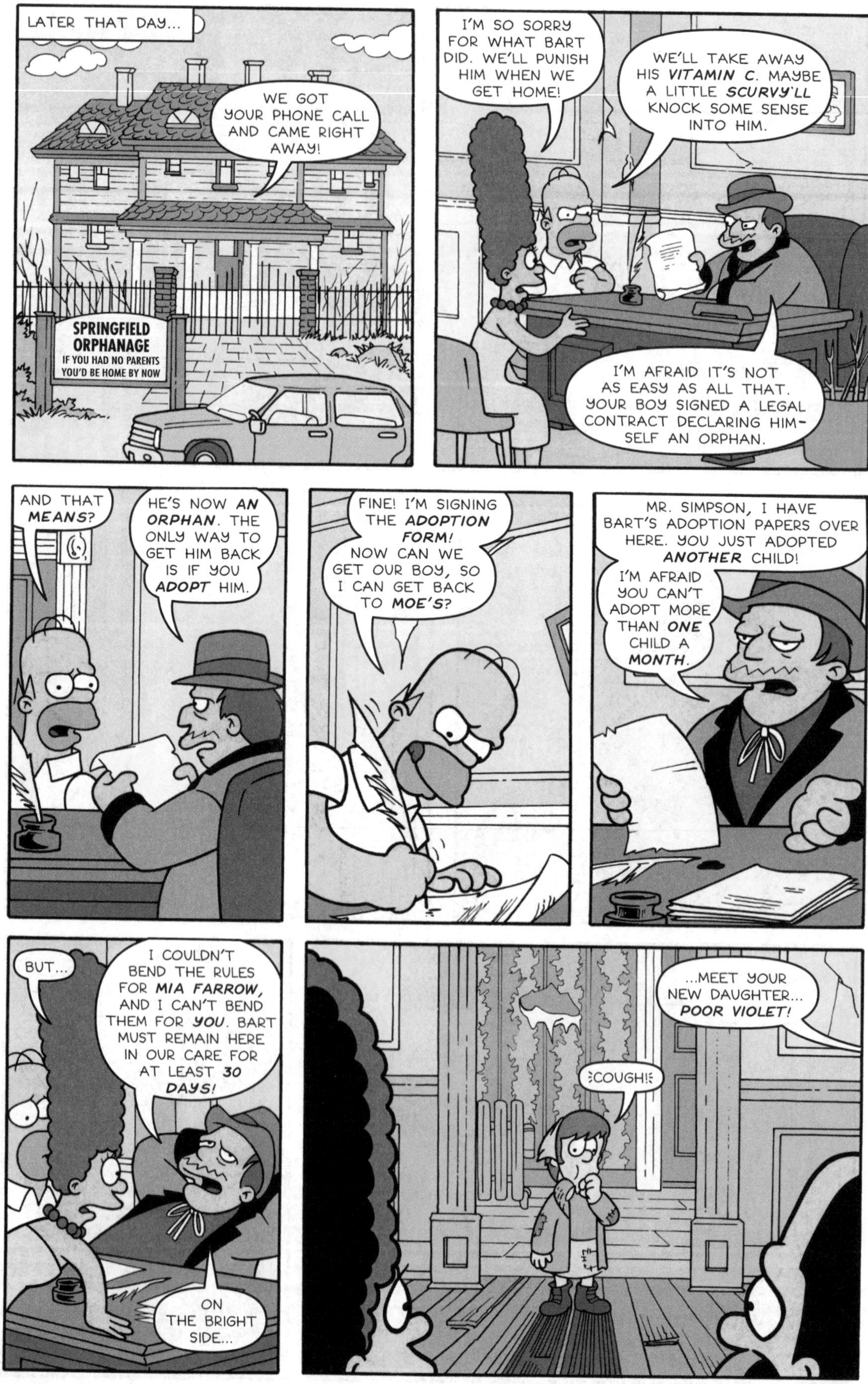
LATER THAT DAY...
WE GOT YOUR PHONE CALL AND CAME RIGHT AWAY!
SPRINGFIELD ORPHANAGE
IF YOU HAD NO PARENTS YOU'D BE HOME BY NOW
I'M SO SORRY FOR WHAT BART DID. WE'LL PUNISH HIM WHEN WE GET HOME!
WE'LL TAKE AWAY HIS VITAMIN C. MAYBE A LITTLE SCURVY'LL KNOCK SOME SENSE INTO HIM.
I'M AFRAID IT'S NOT AS EASY AS ALL THAT. YOUR BOY SIGNED A LEGAL CONTRACT DECLARING HIM-SELF AN ORPHAN.
AND THAT MEANS?
HE'S NOW AN ORPHAN. THE ONLY WAY TO GET HIM BACK IS IF YOU ADOPT HIM.
FINE! I'M SIGNING THE ADOPTION FORM! NOW CAN WE GET OUR BOY, SO I CAN GET BACK TO MOE'S?
MR. SIMPSON, I HAVE BART'S ADOPTION PAPERS OVER HERE. YOU JUST ADOPTED ANOTHER CHILD!
I'M AFRAID YOU CAN'T ADOPT MORE THAN ONE CHILD A MONTH.
BUT...
I COULDN'T BEND THE RULES FOR MIA FARROW, AND I CAN'T BEND THEM FOR YOU. BART MUST REMAIN HERE IN OUR CARE FOR AT LEAST 30 DAYS!
ON THE BRIGHT SIDE...
...MEET YOUR NEW DAUGHTER... POOR VIOLET!
COUGH!

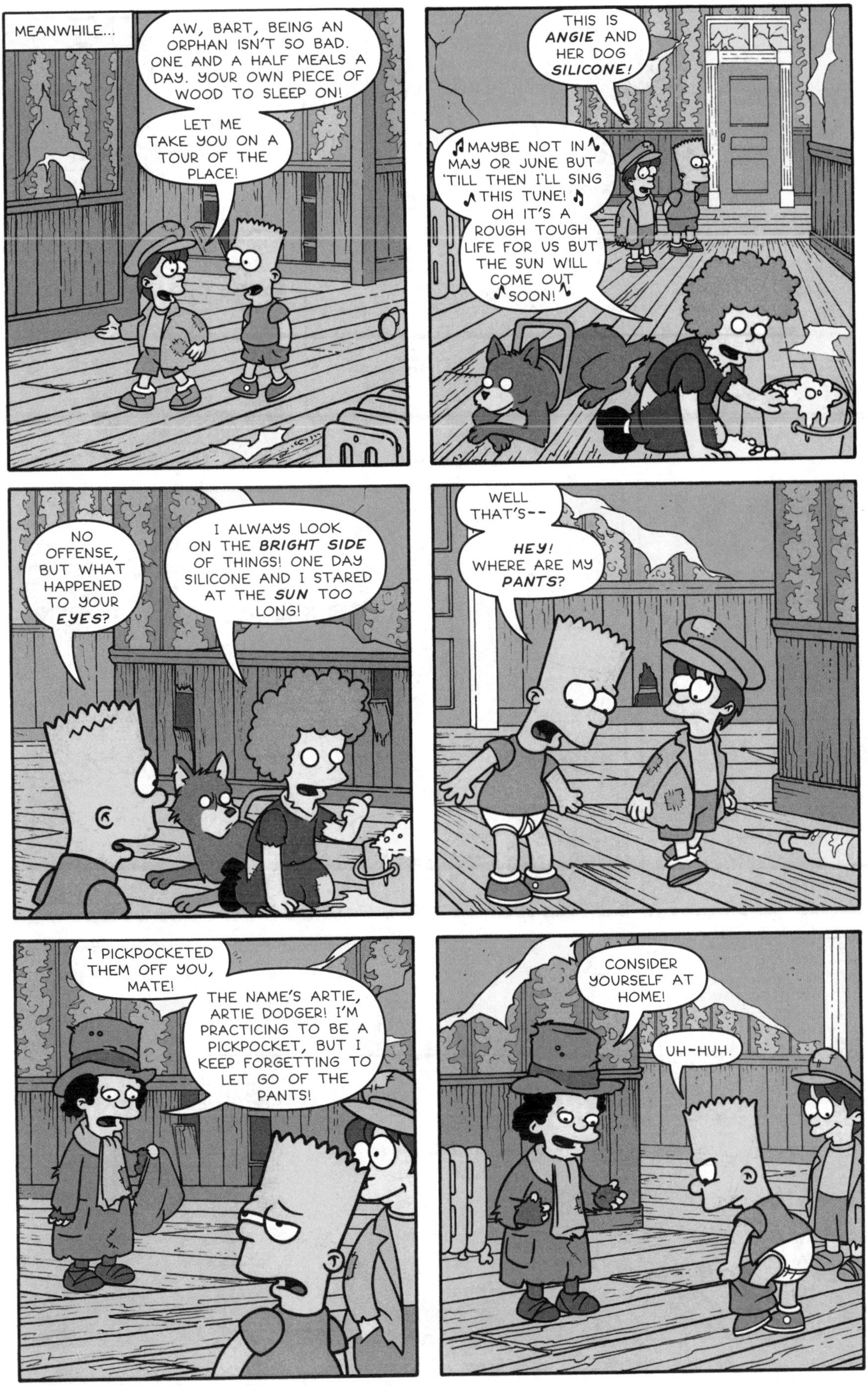
MEANWHILE...
AW, BART, BEING AN ORPHAN ISN'T SO BAD. ONE AND A HALF MEALS A DAY. YOUR OWN PIECE OF WOOD TO SLEEP ON!
LET ME TAKE YOU ON A TOUR OF THE PLACE!
THIS IS ANGIE AND HER DOG SILICONE!
♪ MAYBE NOT IN ♪ MAY OR JUNE BUT 'TILL THEN I'LL SING ♪ THIS TUNE! ♪ OH IT'S A ROUGH TOUGH LIFE FOR US BUT THE SUN WILL COME OUT ♪ SOON! ♪
NO OFFENSE, BUT WHAT HAPPENED TO YOUR EYES?
I ALWAYS LOOK ON THE BRIGHT SIDE OF THINGS! ONE DAY SILICONE AND I STARED AT THE SUN TOO LONG!
WELL THAT'S--
HEY! WHERE ARE MY PANTS?
I PICKPOCKETED THEM OFF YOU, MATE!
THE NAME'S ARTIE, ARTIE DODGER! I'M PRACTICING TO BE A PICKPOCKET, BUT I KEEP FORGETTING TO LET GO OF THE PANTS!
CONSIDER YOURSELF AT HOME!
UH-HUH.

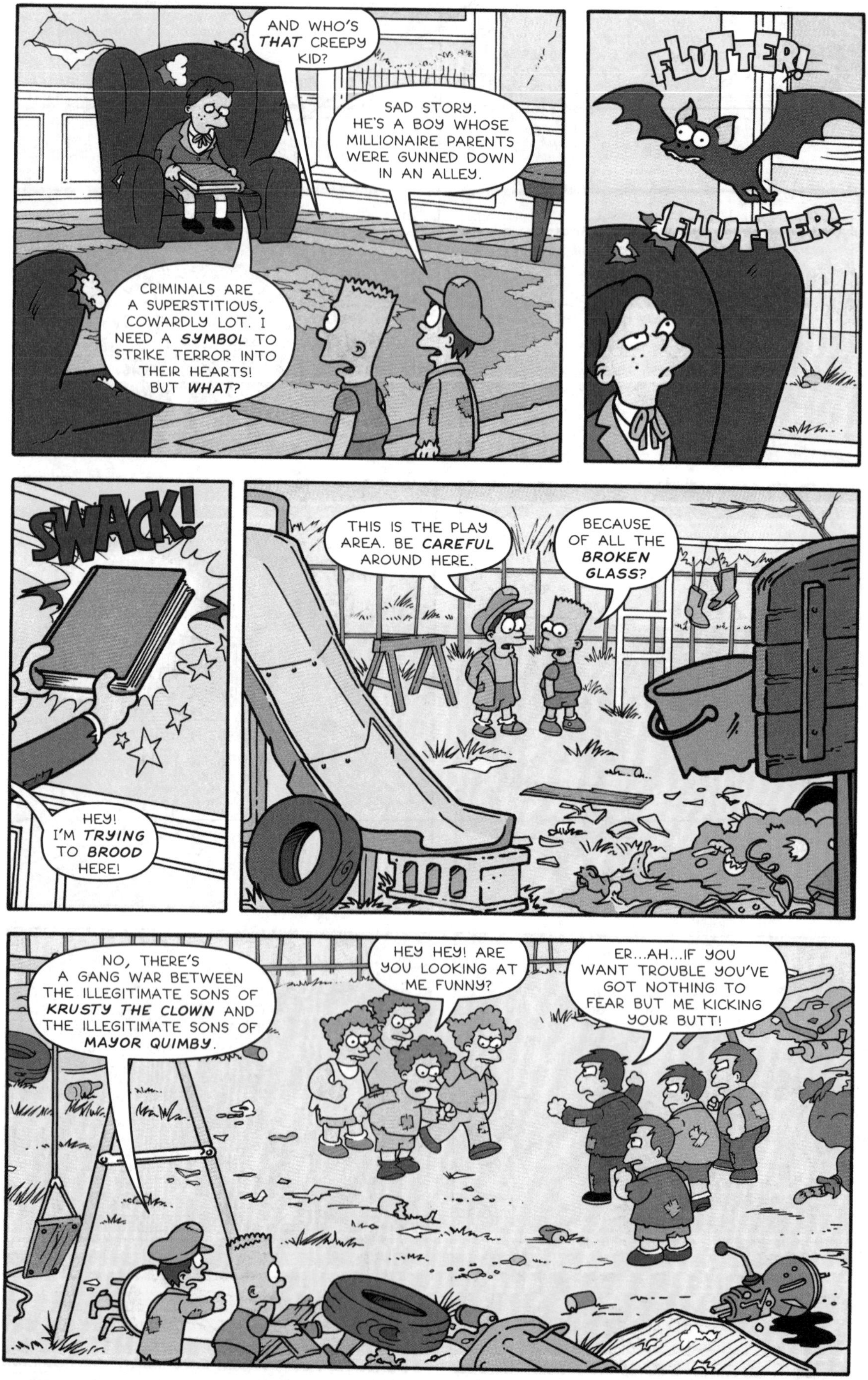

AND WHO'S THAT CREEPY KID?
SAD STORY. HE'S A BOY WHOSE MILLIONAIRE PARENTS WERE GUNNED DOWN IN AN ALLEY.
CRIMINALS ARE A SUPERSTITIOUS, COWARDLY LOT. I NEED A SYMBOL TO STRIKE TERROR INTO THEIR HEARTS! BUT WHAT?
FLUTTER!
FLUTTER!
SWACK!
HEY! I'M TRYING TO BROOD HERE!
THIS IS THE PLAY AREA. BE CAREFUL AROUND HERE.
BECAUSE OF ALL THE BROKEN GLASS?
NO, THERE'S A GANG WAR BETWEEN THE ILLEGITIMATE SONS OF KRUSTY THE CLOWN AND THE ILLEGITIMATE SONS OF MAYOR QUIMBY.
HEY HEY! ARE YOU LOOKING AT ME FUNNY?
ER...AH...IF YOU WANT TROUBLE YOU'VE GOT NOTHING TO FEAR BUT ME KICKING YOUR BUTT!

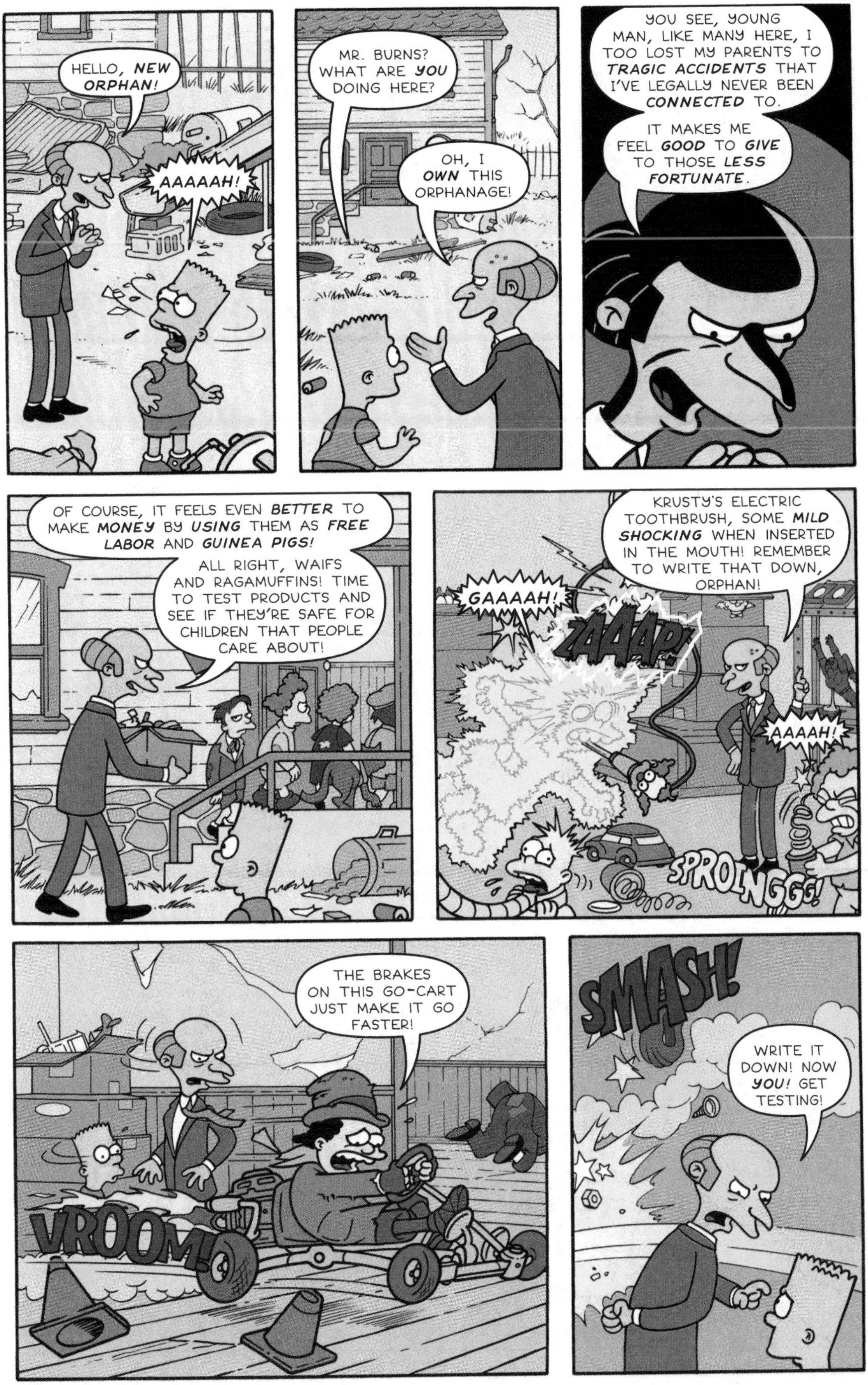
HELLO, NEW ORPHAN!
AAAAAH!
MR. BURNS? WHAT ARE YOU DOING HERE?
OH, I OWN THIS ORPHANAGE!
YOU SEE, YOUNG MAN, LIKE MANY HERE, I TOO LOST MY PARENTS TO TRAGIC ACCIDENTS THAT I'VE LEGALLY NEVER BEEN CONNECTED TO.
IT MAKES ME FEEL GOOD TO GIVE TO THOSE LESS FORTUNATE.
OF COURSE, IT FEELS EVEN BETTER TO MAKE MONEY BY USING THEM AS FREE LABOR AND GUINEA PIGS!
ALL RIGHT, WAIFS AND RAGAMUFFINS! TIME TO TEST PRODUCTS AND SEE IF THEY'RE SAFE FOR CHILDREN THAT PEOPLE CARE ABOUT!
KRUSTY'S ELECTRIC TOOTHBRUSH, SOME MILD SHOCKING WHEN INSERTED IN THE MOUTH! REMEMBER TO WRITE THAT DOWN, ORPHAN!
GAAAAH!
ZAAAP!
AAAAH!
SPROINGGG!
THE BRAKES ON THIS GO-CART JUST MAKE IT GO FASTER!
VROOM!
SMASH!
WRITE IT DOWN! NOW YOU! GET TESTING!

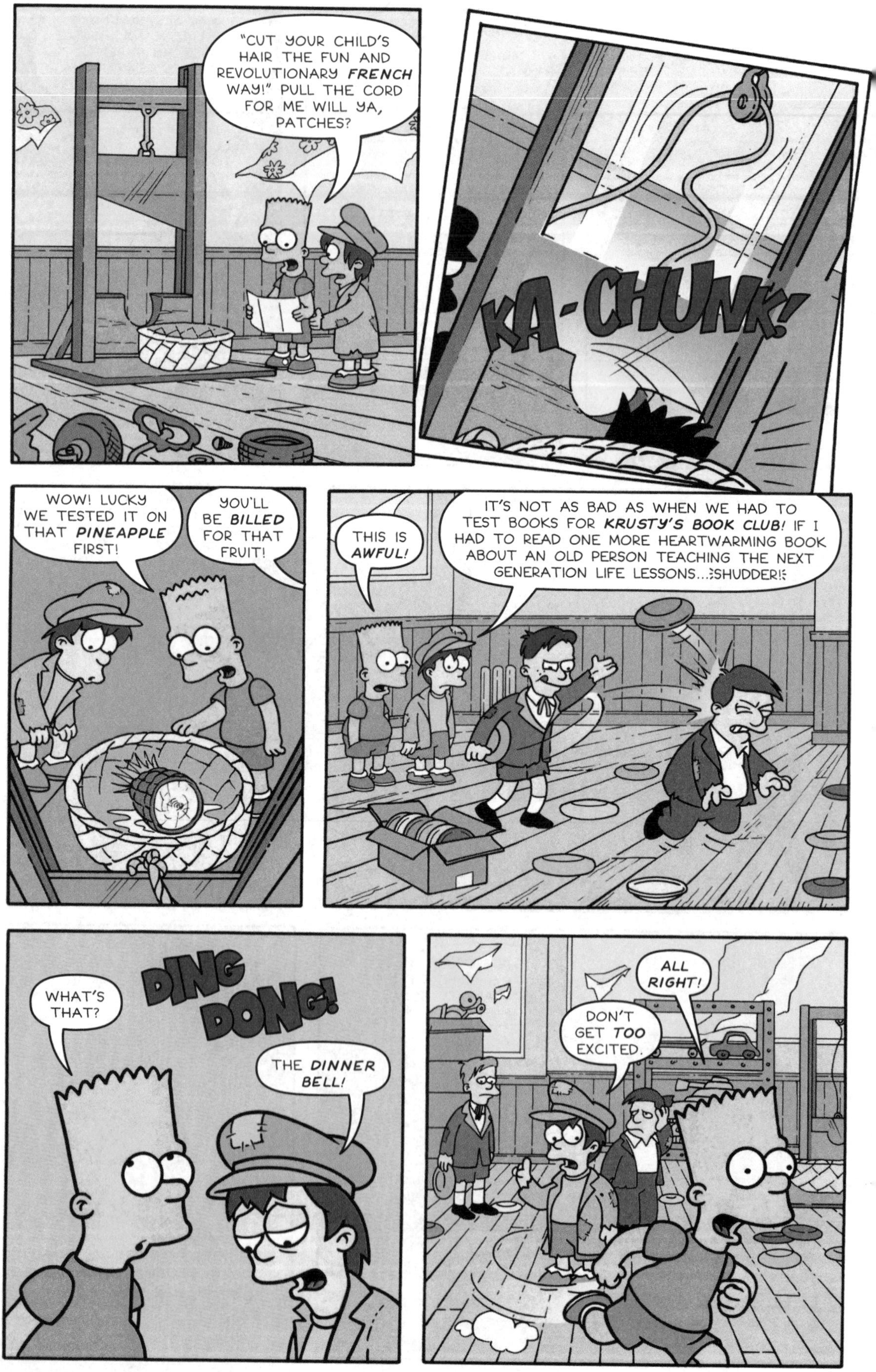
"CUT YOUR CHILD'S HAIR THE FUN AND REVOLUTIONARY *FRENCH* WAY!" PULL THE CORD FOR ME WILL YA, PATCHES?
KA-CHUNK!
WOW! LUCKY WE TESTED IT ON THAT *PINEAPPLE* FIRST!
YOU'LL BE *BILLED* FOR THAT FRUIT!
THIS IS *AWFUL!*
IT'S NOT AS BAD AS WHEN WE HAD TO TEST BOOKS FOR *KRUSTY'S BOOK CLUB!* IF I HAD TO READ ONE MORE HEARTWARMING BOOK ABOUT AN OLD PERSON TEACHING THE NEXT GENERATION LIFE LESSONS... SHUDDER!
WHAT'S THAT?
DING DONG!
THE *DINNER* BELL!
ALL *RIGHT!*
DON'T GET *TOO* EXCITED.

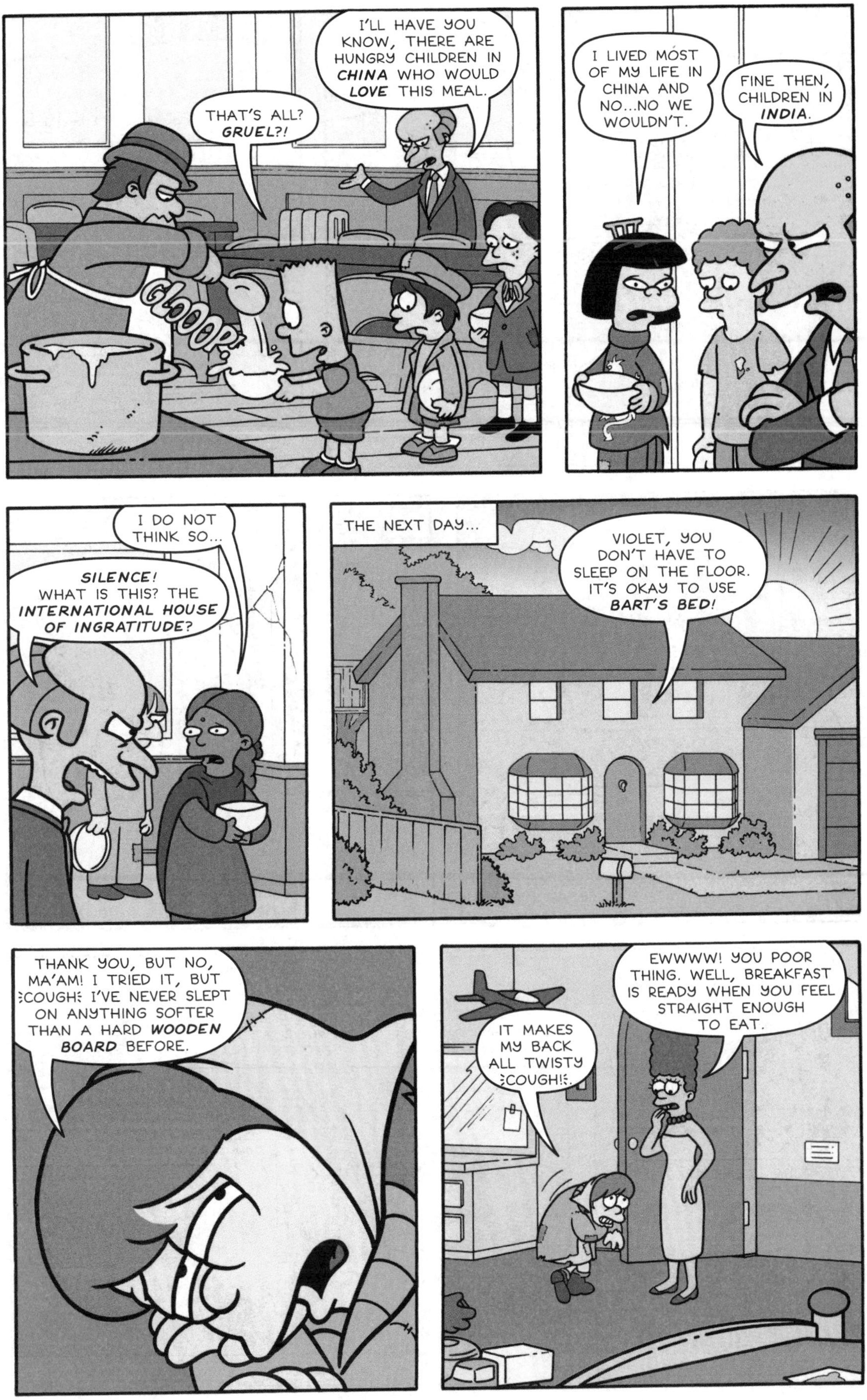

THAT'S ALL? **GRUEL?!**
I'LL HAVE YOU KNOW, THERE ARE HUNGRY CHILDREN IN **CHINA** WHO WOULD **LOVE** THIS MEAL.
GLOOOP!
I LIVED MOST OF MY LIFE IN CHINA AND NO...NO WE WOULDN'T.
FINE THEN, CHILDREN IN **INDIA**.
I DO NOT THINK SO...
SILENCE! WHAT IS THIS? THE **INTERNATIONAL HOUSE OF INGRATITUDE?**
THE NEXT DAY...
VIOLET, YOU DON'T HAVE TO SLEEP ON THE FLOOR. IT'S OKAY TO USE **BART'S BED!**
THANK YOU, BUT NO, MA'AM! I TRIED IT, BUT COUGH! I'VE NEVER SLEPT ON ANYTHING SOFTER THAN A HARD **WOODEN BOARD** BEFORE.
IT MAKES MY BACK ALL TWISTY COUGH!.
EWWWW! YOU POOR THING. WELL, BREAKFAST IS READY WHEN YOU FEEL STRAIGHT ENOUGH TO EAT.

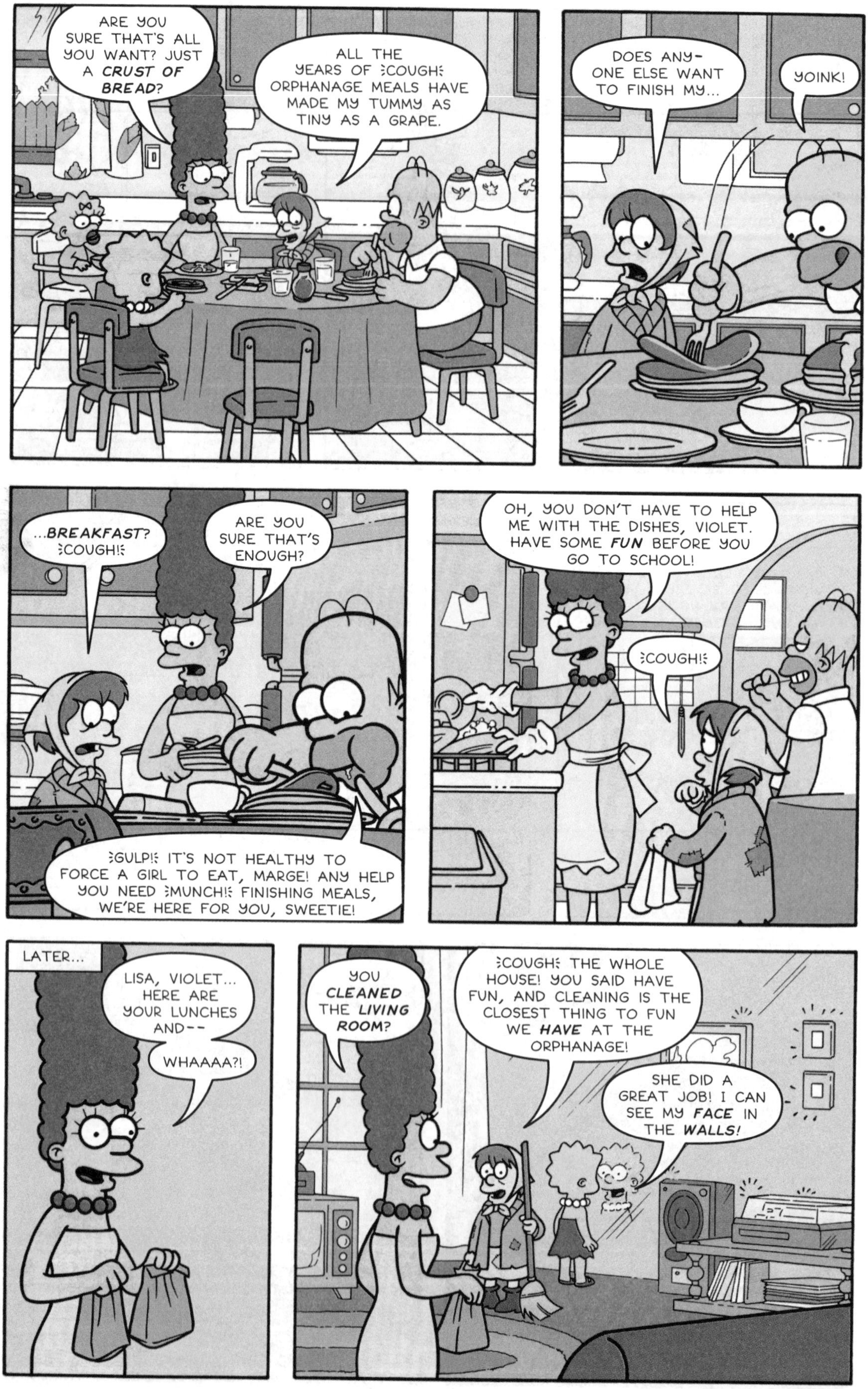

ARE YOU SURE THAT'S ALL YOU WANT? JUST A *CRUST OF BREAD*?
ALL THE YEARS OF ⦚COUGH⦚ ORPHANAGE MEALS HAVE MADE MY TUMMY AS TINY AS A GRAPE.
DOES ANY-ONE ELSE WANT TO FINISH MY...
YOINK!
...*BREAKFAST*? ⦚COUGH!⦚
ARE YOU SURE THAT'S ENOUGH?
⦚GULP!⦚ IT'S NOT HEALTHY TO FORCE A GIRL TO EAT, MARGE! ANY HELP YOU NEED ⦚MUNCH!⦚ FINISHING MEALS, WE'RE HERE FOR YOU, SWEETIE!
OH, YOU DON'T HAVE TO HELP ME WITH THE DISHES, VIOLET. HAVE SOME *FUN* BEFORE YOU GO TO SCHOOL!
⦚COUGH!⦚
LATER...
LISA, VIOLET... HERE ARE YOUR LUNCHES AND--
WHAAAA?!
YOU *CLEANED* THE *LIVING ROOM*?
⦚COUGH⦚ THE WHOLE HOUSE! YOU SAID HAVE FUN, AND CLEANING IS THE CLOSEST THING TO FUN WE *HAVE* AT THE ORPHANAGE!
SHE DID A GREAT JOB! I CAN SEE MY *FACE* IN THE *WALLS!*

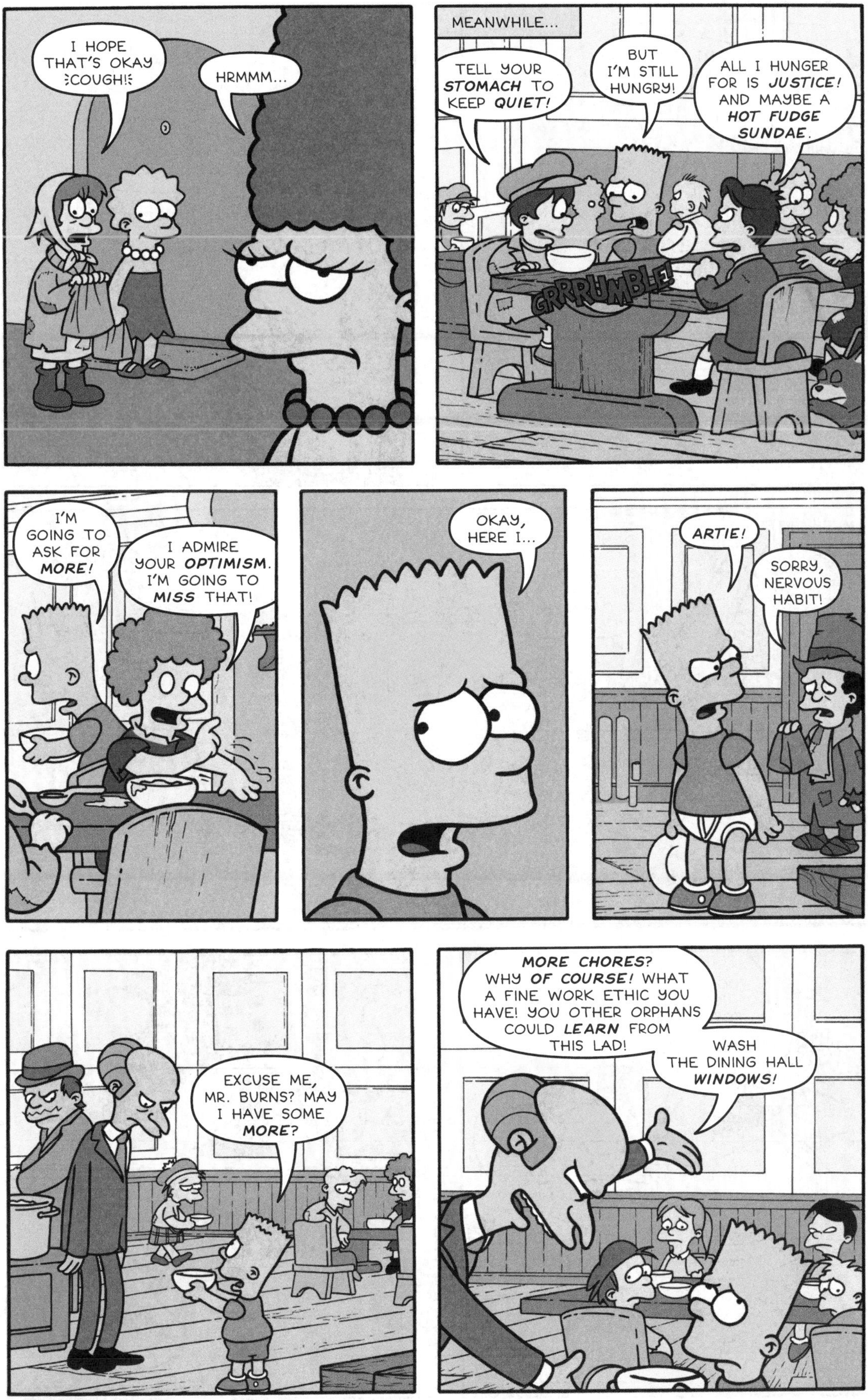
I HOPE THAT'S OKAY *COUGH!*
HRMMM...
MEANWHILE...
TELL YOUR STOMACH TO KEEP QUIET!
BUT I'M STILL HUNGRY!
ALL I HUNGER FOR IS JUSTICE! AND MAYBE A HOT FUDGE SUNDAE.
GRRRUMBLE!
I'M GOING TO ASK FOR MORE!
I ADMIRE YOUR OPTIMISM. I'M GOING TO MISS THAT!
OKAY, HERE I...
ARTIE!
SORRY, NERVOUS HABIT!
EXCUSE ME, MR. BURNS? MAY I HAVE SOME MORE?
MORE CHORES? WHY OF COURSE! WHAT A FINE WORK ETHIC YOU HAVE! YOU OTHER ORPHANS COULD LEARN FROM THIS LAD!
WASH THE DINING HALL WINDOWS!

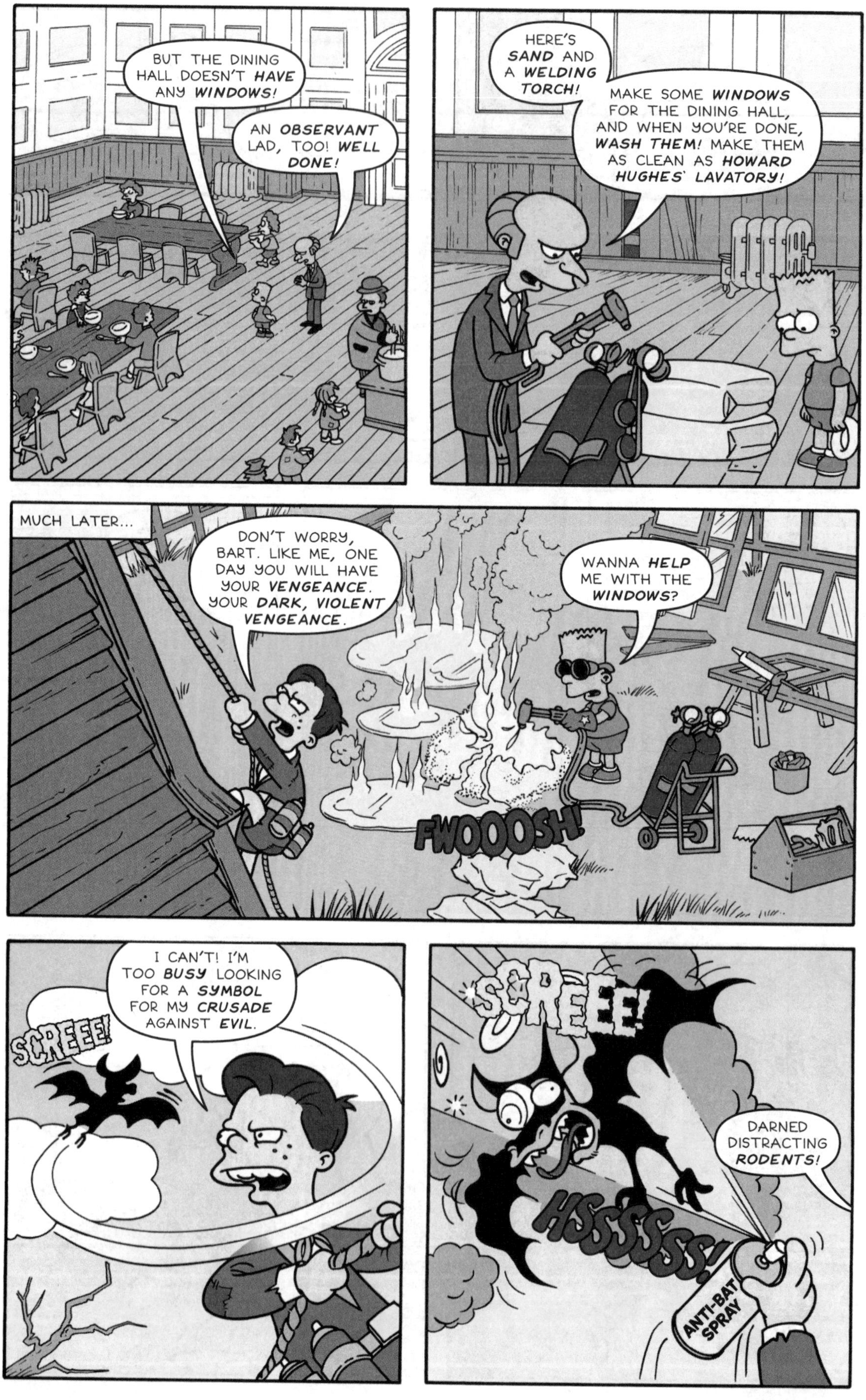

BUT THE DINING HALL DOESN'T HAVE ANY WINDOWS!
AN OBSERVANT LAD, TOO! WELL DONE!
HERE'S SAND AND A WELDING TORCH!
MAKE SOME WINDOWS FOR THE DINING HALL, AND WHEN YOU'RE DONE, WASH THEM! MAKE THEM AS CLEAN AS HOWARD HUGHES' LAVATORY!
MUCH LATER...
DON'T WORRY, BART. LIKE ME, ONE DAY YOU WILL HAVE YOUR VENGEANCE. YOUR DARK, VIOLENT VENGEANCE.
WANNA HELP ME WITH THE WINDOWS?
FWOOOSH!
I CAN'T! I'M TOO BUSY LOOKING FOR A SYMBOL FOR MY CRUSADE AGAINST EVIL.
SCREEE!
SCREEE!
DARNED DISTRACTING RODENTS!
HSSSSSS!
ANTI-BAT SPRAY

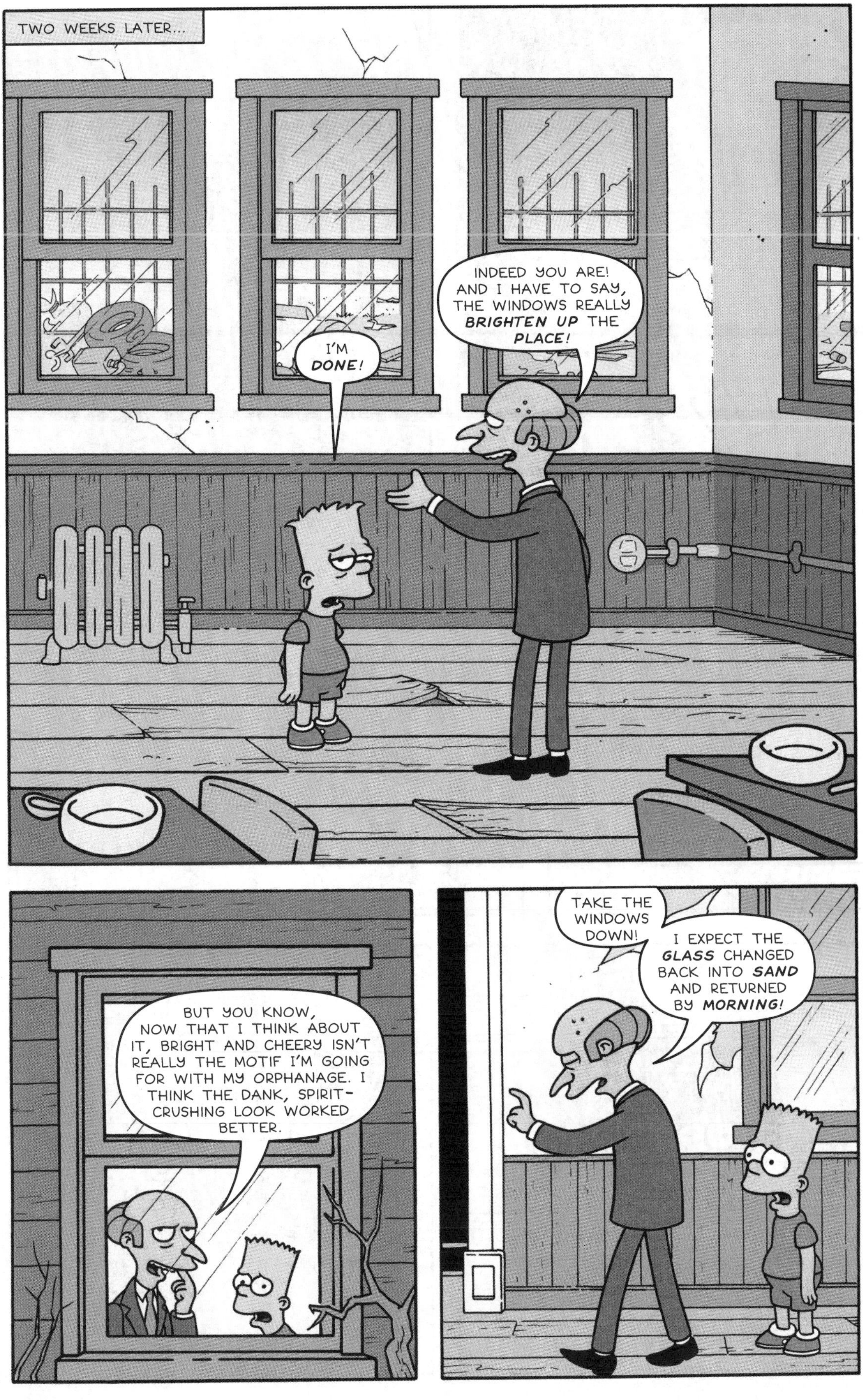

TWO WEEKS LATER...
I'M **DONE**!
INDEED YOU ARE! AND I HAVE TO SAY, THE WINDOWS REALLY **BRIGHTEN UP** THE **PLACE**!
BUT YOU KNOW, NOW THAT I THINK ABOUT IT, BRIGHT AND CHEERY ISN'T REALLY THE MOTIF I'M GOING FOR WITH MY ORPHANAGE. I THINK THE DANK, SPIRIT-CRUSHING LOOK WORKED BETTER.
TAKE THE WINDOWS DOWN!
I EXPECT THE **GLASS** CHANGED BACK INTO **SAND** AND RETURNED BY **MORNING**!

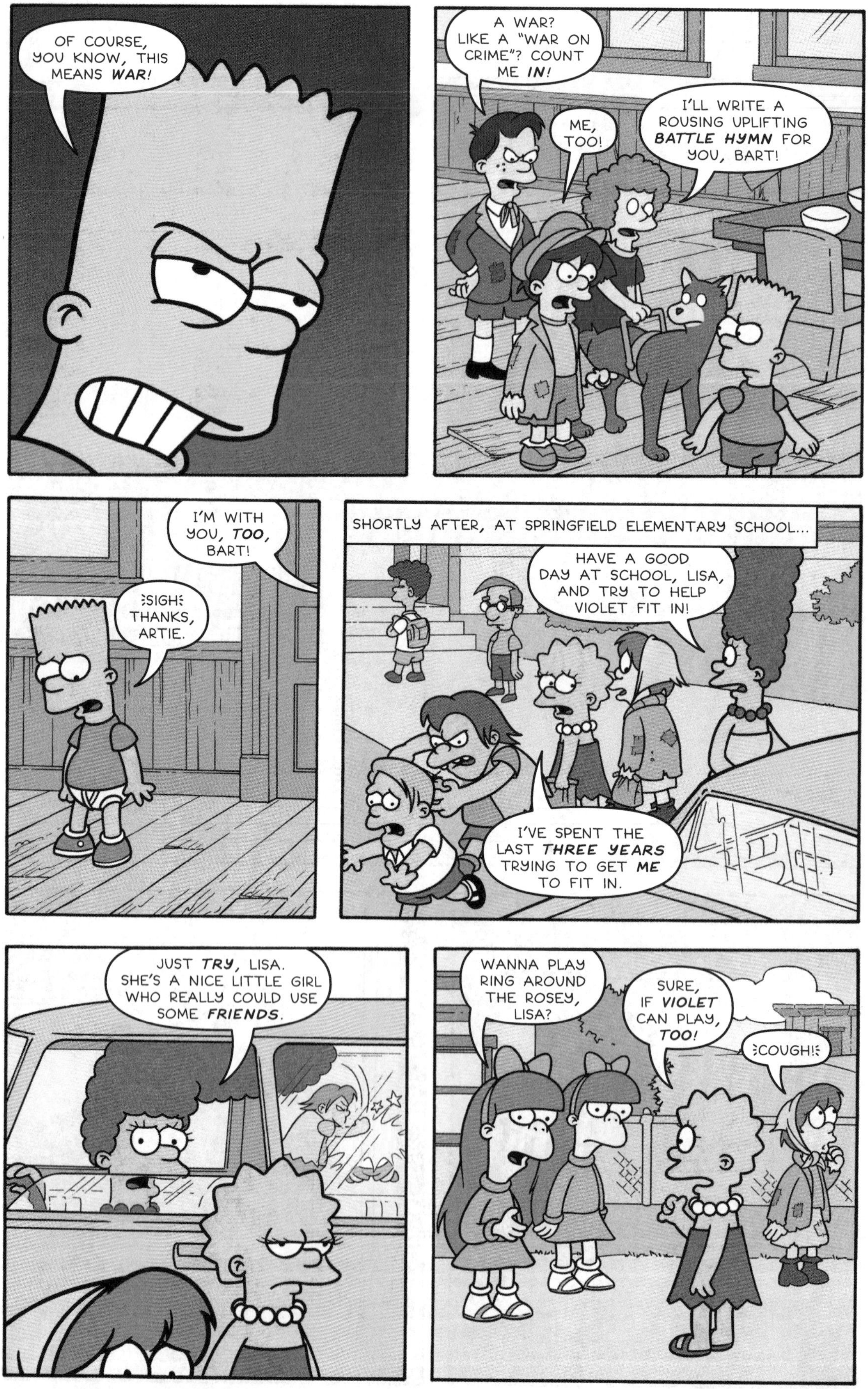

OF COURSE, YOU KNOW, THIS MEANS WAR!
A WAR? LIKE A "WAR ON CRIME"? COUNT ME IN!
ME, TOO!
I'LL WRITE A ROUSING UPLIFTING BATTLE HYMN FOR YOU, BART!
I'M WITH YOU, TOO, BART!
SIGH THANKS, ARTIE.
SHORTLY AFTER, AT SPRINGFIELD ELEMENTARY SCHOOL...
HAVE A GOOD DAY AT SCHOOL, LISA, AND TRY TO HELP VIOLET FIT IN!
I'VE SPENT THE LAST THREE YEARS TRYING TO GET ME TO FIT IN.
JUST TRY, LISA. SHE'S A NICE LITTLE GIRL WHO REALLY COULD USE SOME FRIENDS.
WANNA PLAY RING AROUND THE ROSEY, LISA?
SURE, IF VIOLET CAN PLAY, TOO!
COUGH!

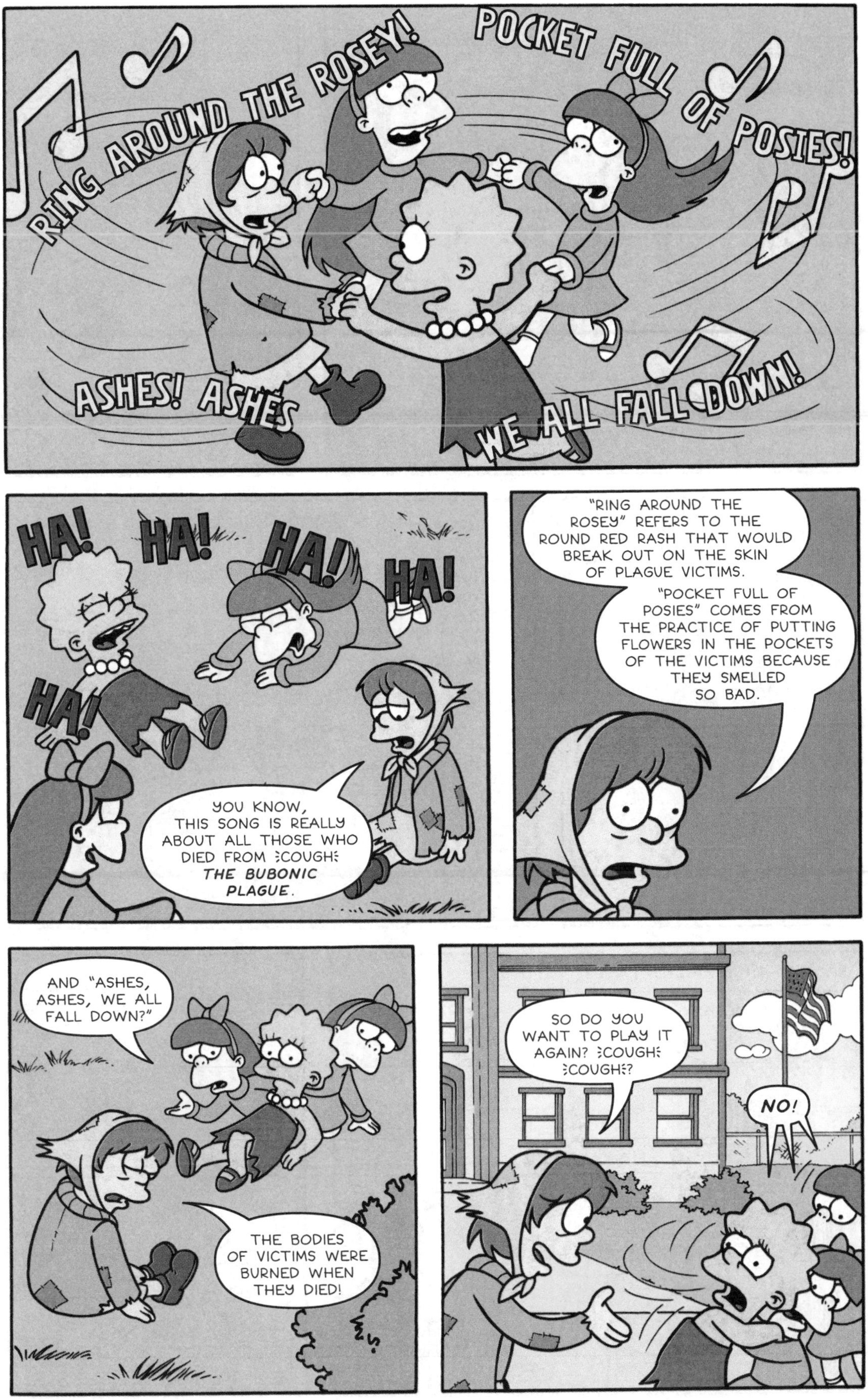
RING AROUND THE ROSEY!
POCKET FULL OF POSIES!
ASHES! ASHES
WE ALL FALL DOWN!
HA! HA! HA! HA! HA!
YOU KNOW, THIS SONG IS REALLY ABOUT ALL THOSE WHO DIED FROM ⁝COUGH⁝ THE BUBONIC PLAGUE.
"RING AROUND THE ROSEY" REFERS TO THE ROUND RED RASH THAT WOULD BREAK OUT ON THE SKIN OF PLAGUE VICTIMS.
"POCKET FULL OF POSIES" COMES FROM THE PRACTICE OF PUTTING FLOWERS IN THE POCKETS OF THE VICTIMS BECAUSE THEY SMELLED SO BAD.
AND "ASHES, ASHES, WE ALL FALL DOWN?"
THE BODIES OF VICTIMS WERE BURNED WHEN THEY DIED!
SO DO YOU WANT TO PLAY IT AGAIN? ⁝COUGH⁝ ⁝COUGH⁝?
NO!

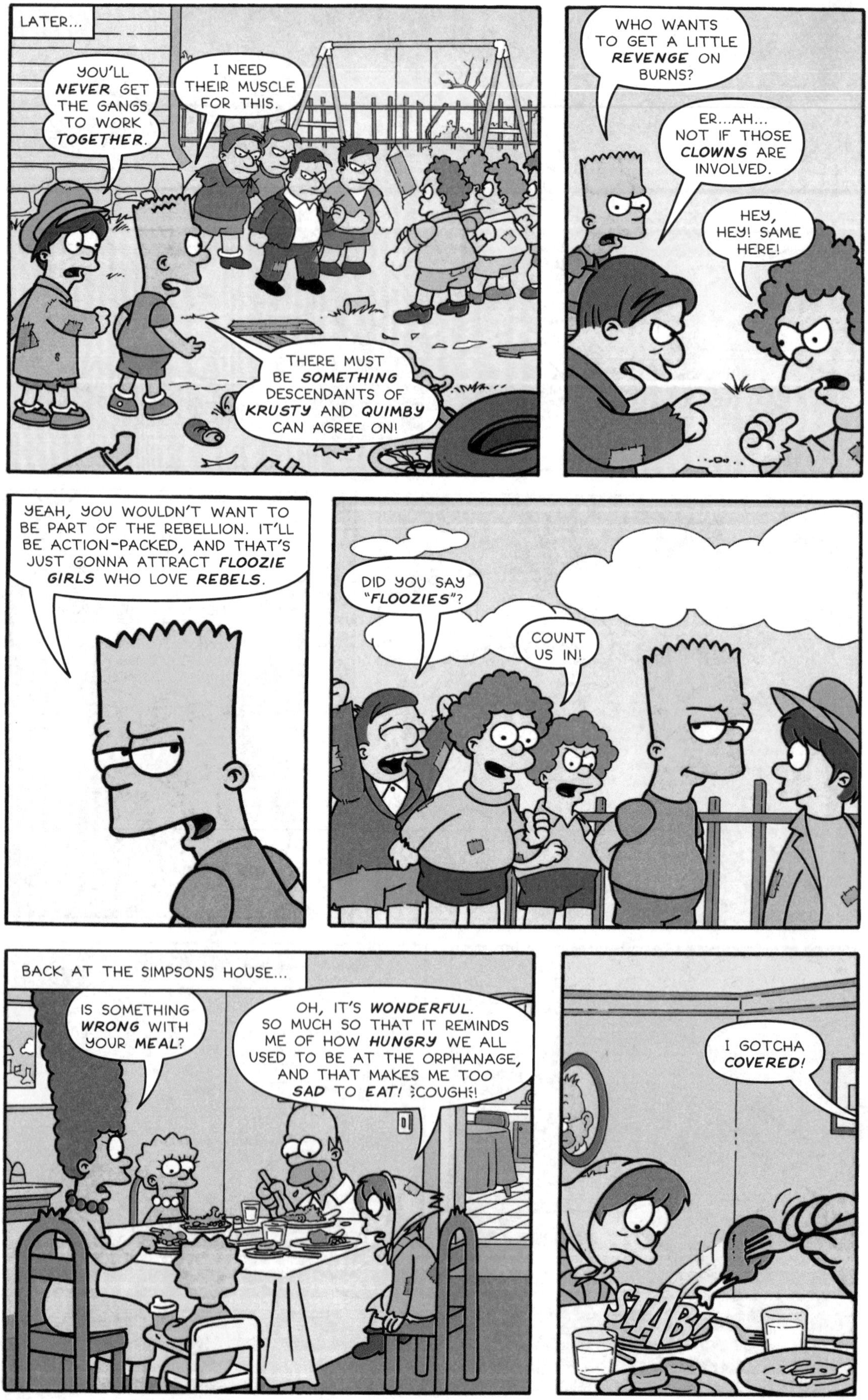
LATER...
YOU'LL NEVER GET THE GANGS TO WORK TOGETHER.
I NEED THEIR MUSCLE FOR THIS.
THERE MUST BE SOMETHING DESCENDANTS OF KRUSTY AND QUIMBY CAN AGREE ON!
WHO WANTS TO GET A LITTLE REVENGE ON BURNS?
ER...AH... NOT IF THOSE CLOWNS ARE INVOLVED.
HEY, HEY! SAME HERE!
YEAH, YOU WOULDN'T WANT TO BE PART OF THE REBELLION. IT'LL BE ACTION-PACKED, AND THAT'S JUST GONNA ATTRACT FLOOZIE GIRLS WHO LOVE REBELS.
DID YOU SAY "FLOOZIES"?
COUNT US IN!
BACK AT THE SIMPSONS HOUSE...
IS SOMETHING WRONG WITH YOUR MEAL?
OH, IT'S WONDERFUL. SO MUCH SO THAT IT REMINDS ME OF HOW HUNGRY WE ALL USED TO BE AT THE ORPHANAGE, AND THAT MAKES ME TOO SAD TO EAT! *COUGH*!
I GOTCHA COVERED!
STAB!

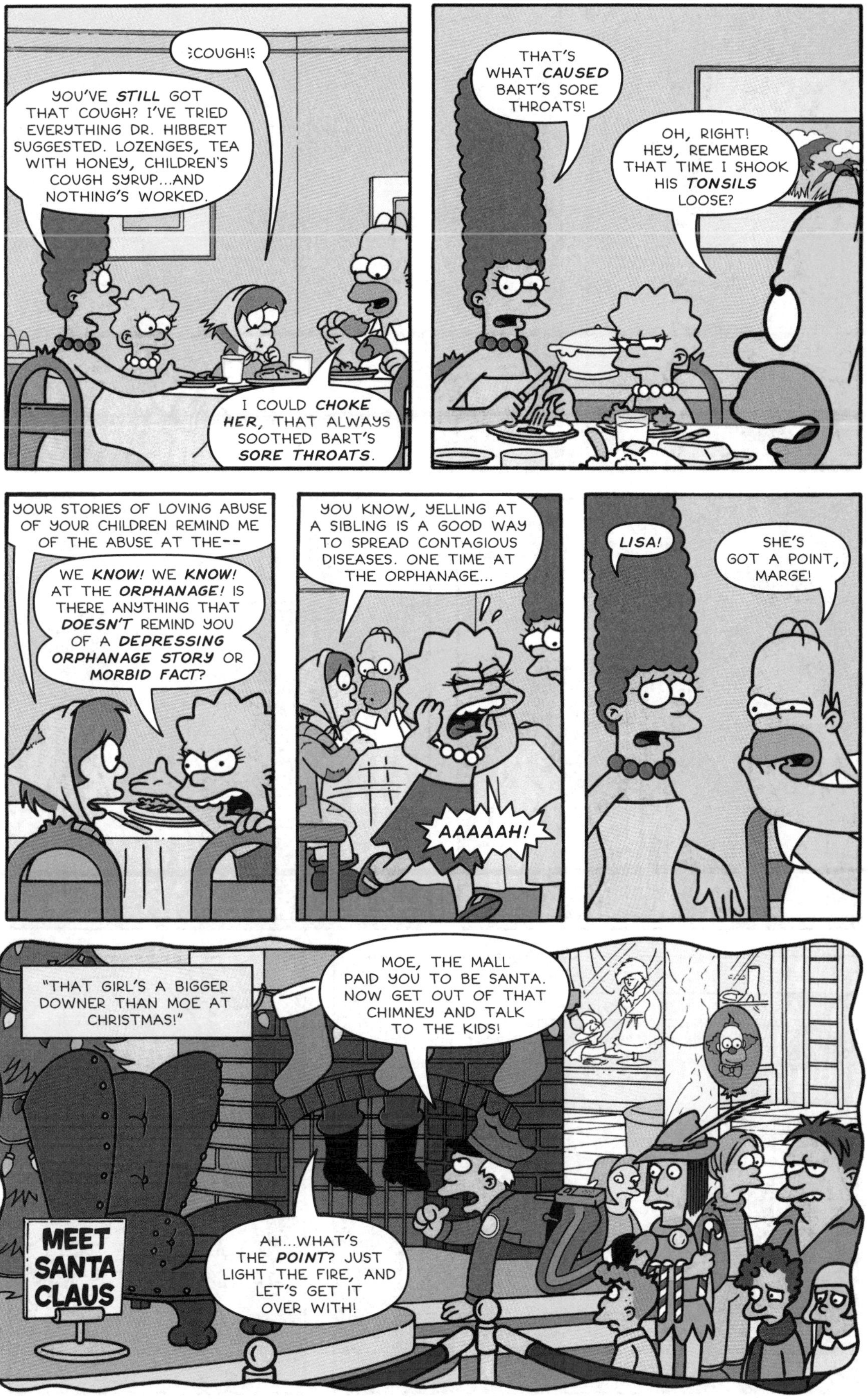

YOU'VE STILL GOT THAT COUGH? I'VE TRIED EVERYTHING DR. HIBBERT SUGGESTED. LOZENGES, TEA WITH HONEY, CHILDREN'S COUGH SYRUP...AND NOTHING'S WORKED.
COUGH!
I COULD CHOKE HER, THAT ALWAYS SOOTHED BART'S SORE THROATS.
THAT'S WHAT CAUSED BART'S SORE THROATS!
OH, RIGHT! HEY, REMEMBER THAT TIME I SHOOK HIS TONSILS LOOSE?
YOUR STORIES OF LOVING ABUSE OF YOUR CHILDREN REMIND ME OF THE ABUSE AT THE--
WE KNOW! WE KNOW! AT THE ORPHANAGE! IS THERE ANYTHING THAT DOESN'T REMIND YOU OF A DEPRESSING ORPHANAGE STORY OR MORBID FACT?
YOU KNOW, YELLING AT A SIBLING IS A GOOD WAY TO SPREAD CONTAGIOUS DISEASES. ONE TIME AT THE ORPHANAGE...
AAAAAH!
LISA!
SHE'S GOT A POINT, MARGE!
"THAT GIRL'S A BIGGER DOWNER THAN MOE AT CHRISTMAS!"
MOE, THE MALL PAID YOU TO BE SANTA. NOW GET OUT OF THAT CHIMNEY AND TALK TO THE KIDS!
AH...WHAT'S THE POINT? JUST LIGHT THE FIRE, AND LET'S GET IT OVER WITH!
MEET SANTA CLAUS

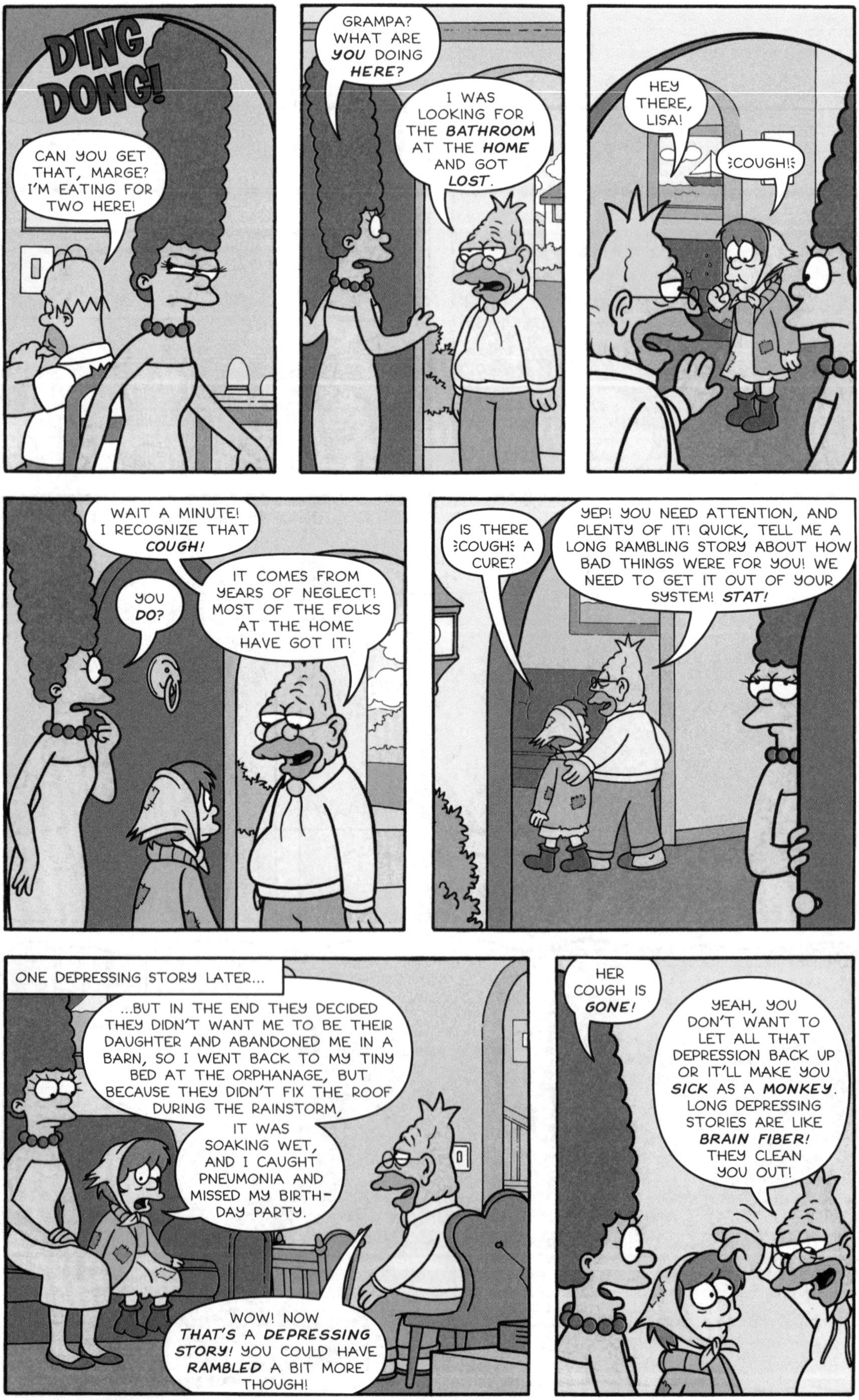
DING DONG!
CAN YOU GET THAT, MARGE? I'M EATING FOR TWO HERE!
GRAMPA? WHAT ARE YOU DOING HERE?
I WAS LOOKING FOR THE BATHROOM AT THE HOME AND GOT LOST.
HEY THERE, LISA!
COUGH!
WAIT A MINUTE! I RECOGNIZE THAT COUGH!
YOU DO?
IT COMES FROM YEARS OF NEGLECT! MOST OF THE FOLKS AT THE HOME HAVE GOT IT!
IS THERE COUGH A CURE?
YEP! YOU NEED ATTENTION, AND PLENTY OF IT! QUICK, TELL ME A LONG RAMBLING STORY ABOUT HOW BAD THINGS WERE FOR YOU! WE NEED TO GET IT OUT OF YOUR SYSTEM! STAT!
ONE DEPRESSING STORY LATER...
...BUT IN THE END THEY DECIDED THEY DIDN'T WANT ME TO BE THEIR DAUGHTER AND ABANDONED ME IN A BARN, SO I WENT BACK TO MY TINY BED AT THE ORPHANAGE, BUT BECAUSE THEY DIDN'T FIX THE ROOF DURING THE RAINSTORM,
IT WAS SOAKING WET, AND I CAUGHT PNEUMONIA AND MISSED MY BIRTH-DAY PARTY.
WOW! NOW THAT'S A DEPRESSING STORY! YOU COULD HAVE RAMBLED A BIT MORE THOUGH!
HER COUGH IS GONE!
YEAH, YOU DON'T WANT TO LET ALL THAT DEPRESSION BACK UP OR IT'LL MAKE YOU SICK AS A MONKEY. LONG DEPRESSING STORIES ARE LIKE BRAIN FIBER! THEY CLEAN YOU OUT!

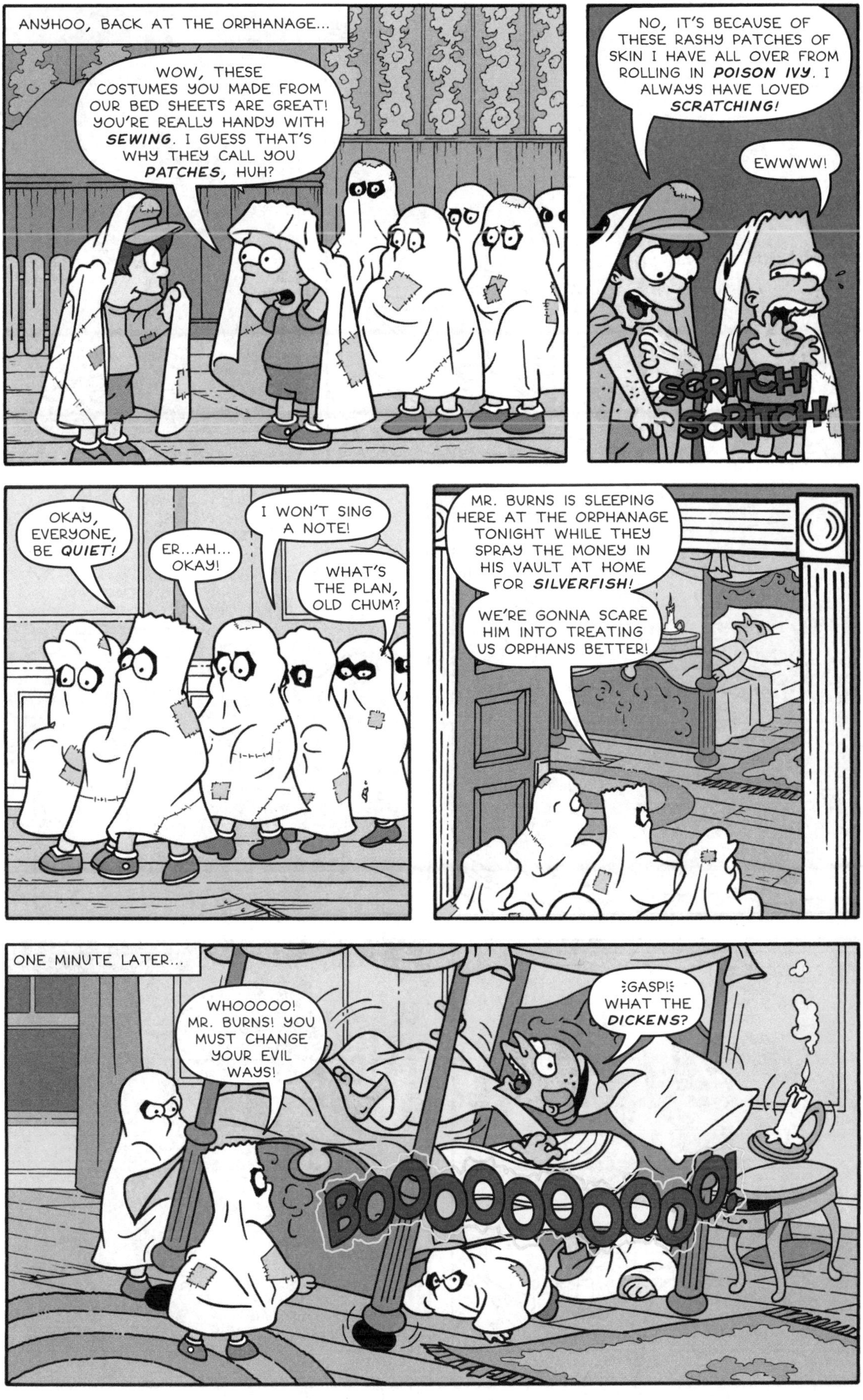
ANYHOO, BACK AT THE ORPHANAGE...
WOW, THESE COSTUMES YOU MADE FROM OUR BED SHEETS ARE GREAT! YOU'RE REALLY HANDY WITH SEWING. I GUESS THAT'S WHY THEY CALL YOU PATCHES, HUH?
NO, IT'S BECAUSE OF THESE RASHY PATCHES OF SKIN I HAVE ALL OVER FROM ROLLING IN POISON IVY. I ALWAYS HAVE LOVED SCRATCHING!
EWWWW!
SCRITCH! SCRITCH!
OKAY, EVERYONE, BE QUIET!
ER...AH... OKAY!
I WON'T SING A NOTE!
WHAT'S THE PLAN, OLD CHUM?
MR. BURNS IS SLEEPING HERE AT THE ORPHANAGE TONIGHT WHILE THEY SPRAY THE MONEY IN HIS VAULT AT HOME FOR SILVERFISH!
WE'RE GONNA SCARE HIM INTO TREATING US ORPHANS BETTER!
ONE MINUTE LATER...
WHOOOOO! MR. BURNS! YOU MUST CHANGE YOUR EVIL WAYS!
GASP! WHAT THE DICKENS?
BOOOOOOOOOOO!

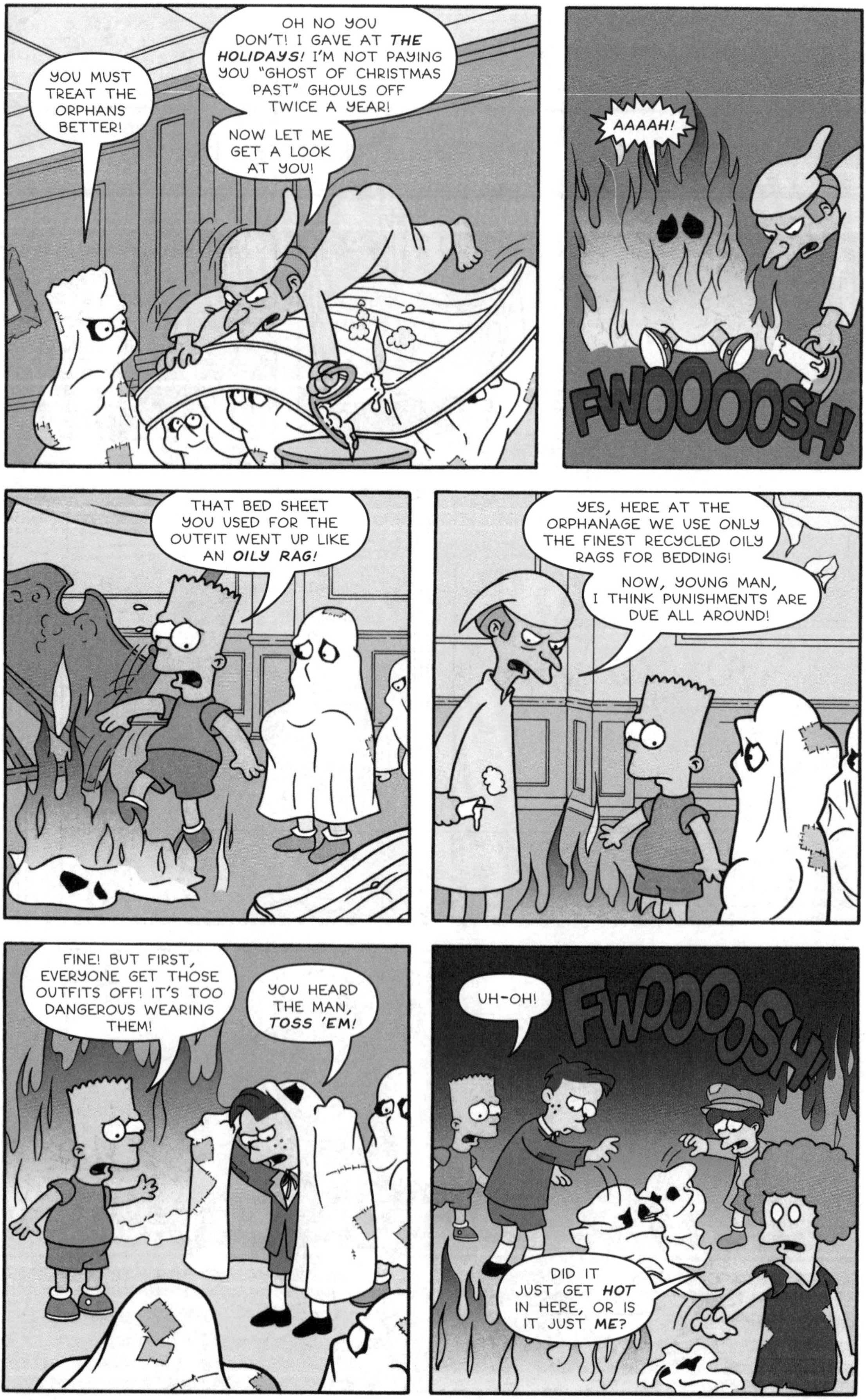
YOU MUST TREAT THE ORPHANS BETTER!
OH NO YOU DON'T! I GAVE AT THE HOLIDAYS! I'M NOT PAYING YOU "GHOST OF CHRISTMAS PAST" GHOULS OFF TWICE A YEAR!
NOW LET ME GET A LOOK AT YOU!
AAAAH!
FWOOOOSH!
THAT BED SHEET YOU USED FOR THE OUTFIT WENT UP LIKE AN OILY RAG!
YES, HERE AT THE ORPHANAGE WE USE ONLY THE FINEST RECYCLED OILY RAGS FOR BEDDING!
NOW, YOUNG MAN, I THINK PUNISHMENTS ARE DUE ALL AROUND!
FINE! BUT FIRST, EVERYONE GET THOSE OUTFITS OFF! IT'S TOO DANGEROUS WEARING THEM!
YOU HEARD THE MAN, TOSS 'EM!
UH-OH!
FWOOOOSH!
DID IT JUST GET HOT IN HERE, OR IS IT JUST ME?

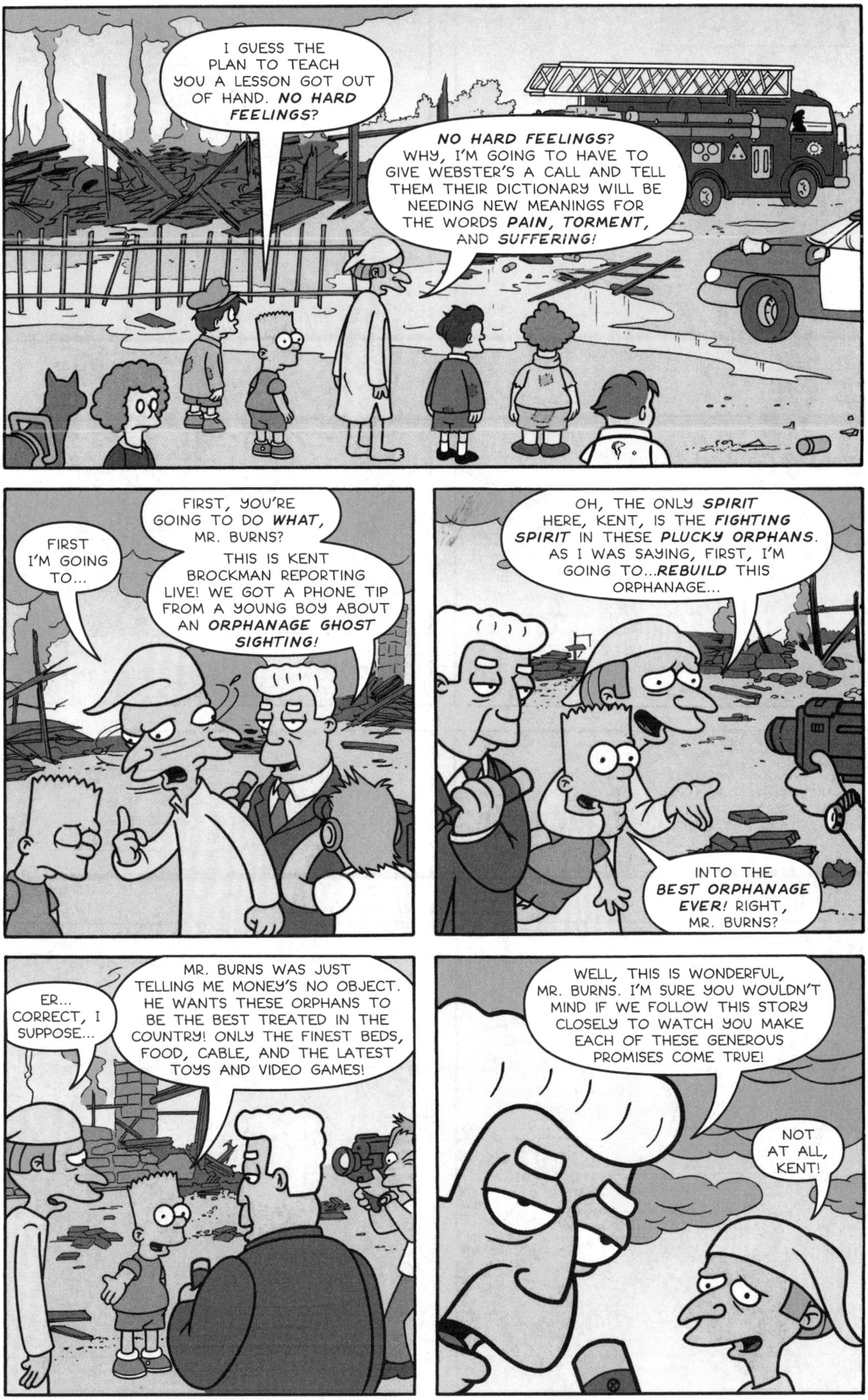
I GUESS THE PLAN TO TEACH YOU A LESSON GOT OUT OF HAND. **NO HARD FEELINGS?**
NO HARD FEELINGS? WHY, I'M GOING TO HAVE TO GIVE WEBSTER'S A CALL AND TELL THEM THEIR DICTIONARY WILL BE NEEDING NEW MEANINGS FOR THE WORDS **PAIN, TORMENT,** AND **SUFFERING!**
FIRST I'M GOING TO...
FIRST, YOU'RE GOING TO DO **WHAT,** MR. BURNS?
THIS IS KENT BROCKMAN REPORTING LIVE! WE GOT A PHONE TIP FROM A YOUNG BOY ABOUT AN **ORPHANAGE GHOST SIGHTING!**
OH, THE ONLY **SPIRIT** HERE, KENT, IS THE **FIGHTING SPIRIT** IN THESE **PLUCKY ORPHANS**. AS I WAS SAYING, FIRST, I'M GOING TO...**REBUILD** THIS ORPHANAGE...
INTO THE **BEST ORPHANAGE EVER!** RIGHT, MR. BURNS?
ER... CORRECT, I SUPPOSE...
MR. BURNS WAS JUST TELLING ME MONEY'S NO OBJECT. HE WANTS THESE ORPHANS TO BE THE BEST TREATED IN THE COUNTRY! ONLY THE FINEST BEDS, FOOD, CABLE, AND THE LATEST TOYS AND VIDEO GAMES!
WELL, THIS IS WONDERFUL, MR. BURNS. I'M SURE YOU WOULDN'T MIND IF WE FOLLOW THIS STORY CLOSELY TO WATCH YOU MAKE EACH OF THESE GENEROUS PROMISES COME TRUE!
NOT AT ALL, KENT!

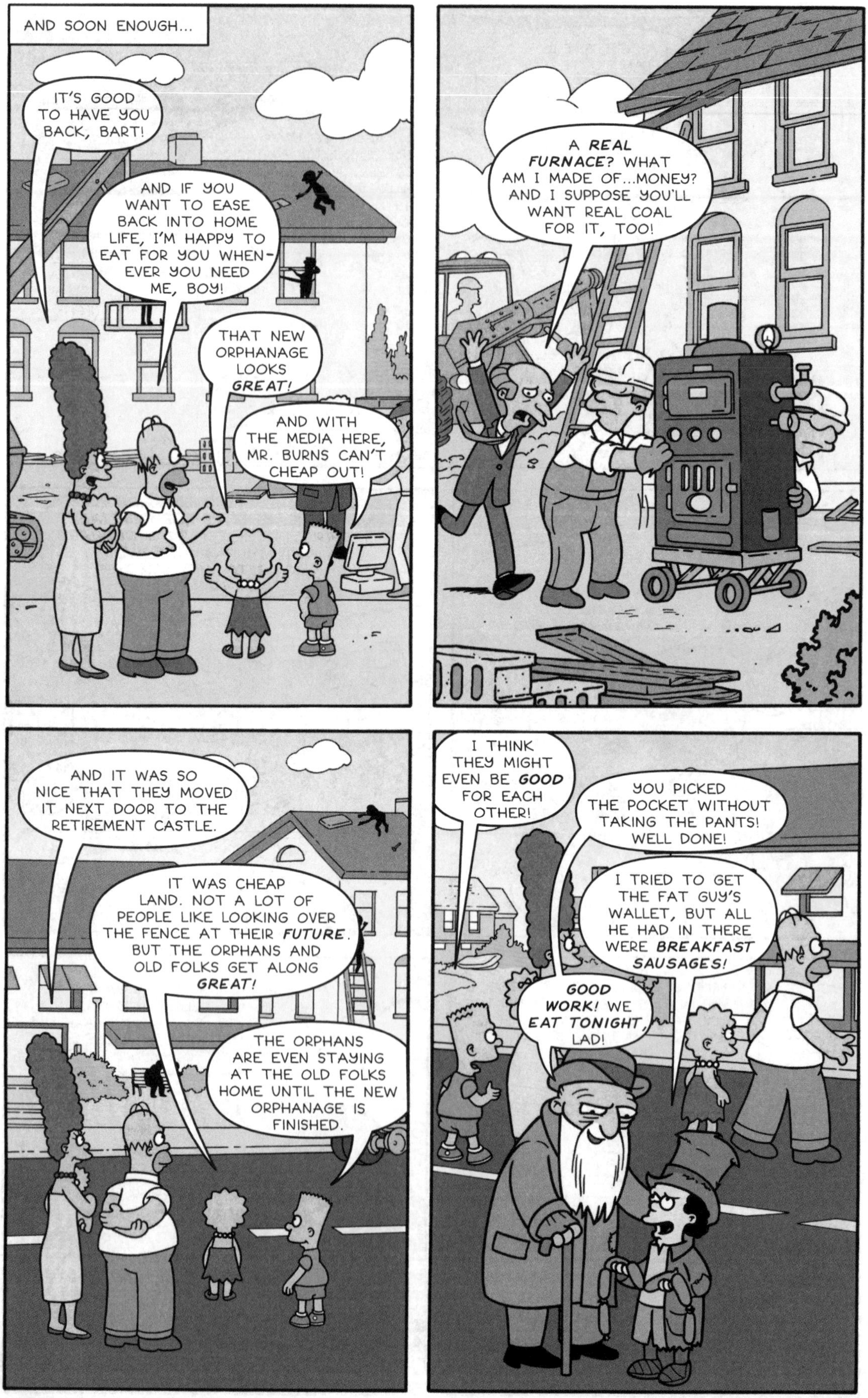
AND SOON ENOUGH...
IT'S GOOD TO HAVE YOU BACK, BART!
AND IF YOU WANT TO EASE BACK INTO HOME LIFE, I'M HAPPY TO EAT FOR YOU WHEN-EVER YOU NEED ME, BOY!
THAT NEW ORPHANAGE LOOKS *GREAT!*
AND WITH THE MEDIA HERE, MR. BURNS CAN'T CHEAP OUT!
A ***REAL FURNACE?*** WHAT AM I MADE OF...MONEY? AND I SUPPOSE YOU'LL WANT REAL COAL FOR IT, TOO!
AND IT WAS SO NICE THAT THEY MOVED IT NEXT DOOR TO THE RETIREMENT CASTLE.
IT WAS CHEAP LAND. NOT A LOT OF PEOPLE LIKE LOOKING OVER THE FENCE AT THEIR *FUTURE*. BUT THE ORPHANS AND OLD FOLKS GET ALONG *GREAT!*
THE ORPHANS ARE EVEN STAYING AT THE OLD FOLKS HOME UNTIL THE NEW ORPHANAGE IS FINISHED.
I THINK THEY MIGHT EVEN BE ***GOOD*** FOR EACH OTHER!
YOU PICKED THE POCKET WITHOUT TAKING THE PANTS! WELL DONE!
I TRIED TO GET THE FAT GUY'S WALLET, BUT ALL HE HAD IN THERE WERE ***BREAKFAST SAUSAGES!***
GOOD WORK! WE ***EAT TONIGHT,*** LAD!

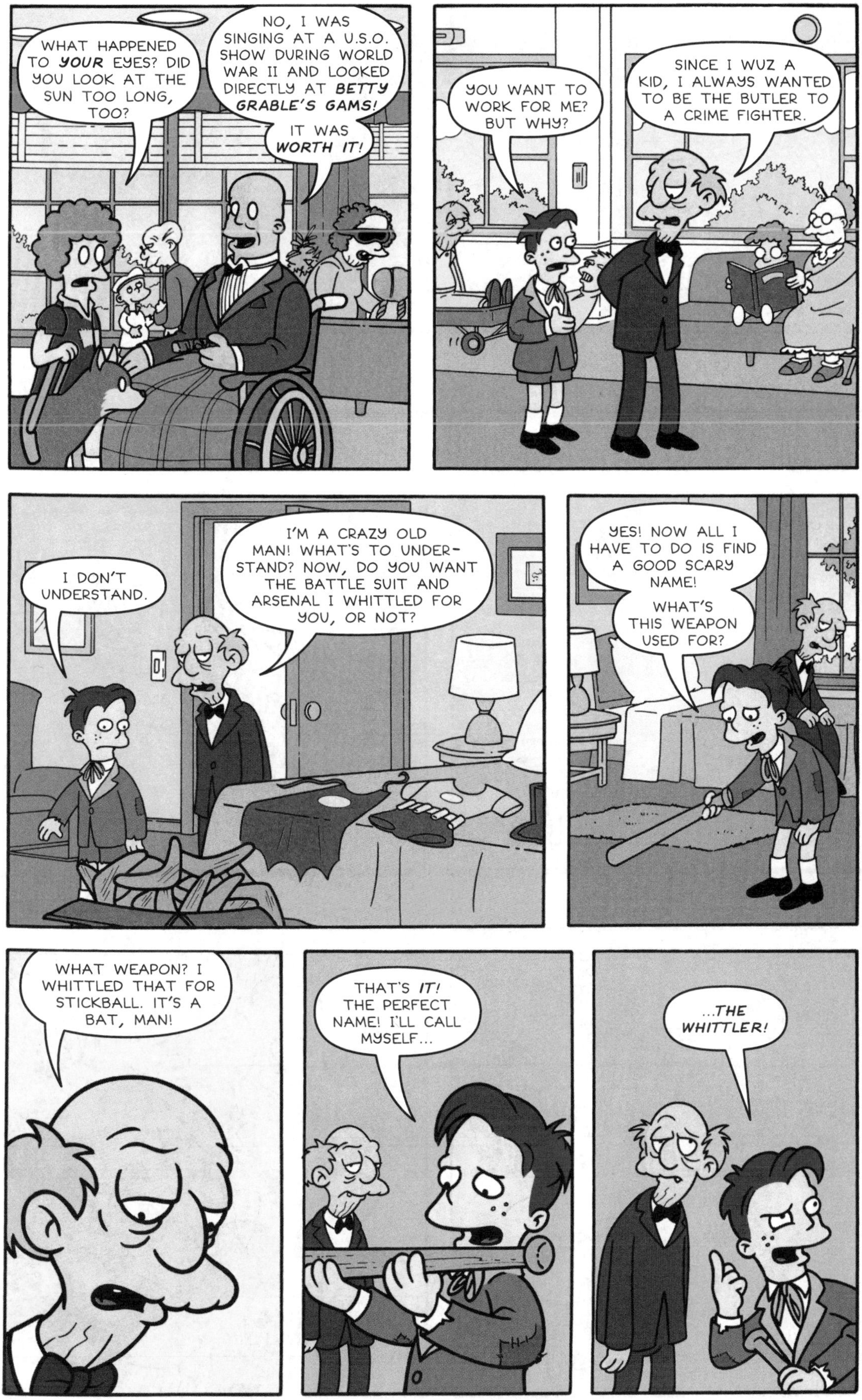
WHAT HAPPENED TO *YOUR* EYES? DID YOU LOOK AT THE SUN TOO LONG, TOO?
NO, I WAS SINGING AT A U.S.O. SHOW DURING WORLD WAR II AND LOOKED DIRECTLY AT *BETTY GRABLE'S GAMS!*
IT WAS *WORTH IT!*
YOU WANT TO WORK FOR ME? BUT WHY?
SINCE I WUZ A KID, I ALWAYS WANTED TO BE THE BUTLER TO A CRIME FIGHTER.
I DON'T UNDERSTAND.
I'M A CRAZY OLD MAN! WHAT'S TO UNDER-STAND? NOW, DO YOU WANT THE BATTLE SUIT AND ARSENAL I WHITTLED FOR YOU, OR NOT?
YES! NOW ALL I HAVE TO DO IS FIND A GOOD SCARY NAME!
WHAT'S THIS WEAPON USED FOR?
WHAT WEAPON? I WHITTLED THAT FOR STICKBALL. IT'S A BAT, MAN!
THAT'S *IT!* THE PERFECT NAME! I'LL CALL MYSELF...
...THE WHITTLER!

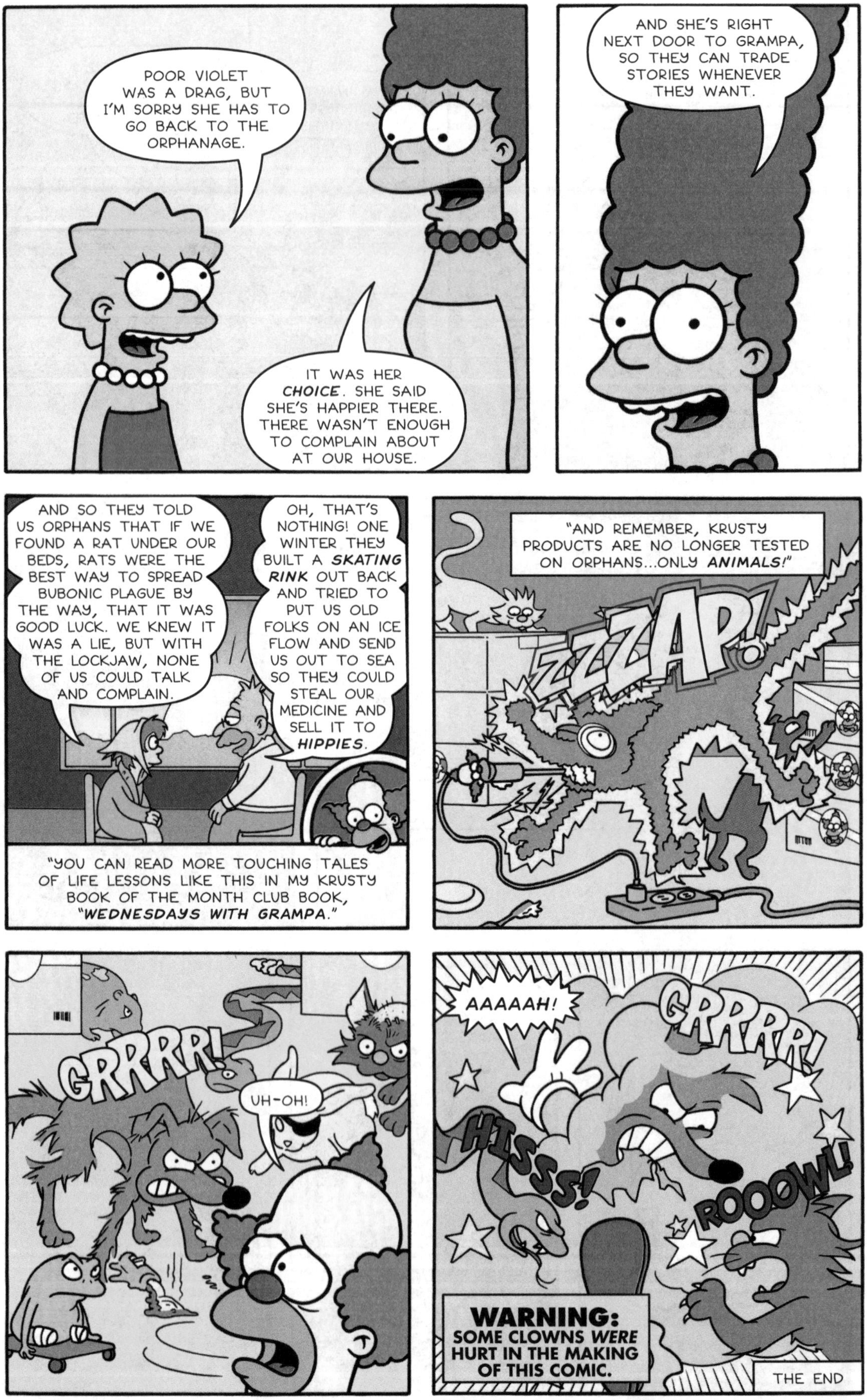
POOR VIOLET WAS A DRAG, BUT I'M SORRY SHE HAS TO GO BACK TO THE ORPHANAGE.
IT WAS HER *CHOICE*. SHE SAID SHE'S HAPPIER THERE. THERE WASN'T ENOUGH TO COMPLAIN ABOUT AT OUR HOUSE.
AND SHE'S RIGHT NEXT DOOR TO GRAMPA, SO THEY CAN TRADE STORIES WHENEVER THEY WANT.
AND SO THEY TOLD US ORPHANS THAT IF WE FOUND A RAT UNDER OUR BEDS, RATS WERE THE BEST WAY TO SPREAD BUBONIC PLAGUE BY THE WAY, THAT IT WAS GOOD LUCK. WE KNEW IT WAS A LIE, BUT WITH THE LOCKJAW, NONE OF US COULD TALK AND COMPLAIN.
OH, THAT'S NOTHING! ONE WINTER THEY BUILT A *SKATING RINK* OUT BACK AND TRIED TO PUT US OLD FOLKS ON AN ICE FLOW AND SEND US OUT TO SEA SO THEY COULD STEAL OUR MEDICINE AND SELL IT TO *HIPPIES*.
"YOU CAN READ MORE TOUCHING TALES OF LIFE LESSONS LIKE THIS IN MY KRUSTY BOOK OF THE MONTH CLUB BOOK, "*WEDNESDAYS WITH GRAMPA*."
"AND REMEMBER, KRUSTY PRODUCTS ARE NO LONGER TESTED ON ORPHANS...ONLY *ANIMALS*!"
ZZZAP!
GRRRR!
UH-OH!
AAAAAH!
GRRRRR!
HISSSS!
ROOOWL!
WARNING:
SOME CLOWNS *WERE* HURT IN THE MAKING OF THIS COMIC.
THE END

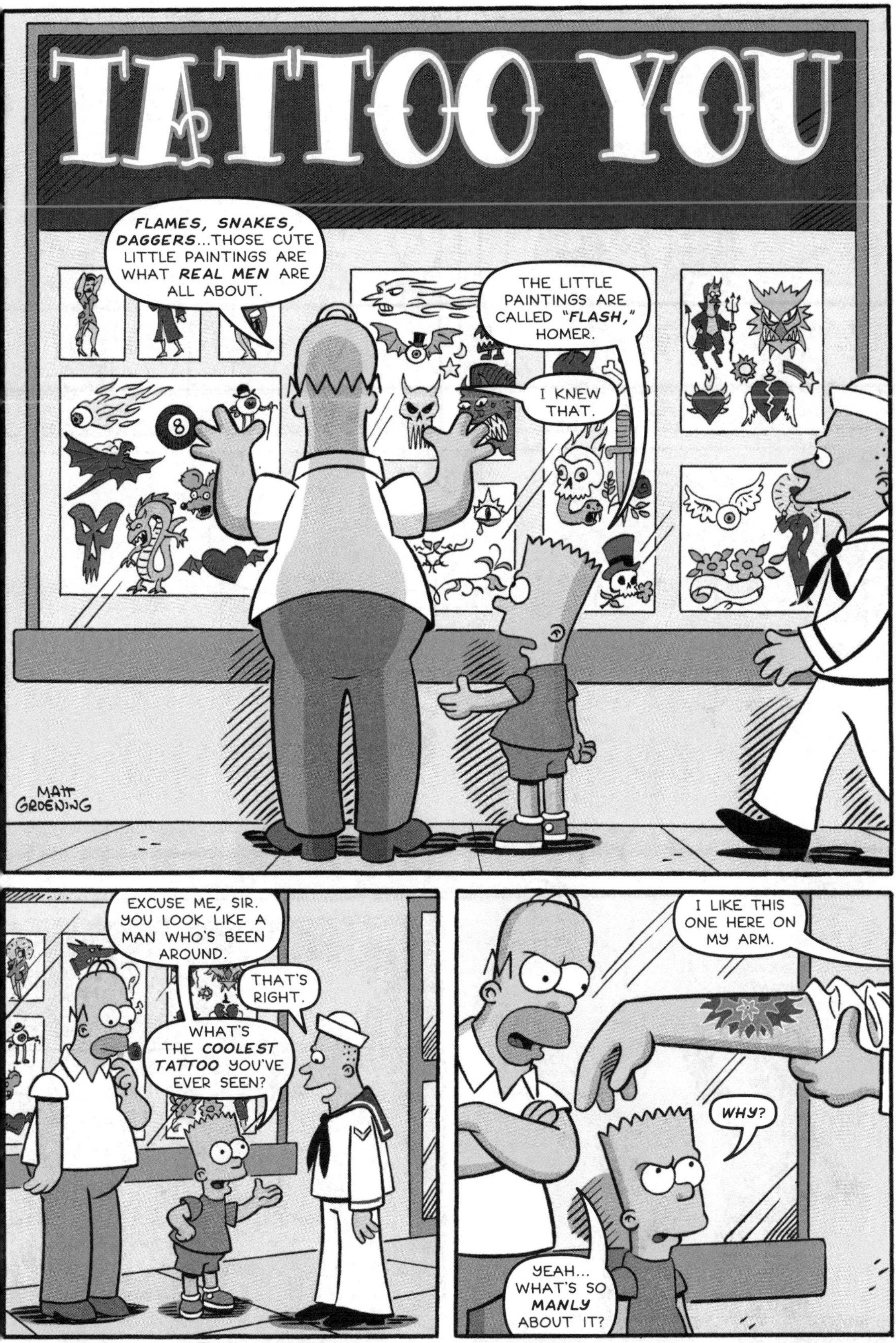
TATTOO YOU
FLAMES, SNAKES, DAGGERS...THOSE CUTE LITTLE PAINTINGS ARE WHAT REAL MEN ARE ALL ABOUT.
THE LITTLE PAINTINGS ARE CALLED "FLASH," HOMER.
I KNEW THAT.
MATT GROENING
EXCUSE ME, SIR. YOU LOOK LIKE A MAN WHO'S BEEN AROUND.
THAT'S RIGHT.
WHAT'S THE COOLEST TATTOO YOU'VE EVER SEEN?
I LIKE THIS ONE HERE ON MY ARM.
WHY?
YEAH... WHAT'S SO MANLY ABOUT IT?

CAROL LAY SCRIPT & ART | **NATHAN HAMILL** COLORS | **KAREN BATES** LETTERS | **BILL MORRISON** EDITOR

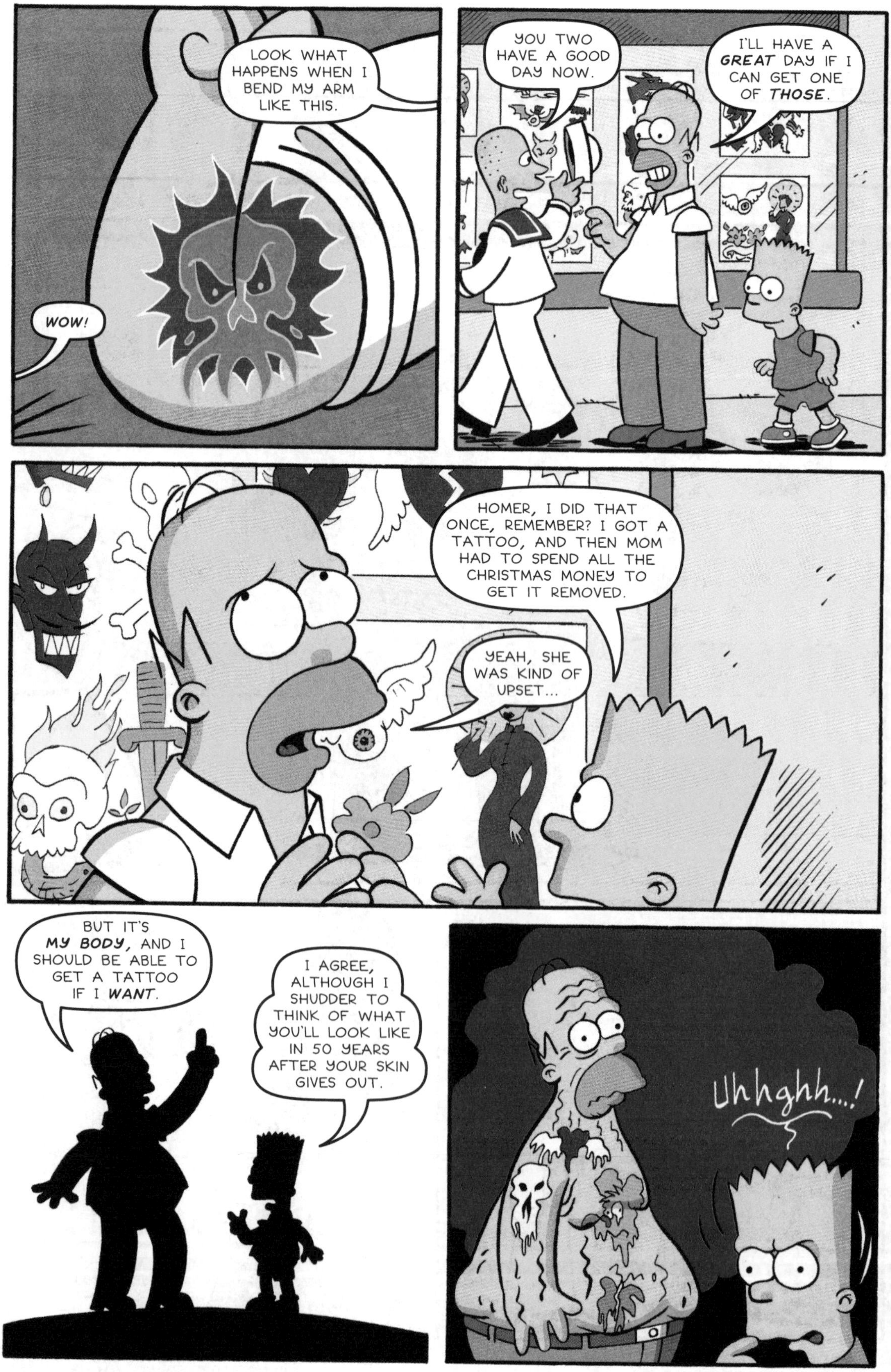

LOOK WHAT HAPPENS WHEN I BEND MY ARM LIKE THIS.
WOW!
YOU TWO HAVE A GOOD DAY NOW.
I'LL HAVE A GREAT DAY IF I CAN GET ONE OF THOSE.
HOMER, I DID THAT ONCE, REMEMBER? I GOT A TATTOO, AND THEN MOM HAD TO SPEND ALL THE CHRISTMAS MONEY TO GET IT REMOVED.
YEAH, SHE WAS KIND OF UPSET...
BUT IT'S MY BODY, AND I SHOULD BE ABLE TO GET A TATTOO IF I WANT.
I AGREE, ALTHOUGH I SHUDDER TO THINK OF WHAT YOU'LL LOOK LIKE IN 50 YEARS AFTER YOUR SKIN GIVES OUT.
Uhhghh...!

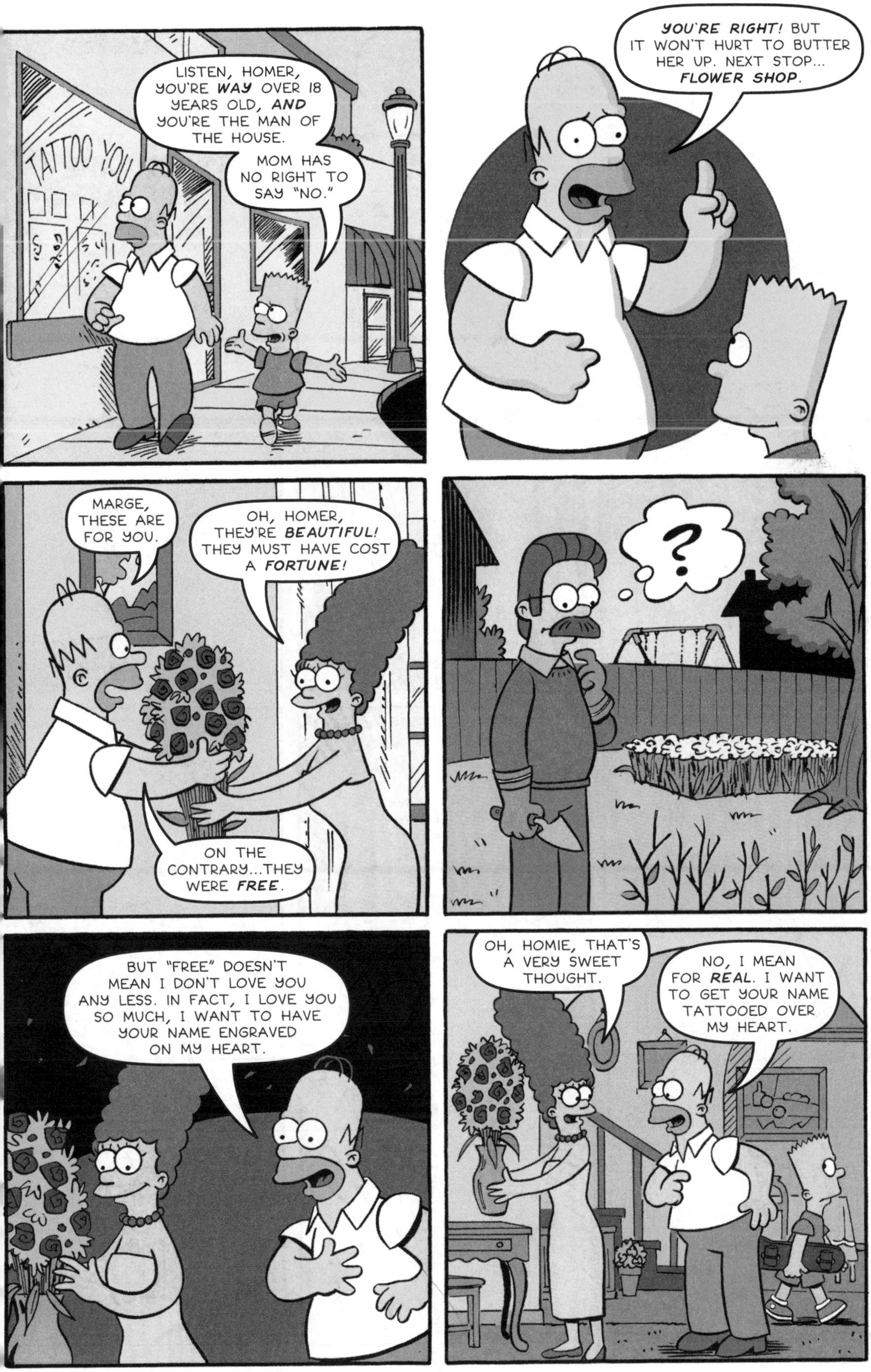
TATTOO YOU
LISTEN, HOMER, YOU'RE WAY OVER 18 YEARS OLD, AND YOU'RE THE MAN OF THE HOUSE.
MOM HAS NO RIGHT TO SAY "NO."
YOU'RE RIGHT! BUT IT WON'T HURT TO BUTTER HER UP. NEXT STOP... FLOWER SHOP.
MARGE, THESE ARE FOR YOU.
OH, HOMER, THEY'RE BEAUTIFUL! THEY MUST HAVE COST A FORTUNE!
ON THE CONTRARY...THEY WERE FREE.
?
BUT "FREE" DOESN'T MEAN I DON'T LOVE YOU ANY LESS. IN FACT, I LOVE YOU SO MUCH, I WANT TO HAVE YOUR NAME ENGRAVED ON MY HEART.
OH, HOMIE, THAT'S A VERY SWEET THOUGHT.
NO, I MEAN FOR REAL. I WANT TO GET YOUR NAME TATTOOED OVER MY HEART.

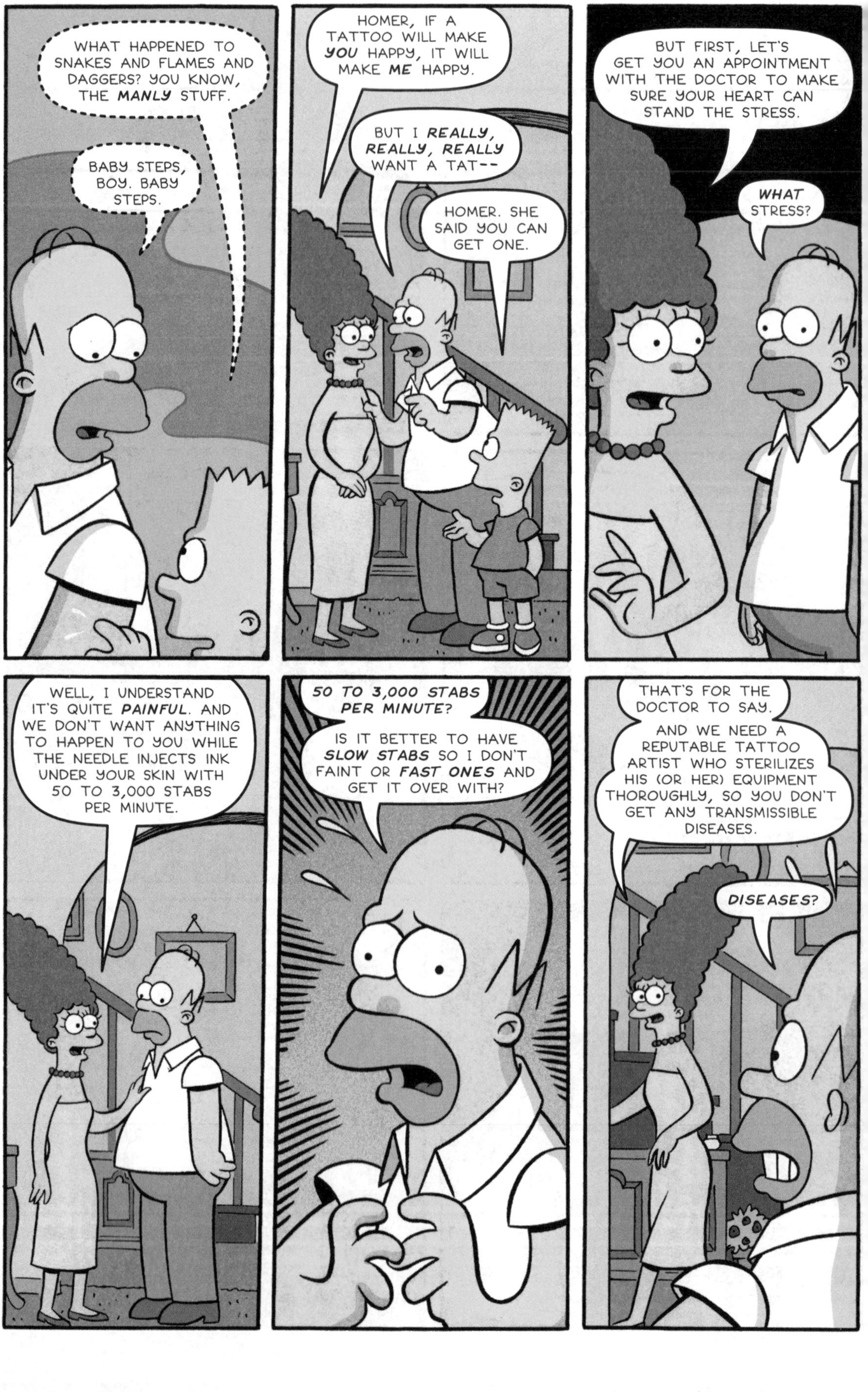
WHAT HAPPENED TO SNAKES AND FLAMES AND DAGGERS? YOU KNOW, THE **MANLY** STUFF.
BABY STEPS, BOY. BABY STEPS.
HOMER, IF A TATTOO WILL MAKE **YOU** HAPPY, IT WILL MAKE **ME** HAPPY.
BUT I **REALLY, REALLY, REALLY** WANT A TAT--
HOMER. SHE SAID YOU CAN GET ONE.
BUT FIRST, LET'S GET YOU AN APPOINTMENT WITH THE DOCTOR TO MAKE SURE YOUR HEART CAN STAND THE STRESS.
WHAT STRESS?
WELL, I UNDERSTAND IT'S QUITE **PAINFUL**. AND WE DON'T WANT ANYTHING TO HAPPEN TO YOU WHILE THE NEEDLE INJECTS INK UNDER YOUR SKIN WITH 50 TO 3,000 STABS PER MINUTE.
50 TO 3,000 STABS PER MINUTE?
IS IT BETTER TO HAVE **SLOW STABS** SO I DON'T FAINT OR **FAST ONES** AND GET IT OVER WITH?
THAT'S FOR THE DOCTOR TO SAY.
AND WE NEED A REPUTABLE TATTOO ARTIST WHO STERILIZES HIS (OR HER) EQUIPMENT THOROUGHLY, SO YOU DON'T GET ANY TRANSMISSIBLE DISEASES.
DISEASES?

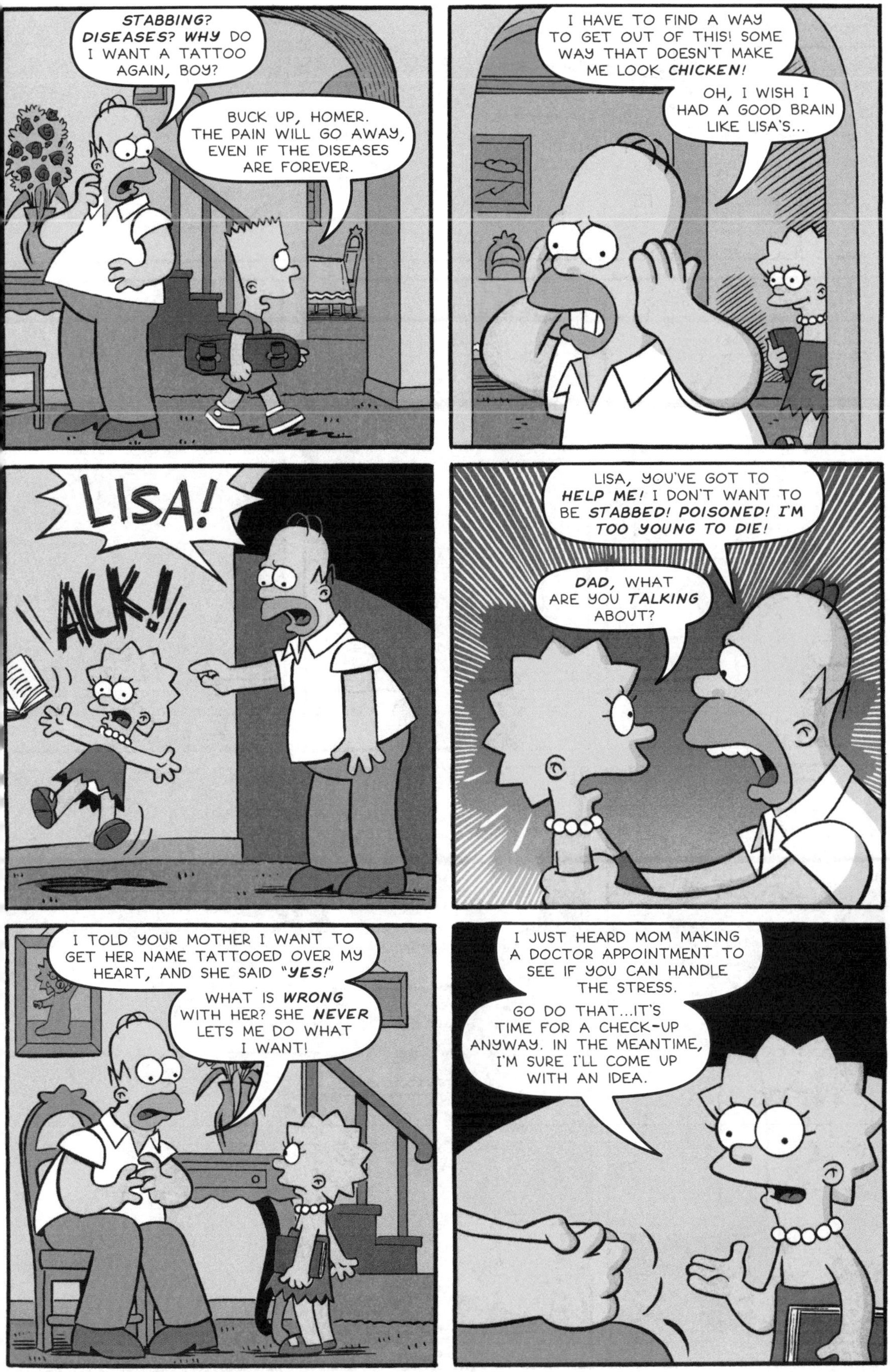

STABBING? DISEASES? WHY DO I WANT A TATTOO AGAIN, BOY?
BUCK UP, HOMER. THE PAIN WILL GO AWAY, EVEN IF THE DISEASES ARE FOREVER.
I HAVE TO FIND A WAY TO GET OUT OF THIS! SOME WAY THAT DOESN'T MAKE ME LOOK CHICKEN!
OH, I WISH I HAD A GOOD BRAIN LIKE LISA'S...
LISA!
ACK!!
LISA, YOU'VE GOT TO HELP ME! I DON'T WANT TO BE STABBED! POISONED! I'M TOO YOUNG TO DIE!
DAD, WHAT ARE YOU TALKING ABOUT?
I TOLD YOUR MOTHER I WANT TO GET HER NAME TATTOOED OVER MY HEART, AND SHE SAID "YES!"
WHAT IS WRONG WITH HER? SHE NEVER LETS ME DO WHAT I WANT!
I JUST HEARD MOM MAKING A DOCTOR APPOINTMENT TO SEE IF YOU CAN HANDLE THE STRESS.
GO DO THAT...IT'S TIME FOR A CHECK-UP ANYWAY. IN THE MEANTIME, I'M SURE I'LL COME UP WITH AN IDEA.

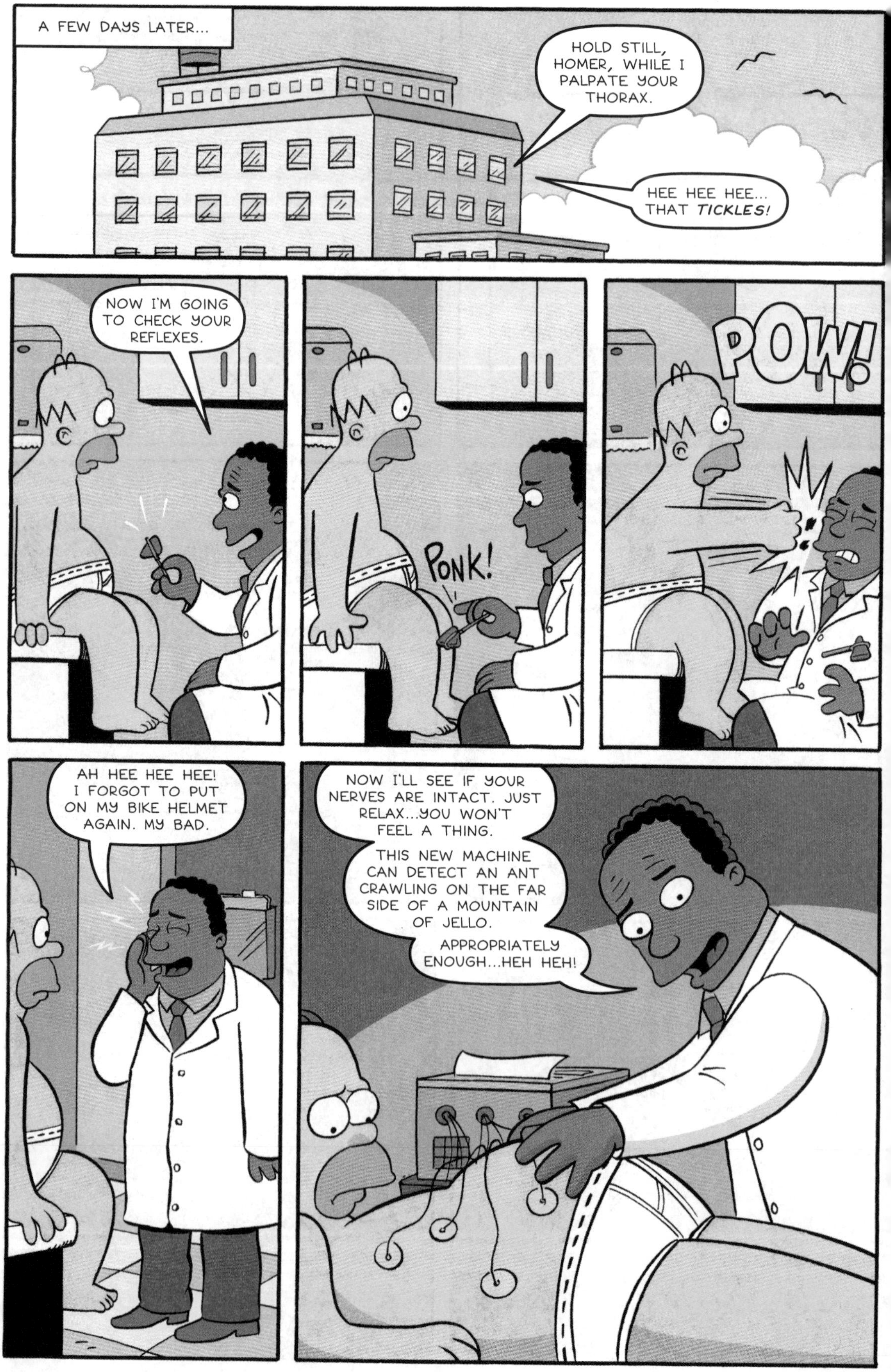
A FEW DAYS LATER...
HOLD STILL, HOMER, WHILE I PALPATE YOUR THORAX.
HEE HEE HEE... THAT *TICKLES!*
NOW I'M GOING TO CHECK YOUR REFLEXES.
PONK!
POW!
AH HEE HEE HEE! I FORGOT TO PUT ON MY BIKE HELMET AGAIN. MY BAD.
NOW I'LL SEE IF YOUR NERVES ARE INTACT. JUST RELAX...YOU WON'T FEEL A THING.
THIS NEW MACHINE CAN DETECT AN ANT CRAWLING ON THE FAR SIDE OF A MOUNTAIN OF JELLO.
APPROPRIATELY ENOUGH...HEH HEH!

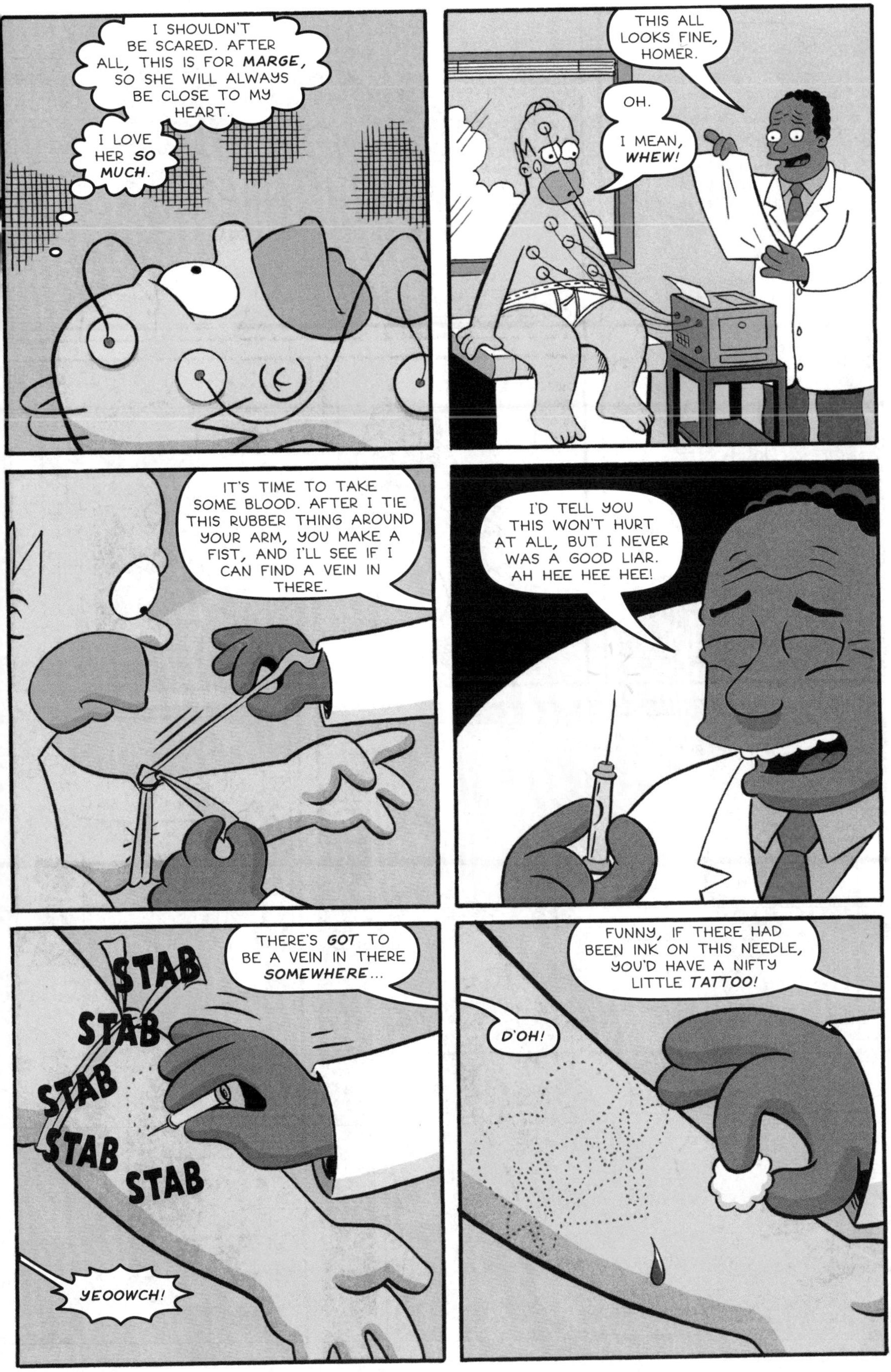
I SHOULDN'T BE SCARED. AFTER ALL, THIS IS FOR **MARGE**, SO SHE WILL ALWAYS BE CLOSE TO MY HEART.
I LOVE HER **SO MUCH**.
THIS ALL LOOKS FINE, HOMER.
OH.
I MEAN, **WHEW!**
IT'S TIME TO TAKE SOME BLOOD. AFTER I TIE THIS RUBBER THING AROUND YOUR ARM, YOU MAKE A FIST, AND I'LL SEE IF I CAN FIND A VEIN IN THERE.
I'D TELL YOU THIS WON'T HURT AT ALL, BUT I NEVER WAS A GOOD LIAR. AH HEE HEE HEE!
THERE'S **GOT** TO BE A VEIN IN THERE **SOMEWHERE**...
STAB
STAB
STAB
STAB
STAB
YEOOWCH!
FUNNY, IF THERE HAD BEEN INK ON THIS NEEDLE, YOU'D HAVE A NIFTY LITTLE **TATTOO!**
D'OH!

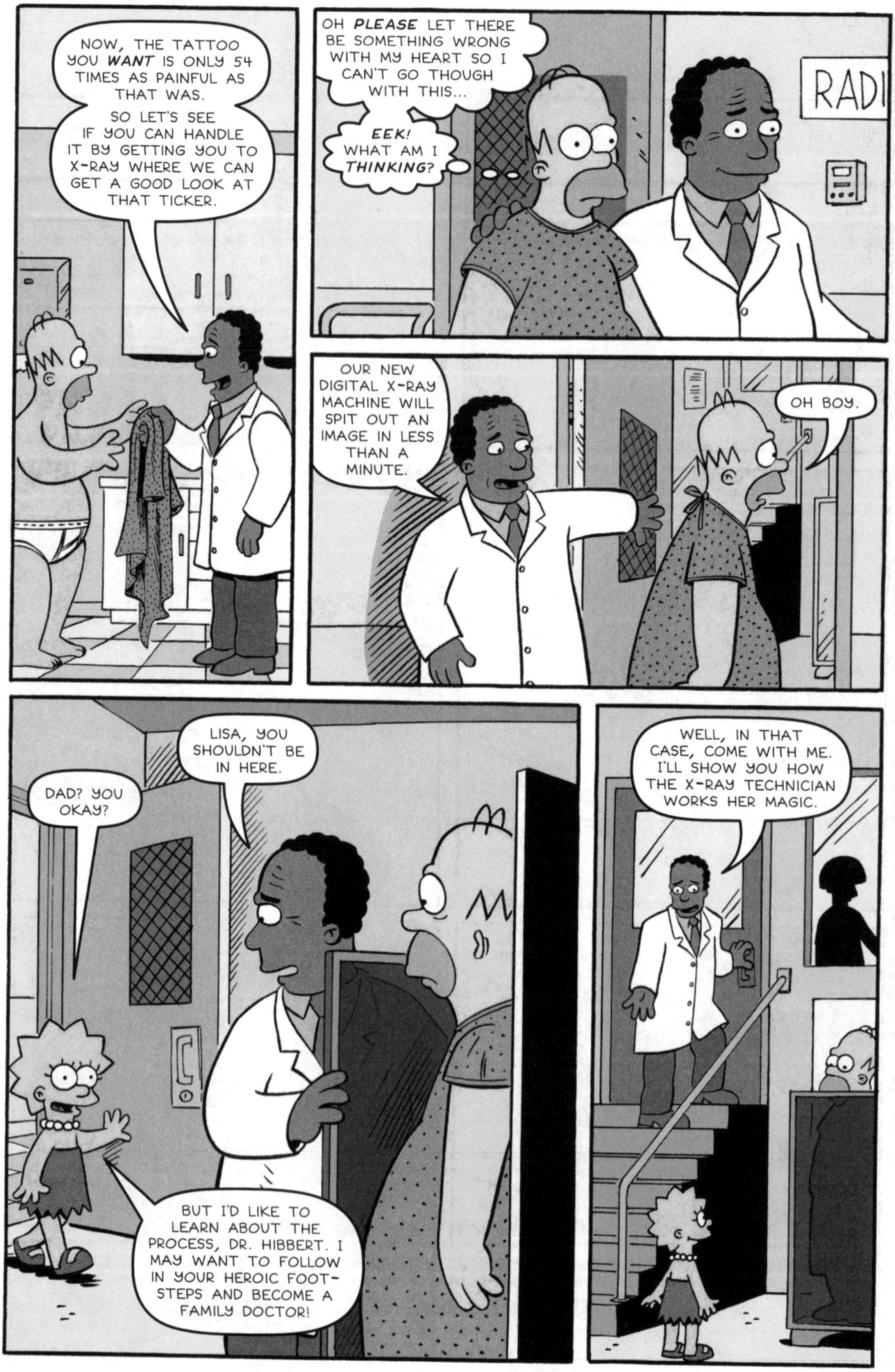
NOW, THE TATTOO YOU *WANT* IS ONLY 54 TIMES AS PAINFUL AS THAT WAS.
SO LET'S SEE IF YOU CAN HANDLE IT BY GETTING YOU TO X-RAY WHERE WE CAN GET A GOOD LOOK AT THAT TICKER.
OH *PLEASE* LET THERE BE SOMETHING WRONG WITH MY HEART SO I CAN'T GO THOUGH WITH THIS...
EEK! WHAT AM I *THINKING*?
RADI
OUR NEW DIGITAL X-RAY MACHINE WILL SPIT OUT AN IMAGE IN LESS THAN A MINUTE.
OH BOY.
DAD? YOU OKAY?
LISA, YOU SHOULDN'T BE IN HERE.
BUT I'D LIKE TO LEARN ABOUT THE PROCESS, DR. HIBBERT. I MAY WANT TO FOLLOW IN YOUR HEROIC FOOT-STEPS AND BECOME A FAMILY DOCTOR!
WELL, IN THAT CASE, COME WITH ME. I'LL SHOW YOU HOW THE X-RAY TECHNICIAN WORKS HER MAGIC.

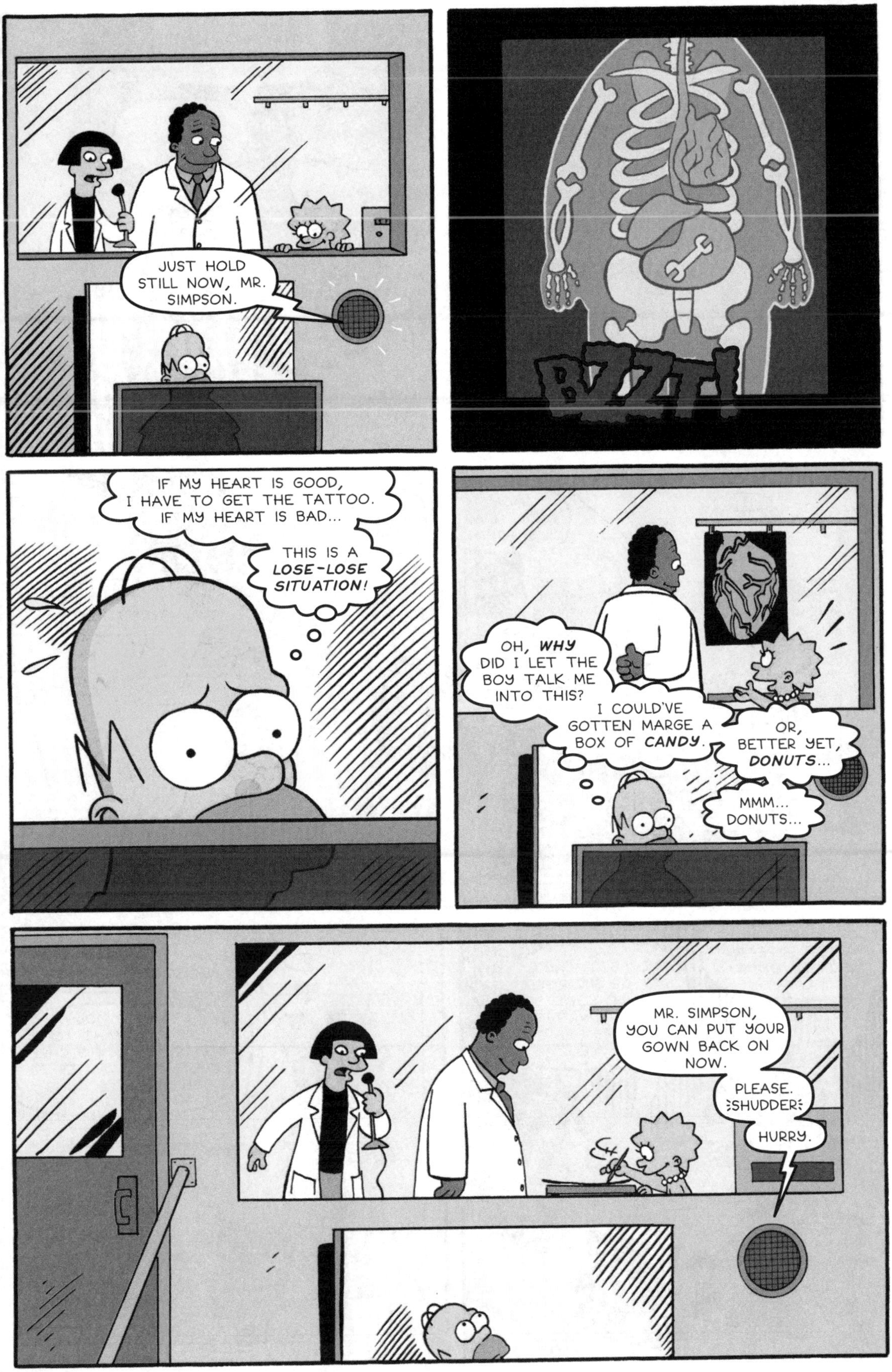
JUST HOLD STILL NOW, MR. SIMPSON.
BZZT!
IF MY HEART IS GOOD, I HAVE TO GET THE TATTOO. IF MY HEART IS BAD...
THIS IS A LOSE-LOSE SITUATION!
OH, WHY DID I LET THE BOY TALK ME INTO THIS?
I COULD'VE GOTTEN MARGE A BOX OF CANDY.
OR, BETTER YET, DONUTS...
MMM... DONUTS...
MR. SIMPSON, YOU CAN PUT YOUR GOWN BACK ON NOW.
PLEASE.
SHUDDER
HURRY.

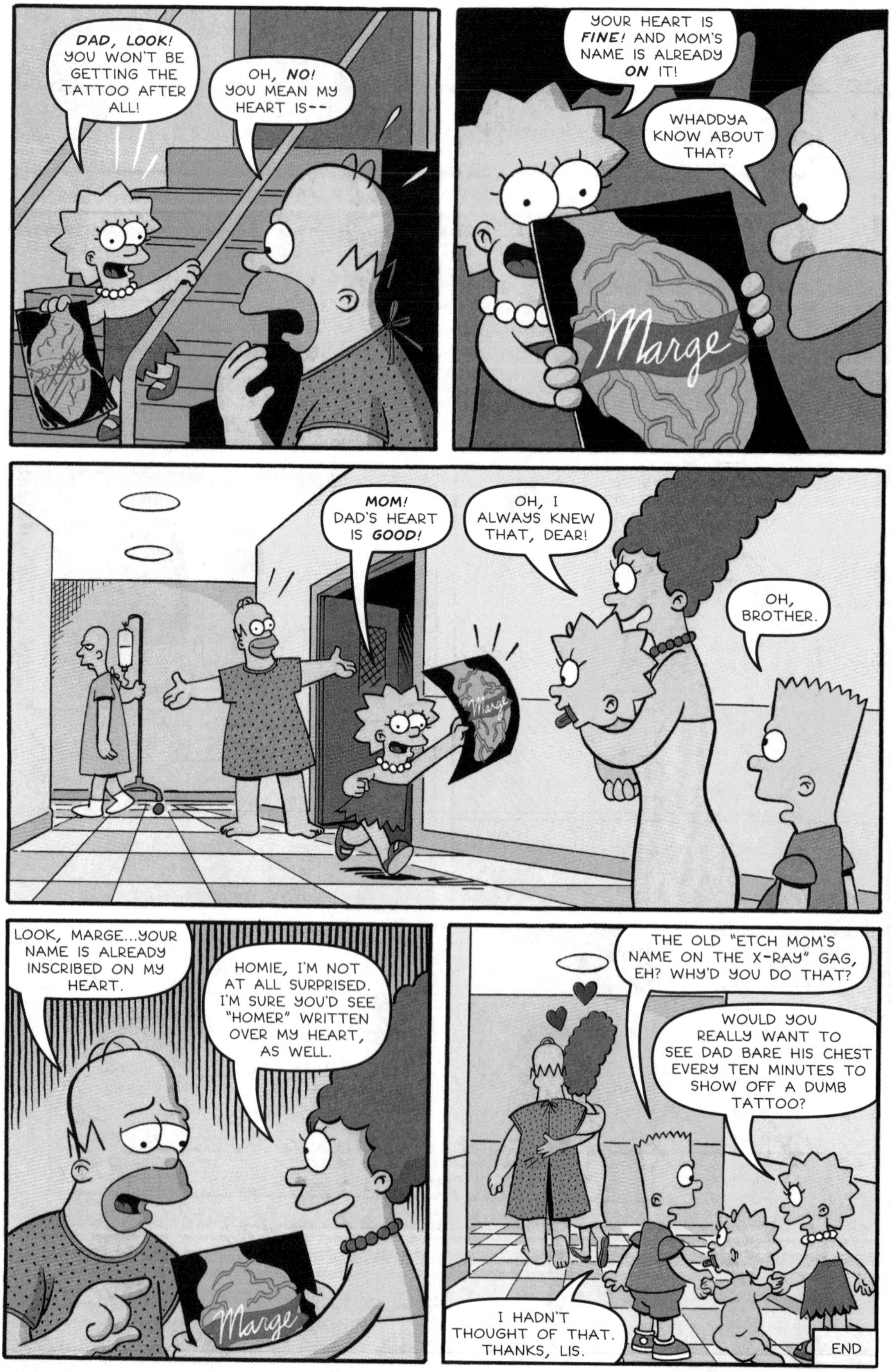

DAD, LOOK! YOU WON'T BE GETTING THE TATTOO AFTER ALL!
OH, NO! YOU MEAN MY HEART IS--
YOUR HEART IS FINE! AND MOM'S NAME IS ALREADY ON IT!
WHADDYA KNOW ABOUT THAT?
Marge
MOM! DAD'S HEART IS GOOD!
OH, I ALWAYS KNEW THAT, DEAR!
OH, BROTHER.
Marge
LOOK, MARGE...YOUR NAME IS ALREADY INSCRIBED ON MY HEART.
HOMIE, I'M NOT AT ALL SURPRISED. I'M SURE YOU'D SEE "HOMER" WRITTEN OVER MY HEART, AS WELL.
Marge
THE OLD "ETCH MOM'S NAME ON THE X-RAY" GAG, EH? WHY'D YOU DO THAT?
WOULD YOU REALLY WANT TO SEE DAD BARE HIS CHEST EVERY TEN MINUTES TO SHOW OFF A DUMB TATTOO?
I HADN'T THOUGHT OF THAT. THANKS, LIS.
END

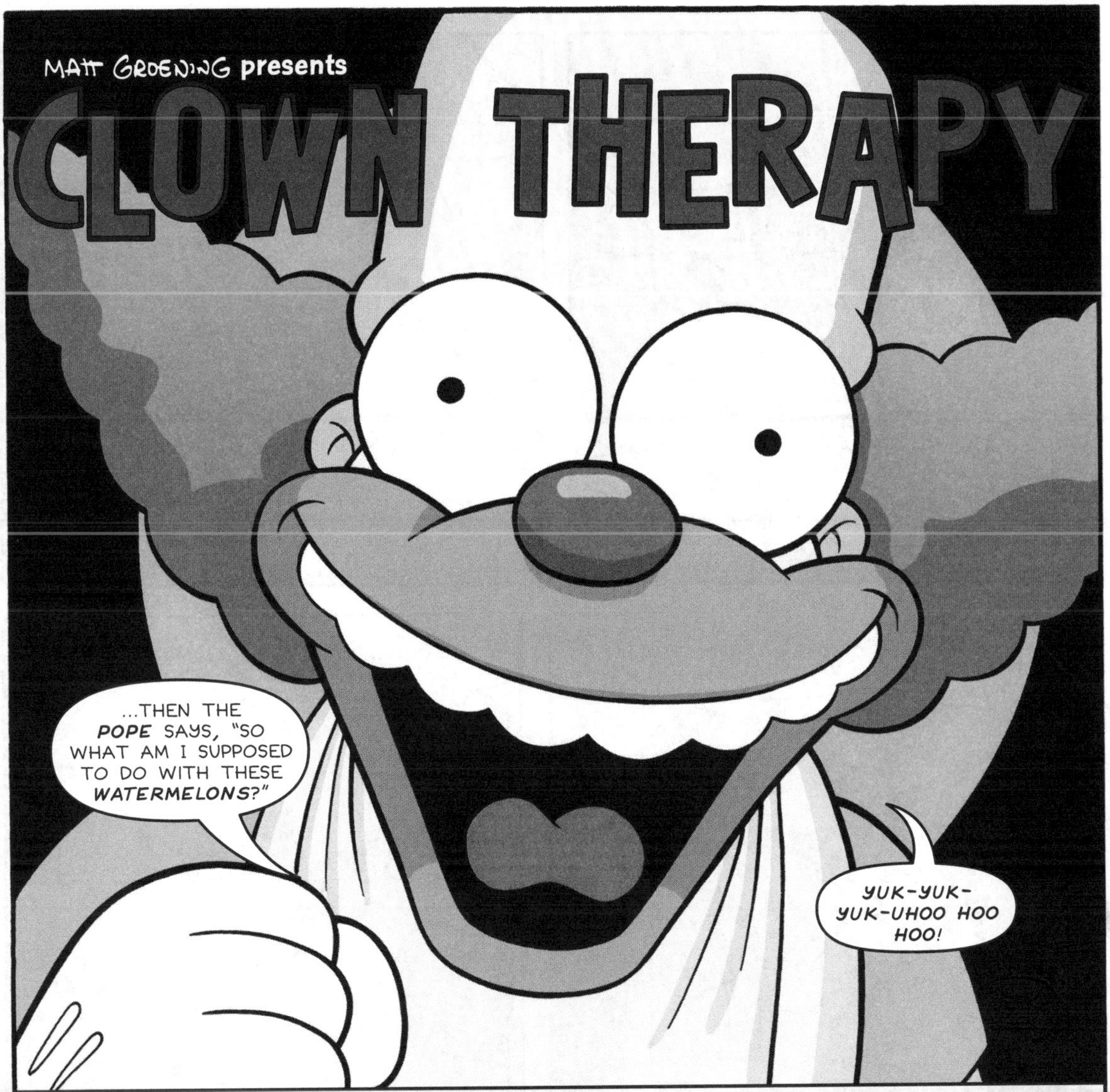
MATT GROENING presents
CLOWN THERAPY
...THEN THE POPE SAYS, "SO WHAT AM I SUPPOSED TO DO WITH THESE WATERMELONS?"
YUK-YUK-YUK-UHOO HOO HOO!

CHUCK DIXON SCRIPT | **PHIL ORTIZ** PENCILS | **MIKE DECARLO** INKS | **ART VILLANUEVA** COLORS | **KAREN BATES** LETTERS | **BILL MORRISON** EDITOR

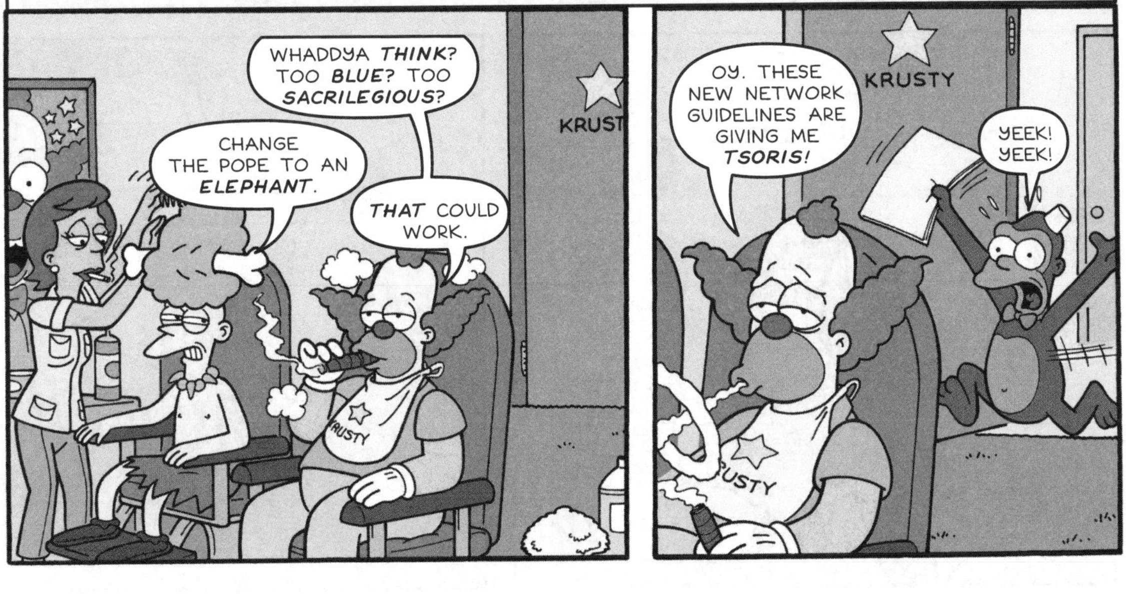
WHADDYA THINK? TOO BLUE? TOO SACRILEGIOUS?
CHANGE THE POPE TO AN ELEPHANT.
THAT COULD WORK.
KRUST
OY. THESE NEW NETWORK GUIDELINES ARE GIVING ME TSORIS!
KRUSTY
YEEK! YEEK!

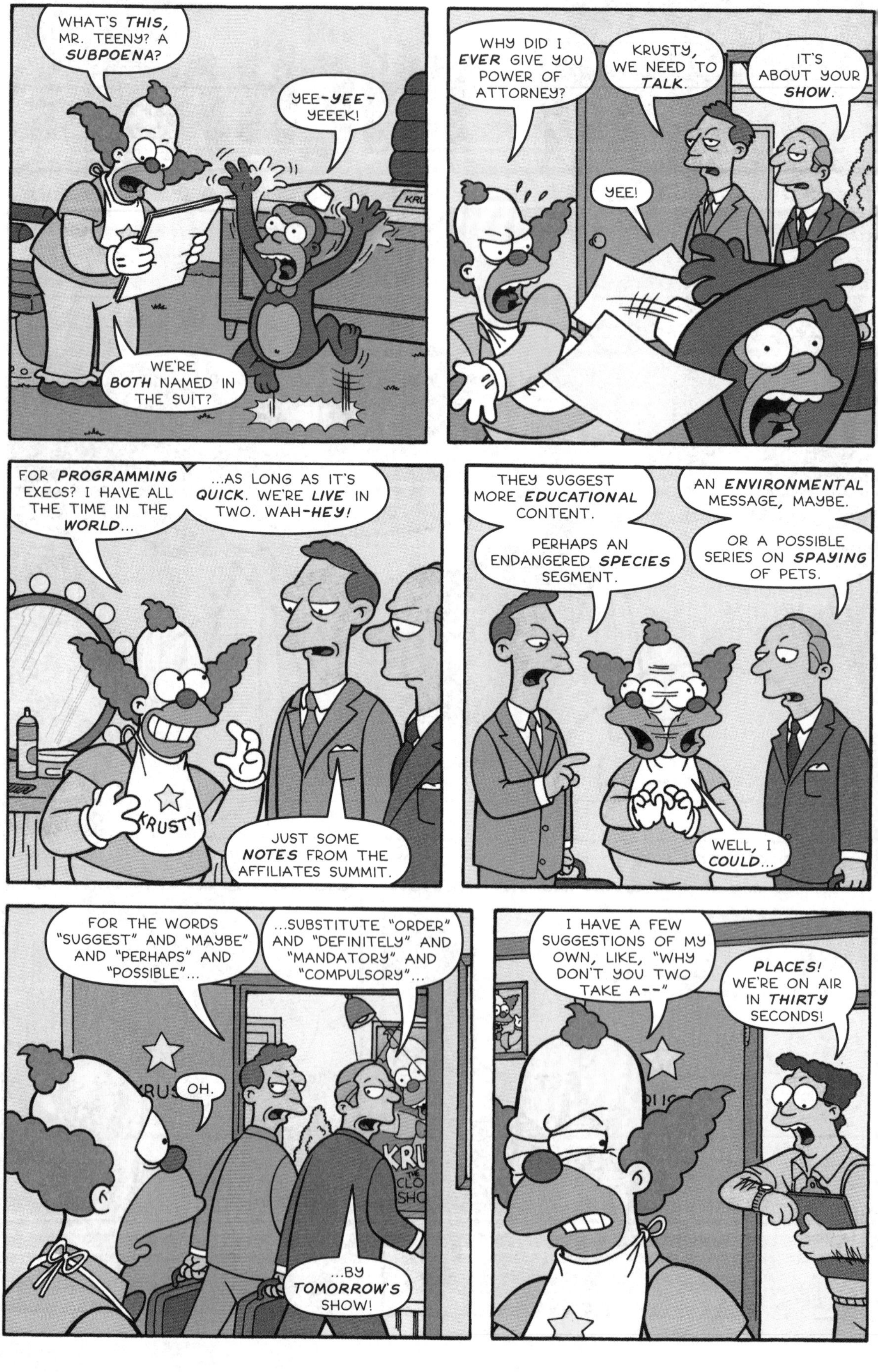
WHAT'S THIS, MR. TEENY? A SUBPOENA?
YEE-YEE-YEEEK!
WE'RE BOTH NAMED IN THE SUIT?
WHY DID I EVER GIVE YOU POWER OF ATTORNEY?
KRUSTY, WE NEED TO TALK.
IT'S ABOUT YOUR SHOW.
YEE!
FOR PROGRAMMING EXECS? I HAVE ALL THE TIME IN THE WORLD...
...AS LONG AS IT'S QUICK. WE'RE LIVE IN TWO. WAH-HEY!
KRUSTY
JUST SOME NOTES FROM THE AFFILIATES SUMMIT.
THEY SUGGEST MORE EDUCATIONAL CONTENT.
AN ENVIRONMENTAL MESSAGE, MAYBE.
PERHAPS AN ENDANGERED SPECIES SEGMENT.
OR A POSSIBLE SERIES ON SPAYING OF PETS.
WELL, I COULD...
FOR THE WORDS "SUGGEST" AND "MAYBE" AND "PERHAPS" AND "POSSIBLE"...
...SUBSTITUTE "ORDER" AND "DEFINITELY" AND "MANDATORY" AND "COMPULSORY"...
OH.
...BY TOMORROW'S SHOW!
I HAVE A FEW SUGGESTIONS OF MY OWN, LIKE, "WHY DON'T YOU TWO TAKE A--"
PLACES! WE'RE ON AIR IN THIRTY SECONDS!

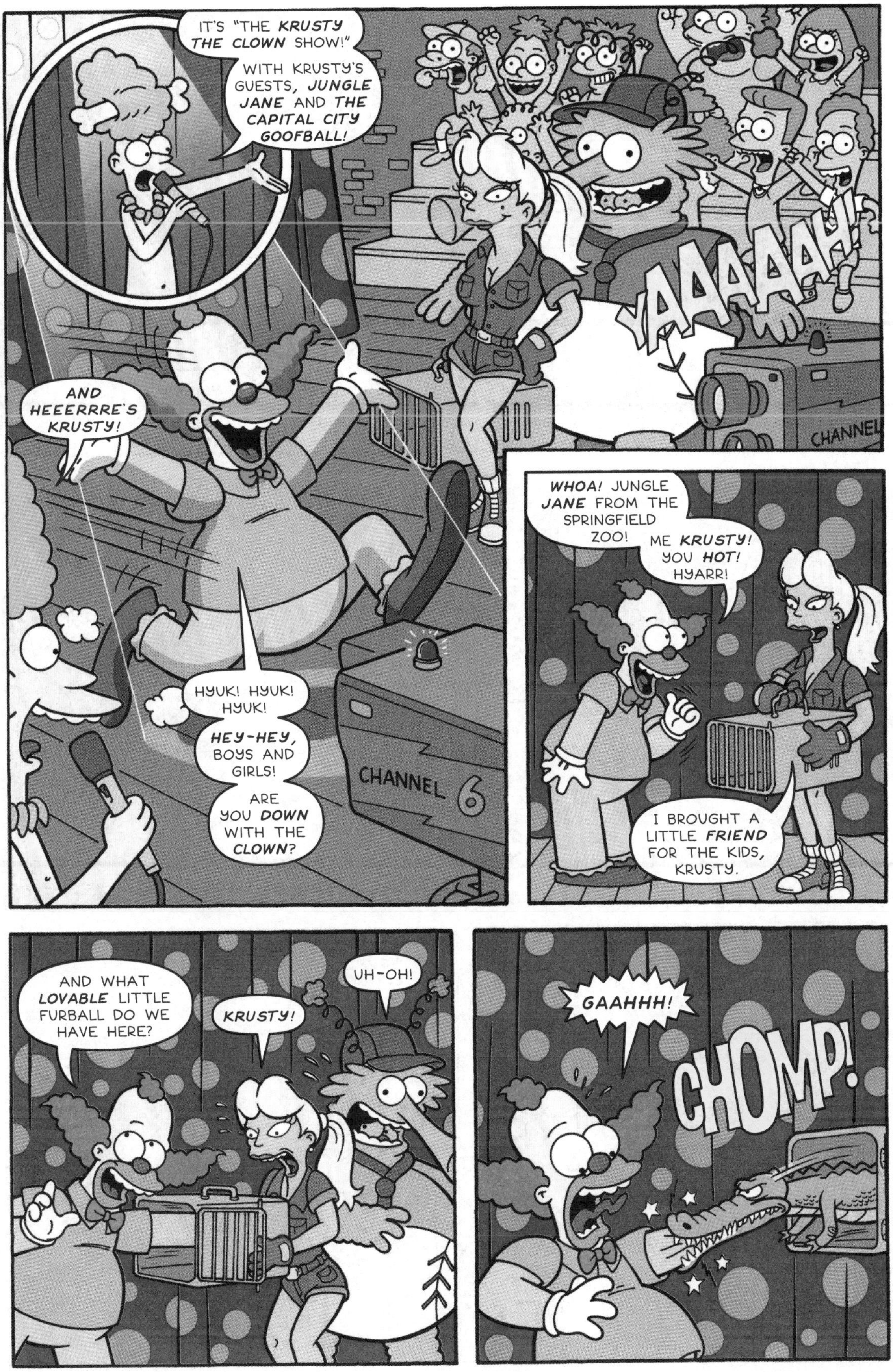
IT'S "THE KRUSTY THE CLOWN SHOW!"
WITH KRUSTY'S GUESTS, JUNGLE JANE AND THE CAPITAL CITY GOOFBALL!
YAAAAAH!
AND HEEERRRE'S KRUSTY!
HYUK! HYUK! HYUK!
HEY-HEY, BOYS AND GIRLS!
ARE YOU DOWN WITH THE CLOWN?
CHANNEL 6
WHOA! JUNGLE JANE FROM THE SPRINGFIELD ZOO!
ME KRUSTY! YOU HOT! HYARR!
I BROUGHT A LITTLE FRIEND FOR THE KIDS, KRUSTY.
AND WHAT LOVABLE LITTLE FURBALL DO WE HAVE HERE?
KRUSTY!
UH-OH!
GAAHHH!
CHOMP!

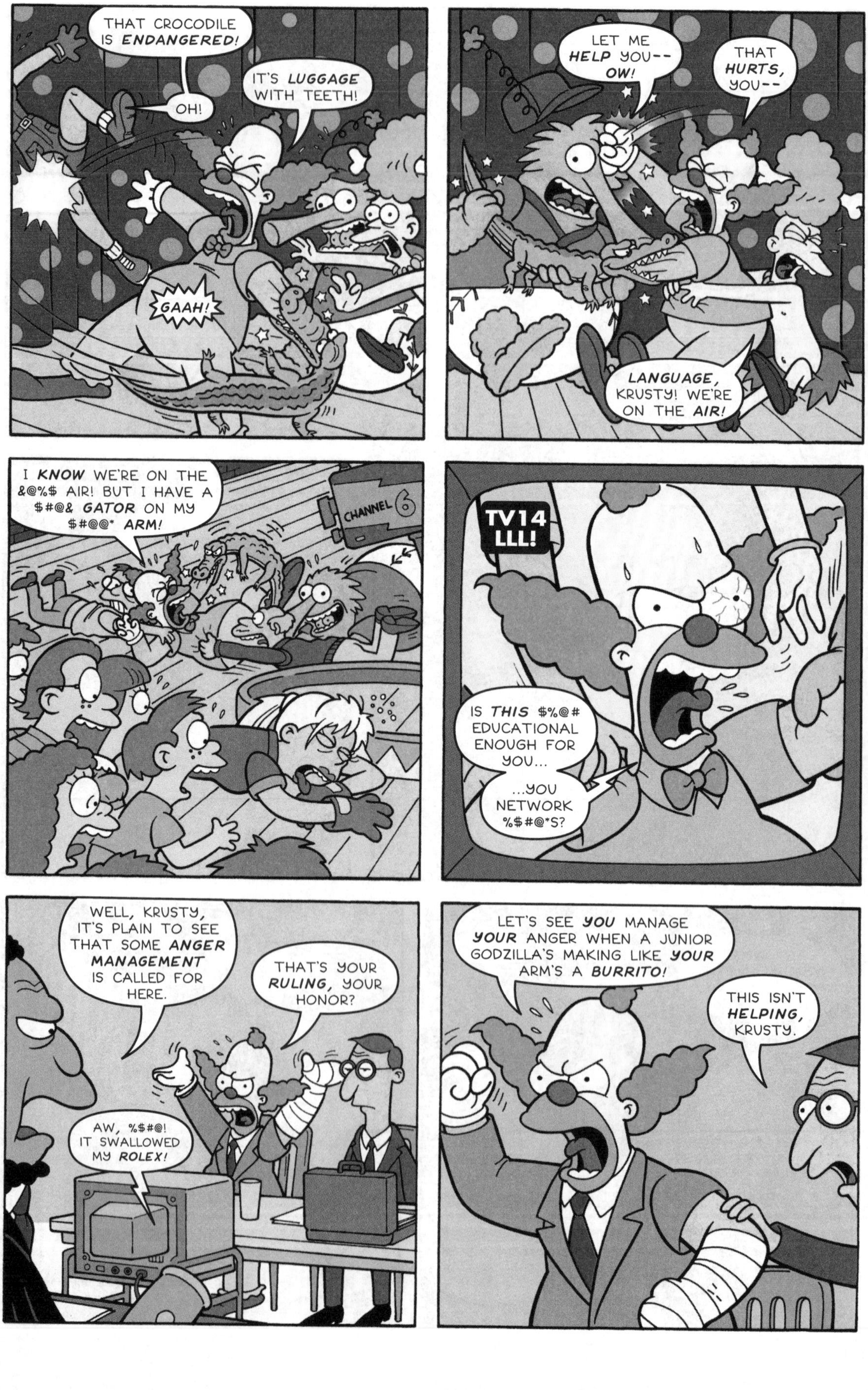
THAT CROCODILE IS ENDANGERED!
OH!
IT'S LUGGAGE WITH TEETH!
GAAH!
LET ME HELP YOU-- OW!
THAT HURTS, YOU--
LANGUAGE, KRUSTY! WE'RE ON THE AIR!
I KNOW WE'RE ON THE &@%$ AIR! BUT I HAVE A $#@& GATOR ON MY $#@@* ARM!
CHANNEL 6
TV14 LLL!
IS THIS $%@# EDUCATIONAL ENOUGH FOR YOU...
...YOU NETWORK %$#@*S?
WELL, KRUSTY, IT'S PLAIN TO SEE THAT SOME ANGER MANAGEMENT IS CALLED FOR HERE.
THAT'S YOUR RULING, YOUR HONOR?
AW, %$#@! IT SWALLOWED MY ROLEX!
LET'S SEE YOU MANAGE YOUR ANGER WHEN A JUNIOR GODZILLA'S MAKING LIKE YOUR ARM'S A BURRITO!
THIS ISN'T HELPING, KRUSTY.

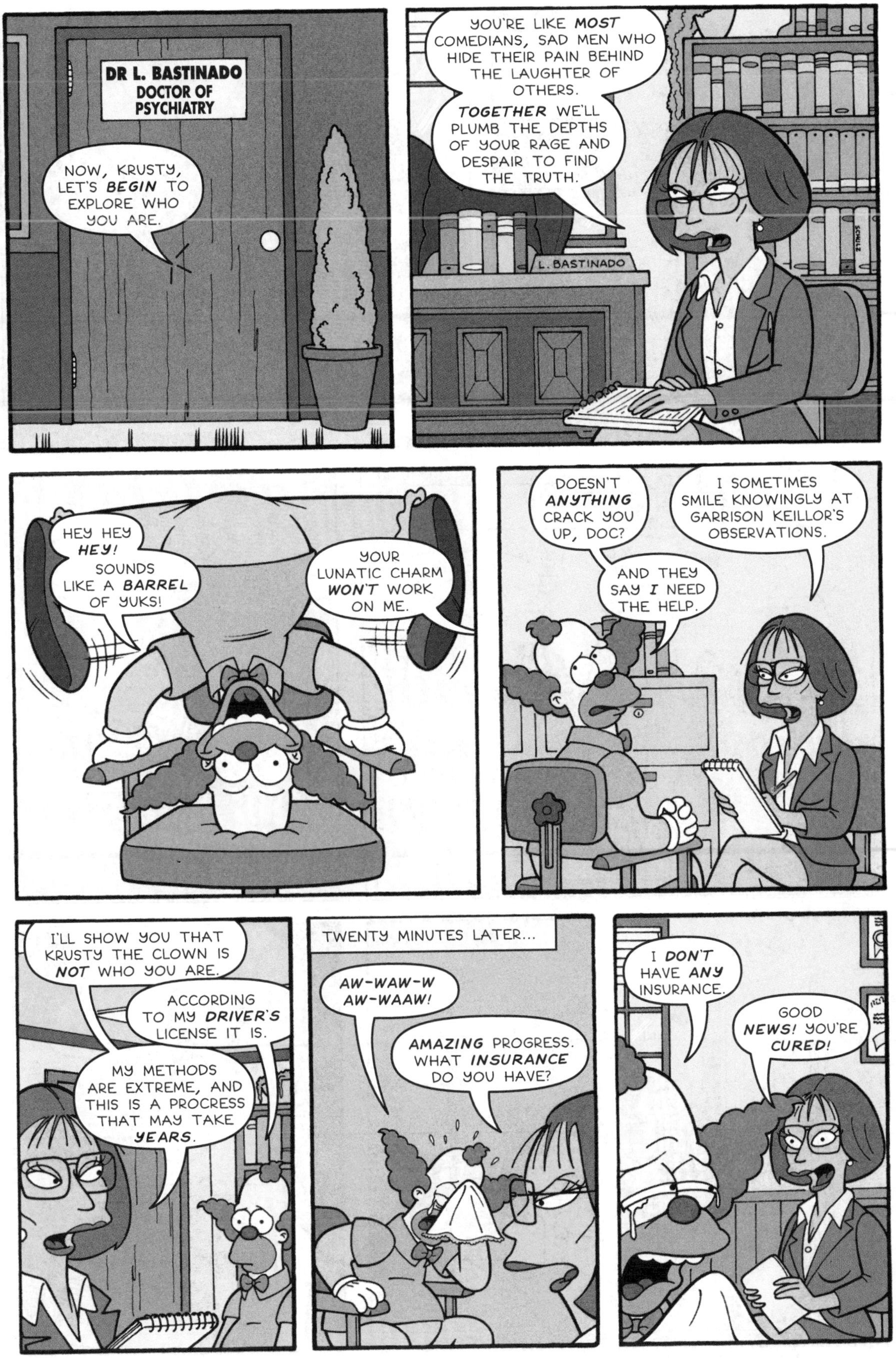
DR L. BASTINADO
DOCTOR OF PSYCHIATRY
NOW, KRUSTY, LET'S BEGIN TO EXPLORE WHO YOU ARE.
YOU'RE LIKE MOST COMEDIANS, SAD MEN WHO HIDE THEIR PAIN BEHIND THE LAUGHTER OF OTHERS.
TOGETHER WE'LL PLUMB THE DEPTHS OF YOUR RAGE AND DESPAIR TO FIND THE TRUTH.
L. BASTINADO
HEY HEY HEY! SOUNDS LIKE A BARREL OF YUKS!
YOUR LUNATIC CHARM WON'T WORK ON ME.
DOESN'T ANYTHING CRACK YOU UP, DOC?
I SOMETIMES SMILE KNOWINGLY AT GARRISON KEILLOR'S OBSERVATIONS.
AND THEY SAY I NEED THE HELP.
I'LL SHOW YOU THAT KRUSTY THE CLOWN IS NOT WHO YOU ARE.
ACCORDING TO MY DRIVER'S LICENSE IT IS.
MY METHODS ARE EXTREME, AND THIS IS A PROCRESS THAT MAY TAKE YEARS.
TWENTY MINUTES LATER...
AW-WAW-W AW-WAAW!
AMAZING PROGRESS. WHAT INSURANCE DO YOU HAVE?
I DON'T HAVE ANY INSURANCE.
GOOD NEWS! YOU'RE CURED!

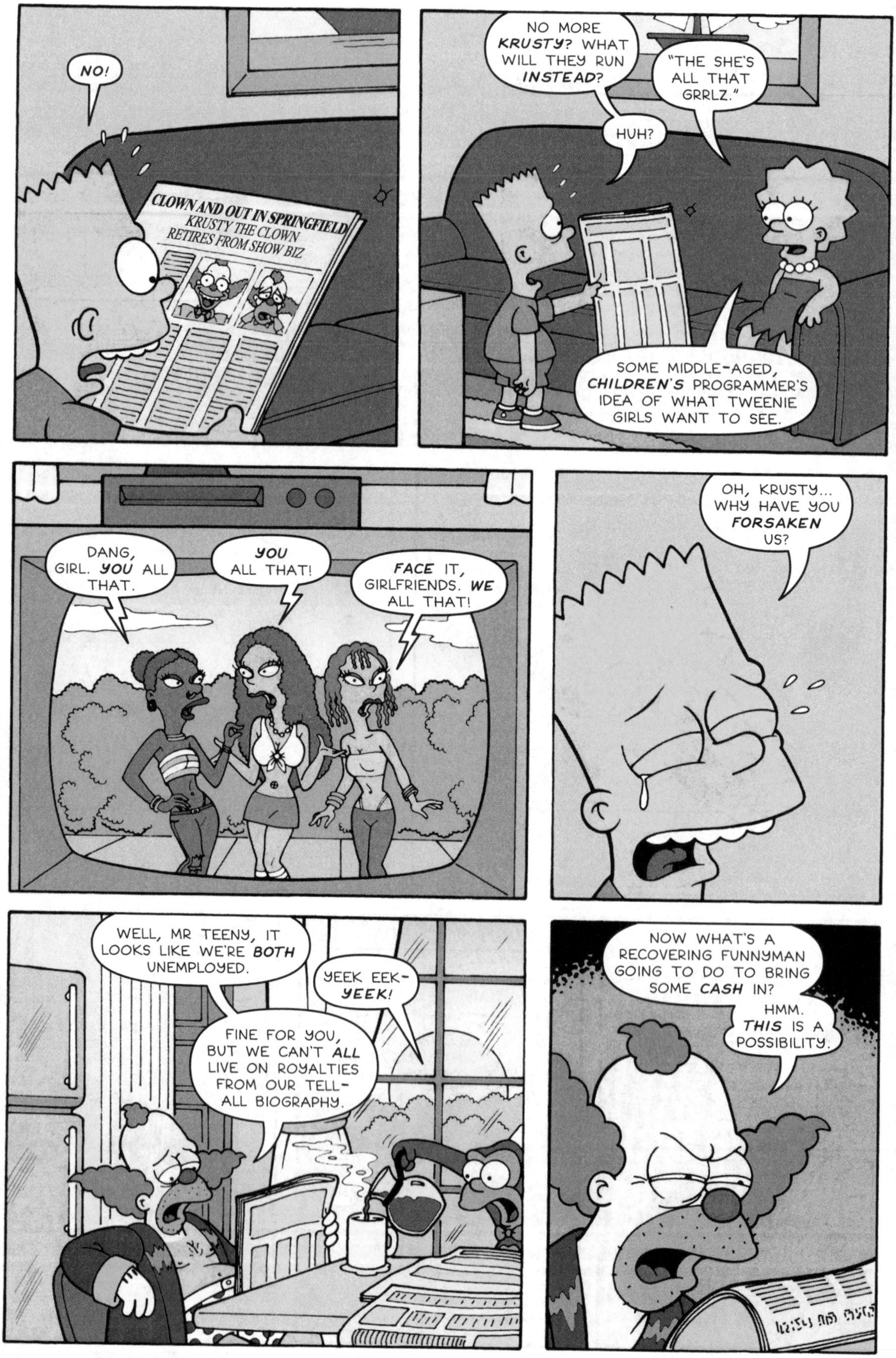
NO!
CLOWN AND OUT IN SPRINGFIELD
KRUSTY THE CLOWN RETIRES FROM SHOW BIZ
NO MORE KRUSTY? WHAT WILL THEY RUN INSTEAD?
"THE SHE'S ALL THAT GRRLZ."
HUH?
SOME MIDDLE-AGED, CHILDREN'S PROGRAMMER'S IDEA OF WHAT TWEENIE GIRLS WANT TO SEE.
DANG, GIRL. YOU ALL THAT.
YOU ALL THAT!
FACE IT, GIRLFRIENDS. WE ALL THAT!
OH, KRUSTY... WHY HAVE YOU FORSAKEN US?
WELL, MR TEENY, IT LOOKS LIKE WE'RE BOTH UNEMPLOYED.
YEEK EEK-YEEK!
FINE FOR YOU, BUT WE CAN'T ALL LIVE ON ROYALTIES FROM OUR TELL-ALL BIOGRAPHY.
NOW WHAT'S A RECOVERING FUNNYMAN GOING TO DO TO BRING SOME CASH IN?
HMM. THIS IS A POSSIBILITY.

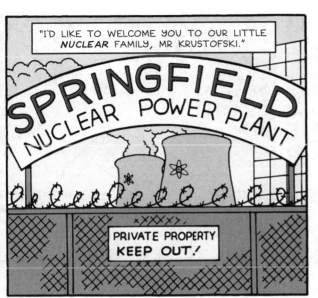

"I'D LIKE TO WELCOME YOU TO OUR LITTLE *NUCLEAR* FAMILY, MR KRUSTOFSKI."

SPRINGFIELD NUCLEAR POWER PLANT

PRIVATE PROPERTY KEEP OUT!

WAS THAT A *JOKE*, MR SMITHERS? BECAUSE I'M UNDER A DOCTOR'S ORDERS NOT TO *LAUGH*.

URM... ¡AHEM¡ MORE A PLAY ON *WORDS*.

HEY, IT'S *KRUSTY!*

HEY, *KRUSTY!* DO SOMETHING *FUNNY!*

NOT *TODAY*, GENTLEMAN.

DARN CLOWN THINKS HE'S *BETTER* THAN US.

I HEARD HE GOT HIRED UNDER *AFFIRMATIVE ACTION*.

THIS IS YOUR *WORK* AREA.

NOTHING FUNNY *HERE*. IT'S *PERFECT*.

WELL, I'LL LEAVE YOU TO YOUR *NUMBER CRUNCHING*.

HRRMM...

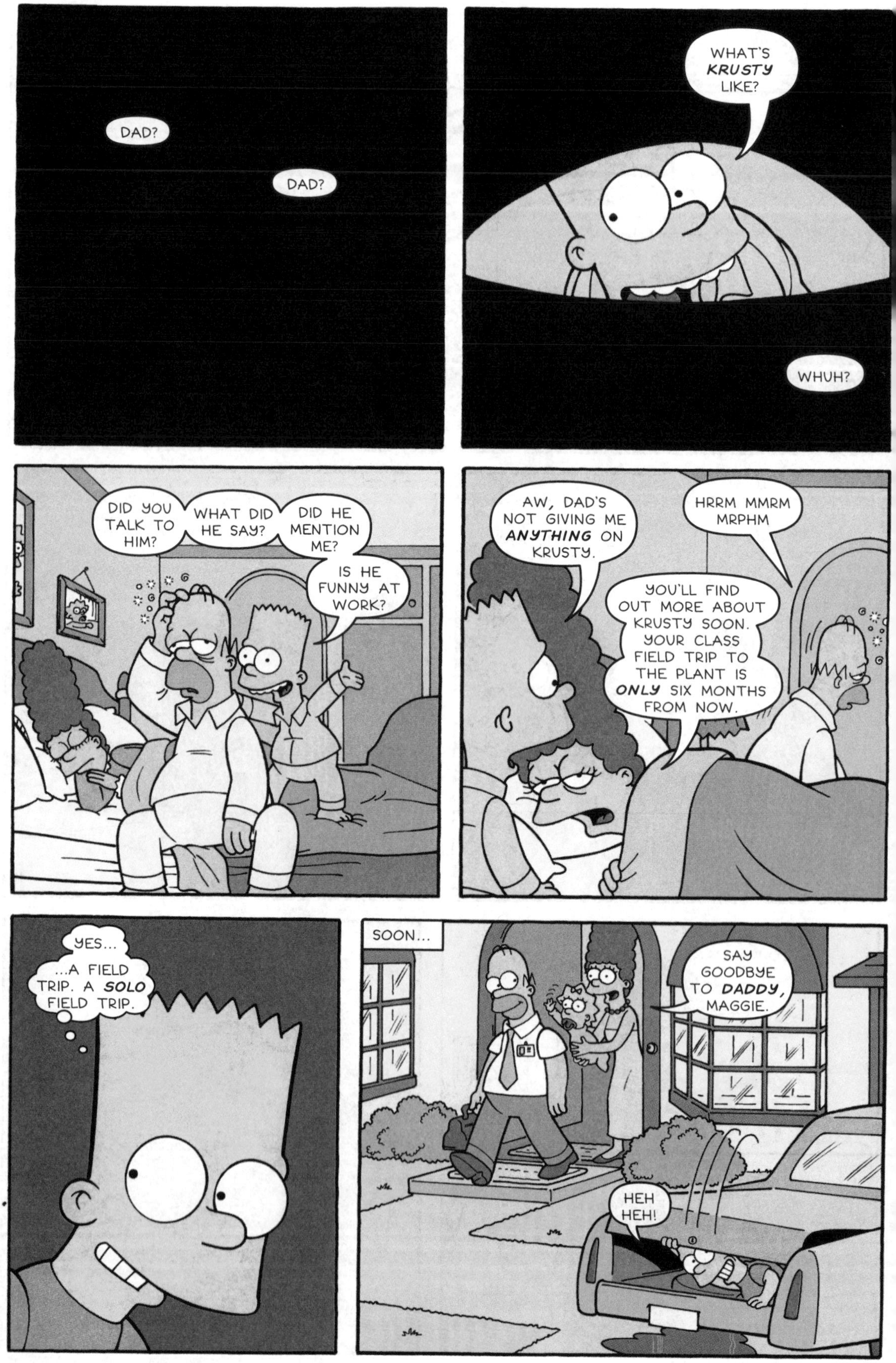
DAD?
DAD?
WHAT'S KRUSTY LIKE?
WHUH?
DID YOU TALK TO HIM?
WHAT DID HE SAY?
DID HE MENTION ME?
IS HE FUNNY AT WORK?
AW, DAD'S NOT GIVING ME ANYTHING ON KRUSTY.
HRRM MMRM MRPHM
YOU'LL FIND OUT MORE ABOUT KRUSTY SOON. YOUR CLASS FIELD TRIP TO THE PLANT IS ONLY SIX MONTHS FROM NOW.
YES...
...A FIELD TRIP. A SOLO FIELD TRIP.
SOON...
SAY GOODBYE TO DADDY, MAGGIE.
HEH HEH!

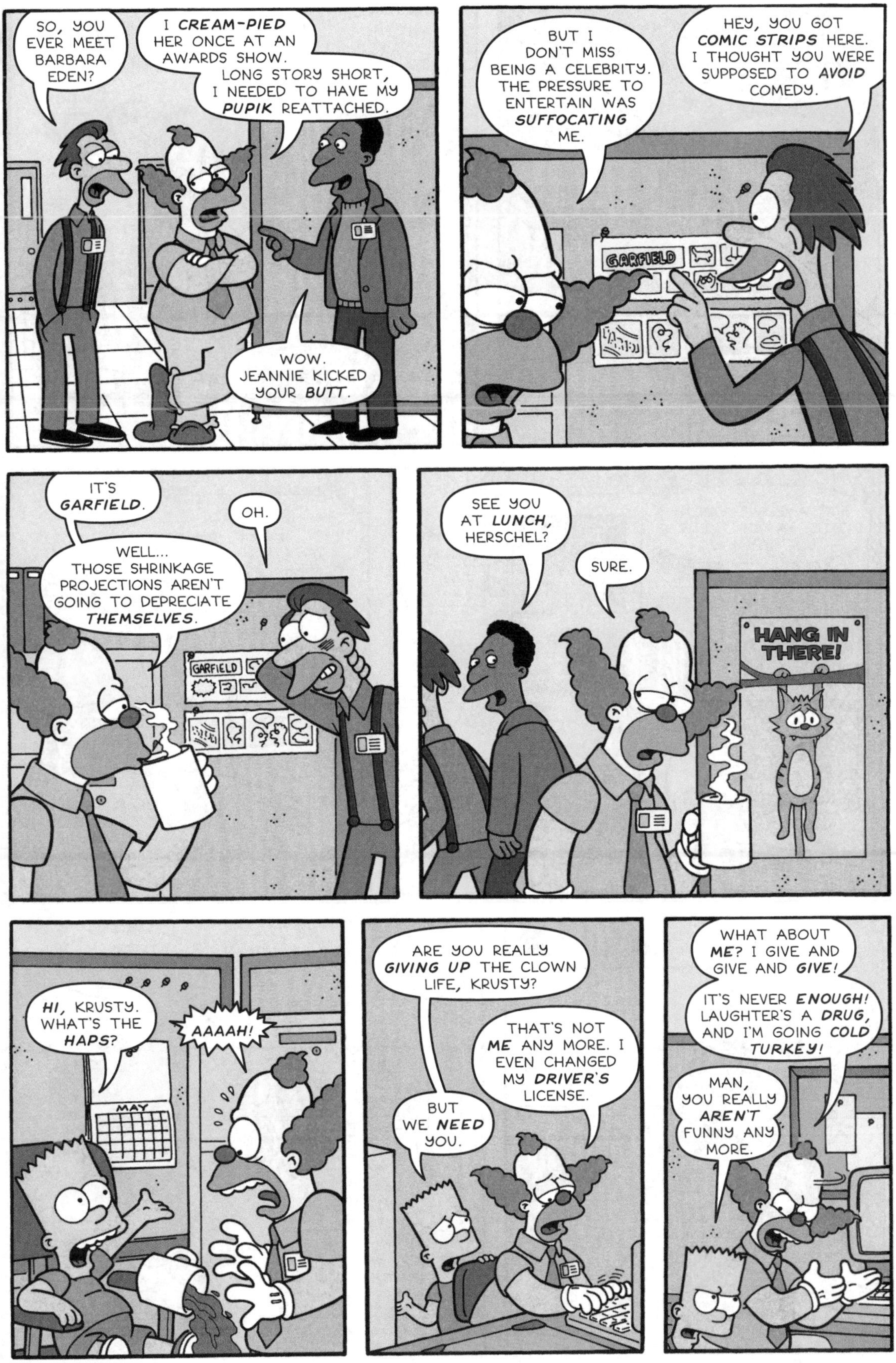
SO, YOU EVER MEET BARBARA EDEN?
I **CREAM-PIED** HER ONCE AT AN AWARDS SHOW.
LONG STORY SHORT, I NEEDED TO HAVE MY **PUPIK** REATTACHED.
WOW. JEANNIE KICKED YOUR **BUTT**.
BUT I DON'T MISS BEING A CELEBRITY. THE PRESSURE TO ENTERTAIN WAS **SUFFOCATING** ME.
HEY, YOU GOT **COMIC STRIPS** HERE. I THOUGHT YOU WERE SUPPOSED TO **AVOID** COMEDY.
GARFIELD
IT'S **GARFIELD**.
OH.
WELL... THOSE SHRINKAGE PROJECTIONS AREN'T GOING TO DEPRECIATE **THEMSELVES**.
GARFIELD
SEE YOU AT **LUNCH**, HERSCHEL?
SURE.
HANG IN THERE!
HI, KRUSTY. WHAT'S THE **HAPS**?
AAAAH!
MAY
ARE YOU REALLY **GIVING UP** THE CLOWN LIFE, KRUSTY?
THAT'S NOT **ME** ANY MORE. I EVEN CHANGED MY **DRIVER'S** LICENSE.
BUT WE **NEED** YOU.
WHAT ABOUT **ME**? I GIVE AND GIVE AND **GIVE**!
IT'S NEVER **ENOUGH**! LAUGHTER'S A **DRUG**, AND I'M GOING **COLD TURKEY**!
MAN, YOU REALLY **AREN'T** FUNNY ANY MORE.

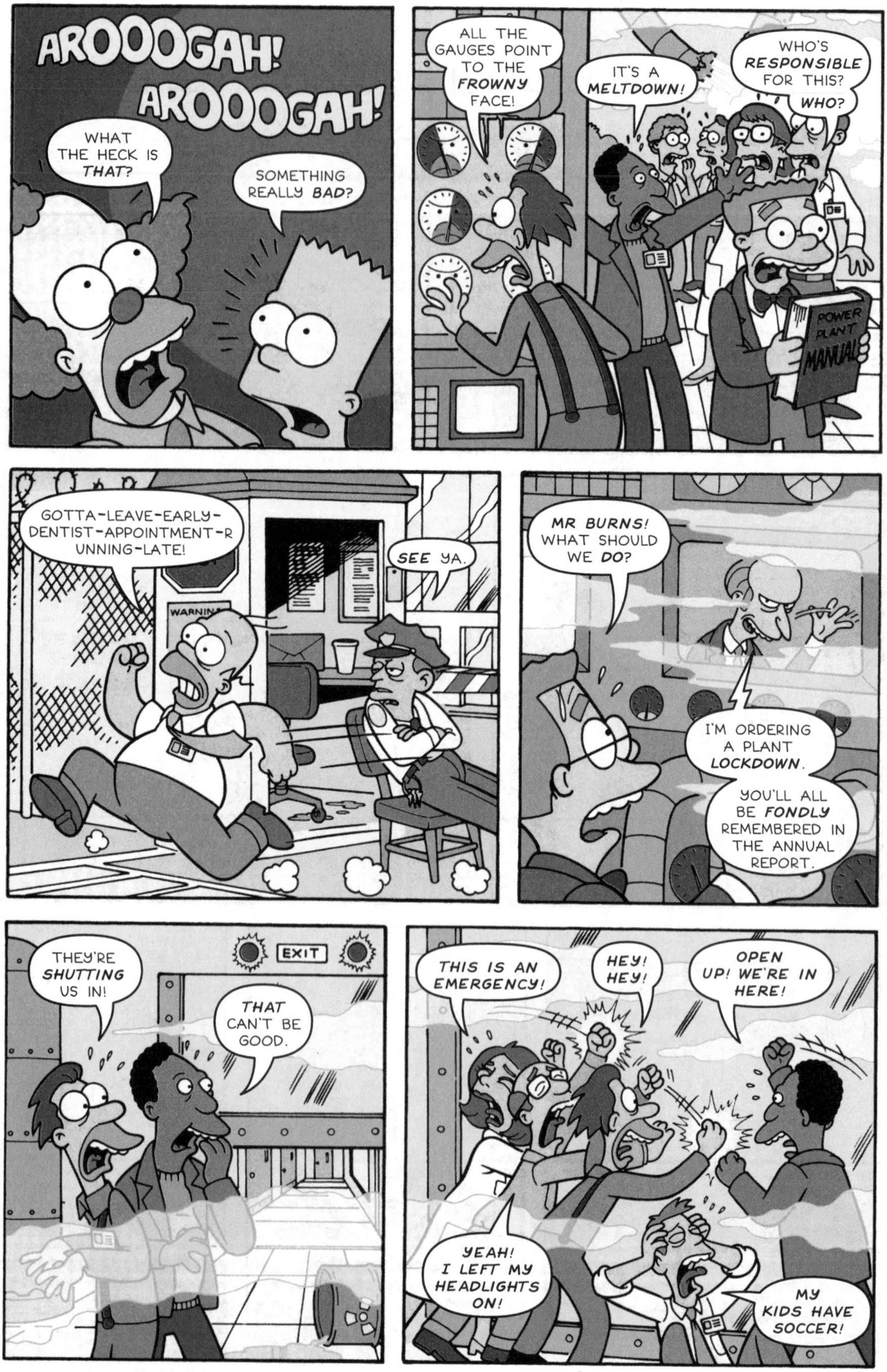
AROOOGAH!
AROOOGAH!
WHAT THE HECK IS *THAT*?
SOMETHING REALLY *BAD*?
ALL THE GAUGES POINT TO THE *FROWNY* FACE!
IT'S A *MELTDOWN*!
WHO'S *RESPONSIBLE* FOR THIS?
WHO?
POWER PLANT MANUAL
GOTTA-LEAVE-EARLY-DENTIST-APPOINTMENT-RUNNING-LATE!
SEE YA.
WARNING
MR BURNS! WHAT SHOULD WE *DO*?
I'M ORDERING A PLANT *LOCKDOWN*.
YOU'LL ALL BE *FONDLY* REMEMBERED IN THE ANNUAL REPORT.
THEY'RE *SHUTTING* US IN!
EXIT
THAT CAN'T BE GOOD.
THIS IS AN EMERGENCY!
HEY! HEY!
OPEN UP! WE'RE IN HERE!
YEAH! I LEFT MY HEADLIGHTS ON!
MY KIDS HAVE SOCCER!

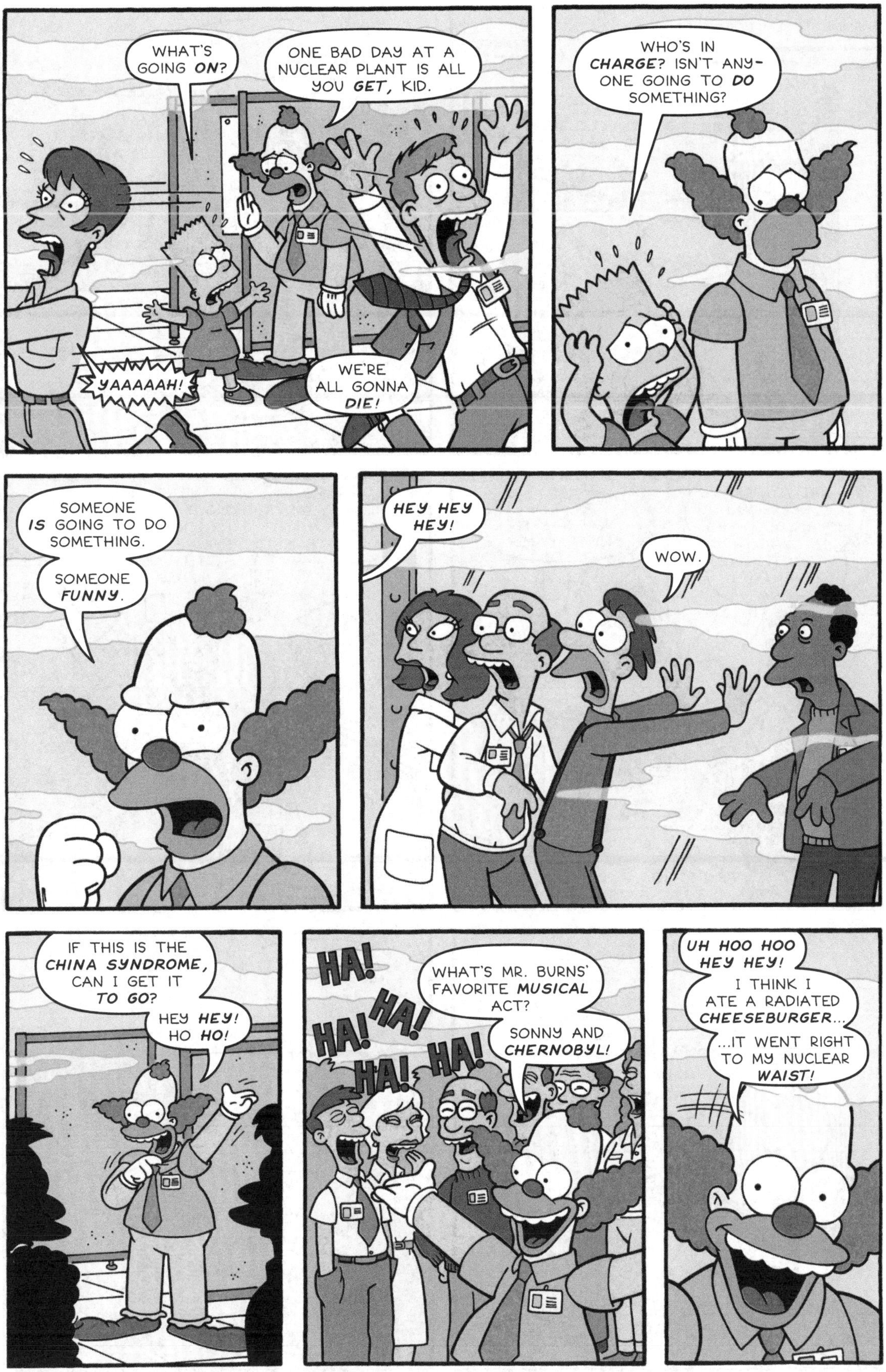
WHAT'S GOING ON?
ONE BAD DAY AT A NUCLEAR PLANT IS ALL YOU GET, KID.
YAAAAAH!
WE'RE ALL GONNA DIE!
WHO'S IN CHARGE? ISN'T ANYONE GOING TO DO SOMETHING?
SOMEONE IS GOING TO DO SOMETHING.
SOMEONE FUNNY.
HEY HEY HEY!
WOW.
IF THIS IS THE CHINA SYNDROME, CAN I GET IT TO GO?
HEY HEY! HO HO!
HA! HA! HA! HA! HA!
WHAT'S MR. BURNS' FAVORITE MUSICAL ACT?
SONNY AND CHERNOBYL!
UH HOO HOO HEY HEY!
I THINK I ATE A RADIATED CHEESEBURGER...
...IT WENT RIGHT TO MY NUCLEAR WAIST!

SOME TIME LATER...

MOVE **ALONG** PEOPLE.

SHOWERS TO THE LEFT. **INSURANCE** WAIVERS TO THE RIGHT!

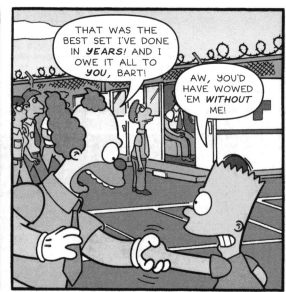

THAT WAS THE BEST SET I'VE DONE IN **YEARS**! AND I OWE IT ALL TO **YOU**, BART!

AW, YOU'D HAVE WOWED 'EM **WITHOUT** ME!

KRUSTOFSKI! I UNDERSTAND YOUR COOL HEAD AND JOCULAR RACONTEURING THWARTED A **PANIC**.

ERRR...IF YOU **SAY** SO, NOSTRADAMUS.

I'D LIKE TO OFFER YOU A **PROMOTION** AND A BIG FAT **RAISE**.

THANKS, BUT **NO** THANKS. I **KNOW** WHERE MY PLACE IS.

AND IF I EVER FORGET, I ONLY HAVE TO LOOK INTO THE SMILING FACE OF A CHILD JUST LIKE **THIS** ONE.

AW...

AND IF I **STILL** CAN'T REMEMBER, I CAN LOOK AT THIS FAT CHECK THE **NETWORK** SENT TO GET ME BACK!

TURNS OUT THE "SHE'S ALL THAT GRRLZ" **WEREN'T** ALL THAT.

WHAT A **LOSS** TO THE NUCLEAR ENERGY INDUSTRY.

YOUR **LOSS** IS MINDLESS CHILDREN'S PROGRAMMING'S **GAIN**.

YAH HA HA HA HA HA!

THE END

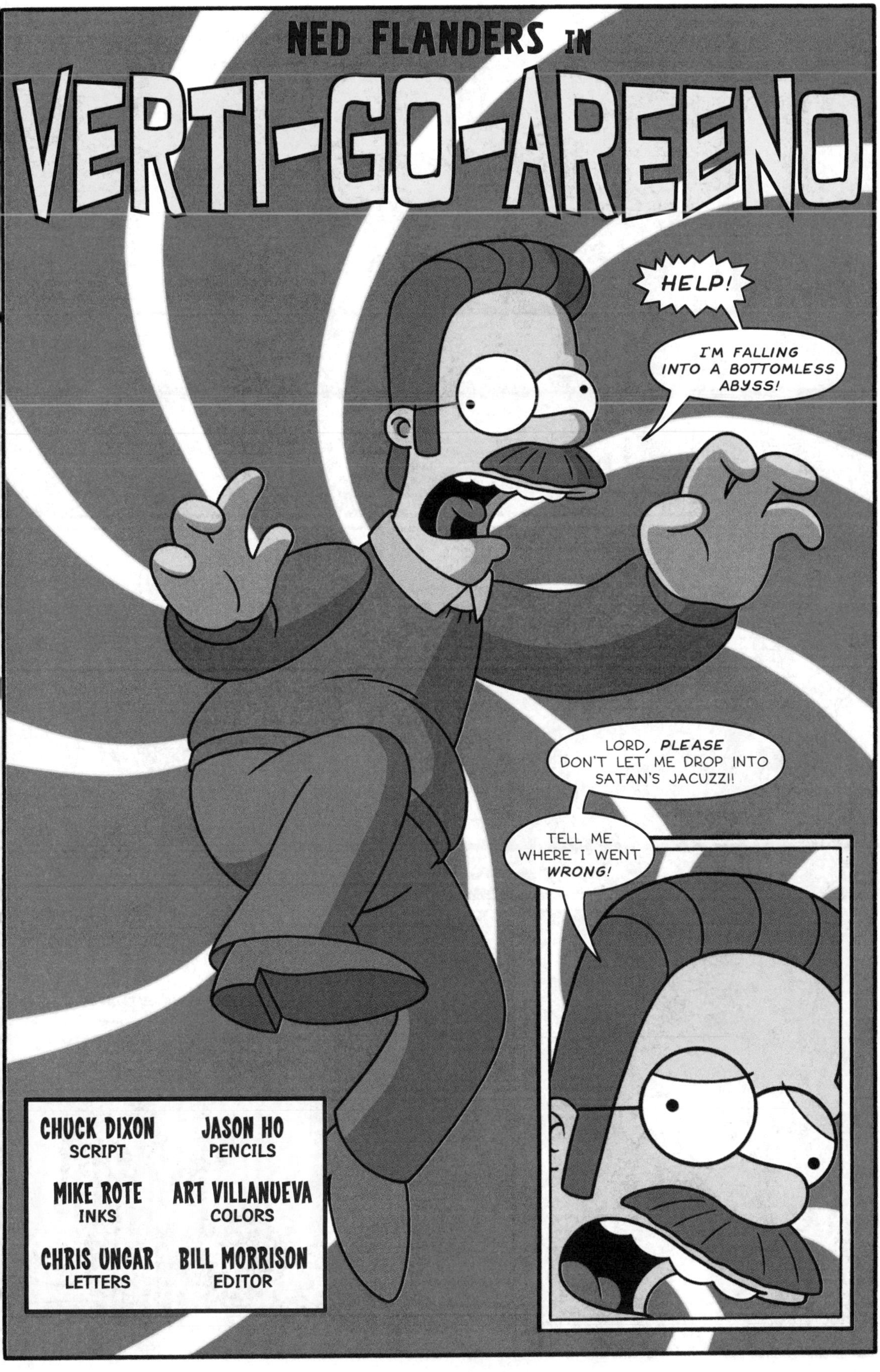
NED FLANDERS IN
VERTI-GO-AREENO
HELP!
I'M FALLING INTO A BOTTOMLESS ABYSS!
LORD, PLEASE DON'T LET ME DROP INTO SATAN'S JACUZZI!
TELL ME WHERE I WENT WRONG!
CHUCK DIXON SCRIPT
JASON HO PENCILS
MIKE ROTE INKS
ART VILLANUEVA COLORS
CHRIS UNGAR LETTERS
BILL MORRISON EDITOR

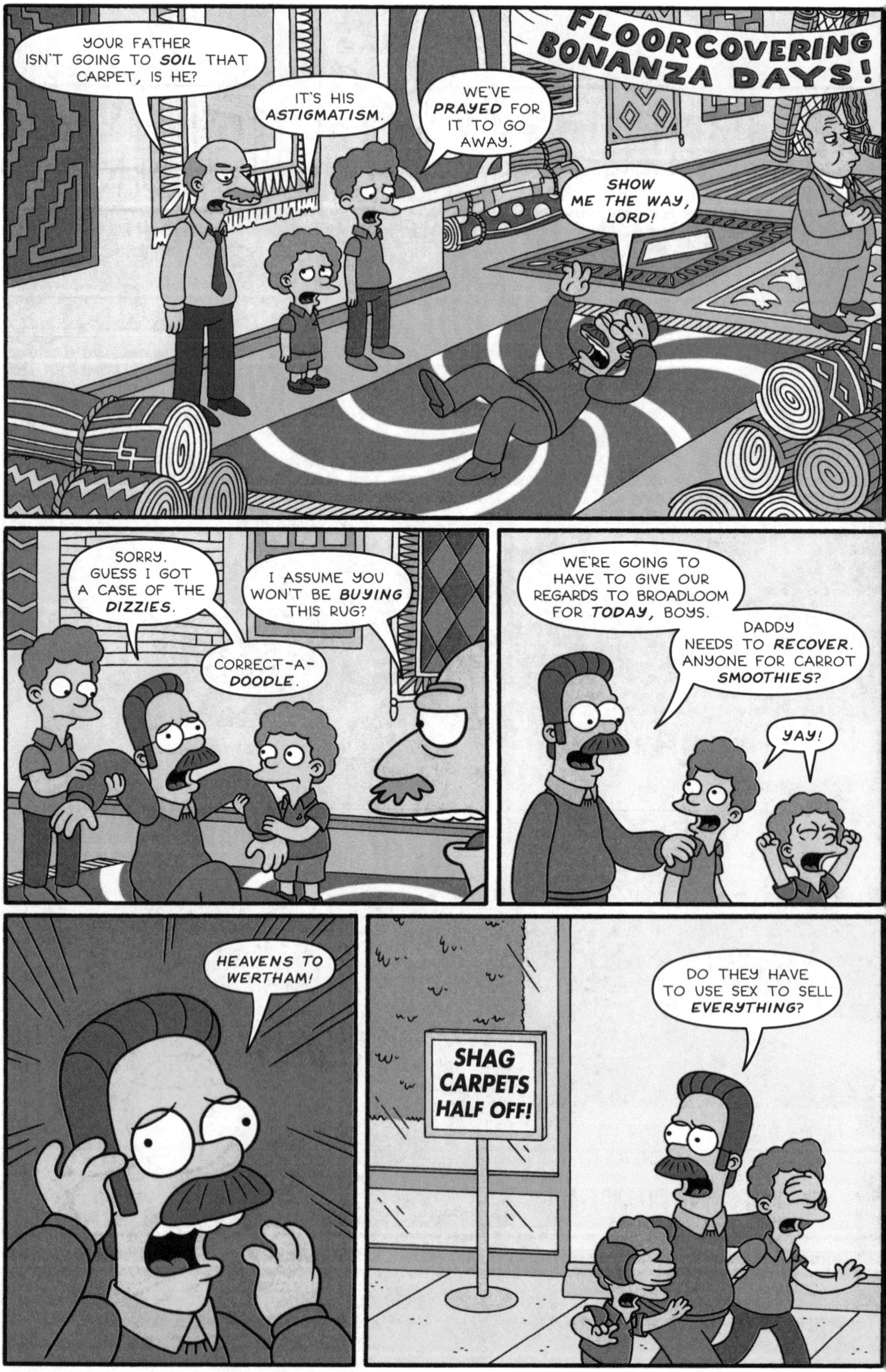
FLOORCOVERING BONANZA DAYS!
YOUR FATHER ISN'T GOING TO SOIL THAT CARPET, IS HE?
IT'S HIS ASTIGMATISM.
WE'VE PRAYED FOR IT TO GO AWAY.
SHOW ME THE WAY, LORD!
SORRY. GUESS I GOT A CASE OF THE DIZZIES.
CORRECT-A-DOODLE.
I ASSUME YOU WON'T BE BUYING THIS RUG?
WE'RE GOING TO HAVE TO GIVE OUR REGARDS TO BROADLOOM FOR TODAY, BOYS.
DADDY NEEDS TO RECOVER. ANYONE FOR CARROT SMOOTHIES?
YAY!
HEAVENS TO WERTHAM!
SHAG CARPETS HALF OFF!
DO THEY HAVE TO USE SEX TO SELL EVERYTHING?

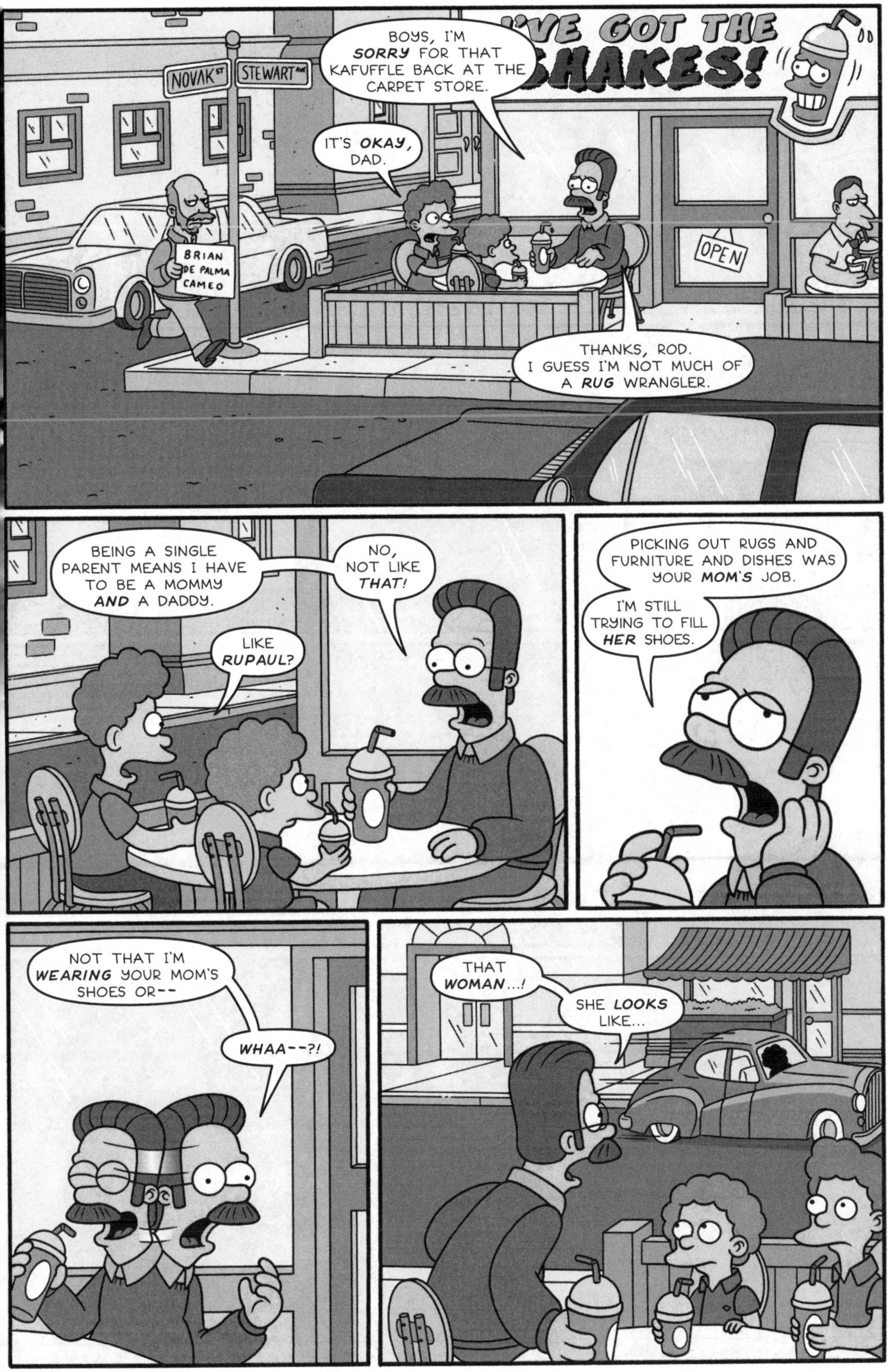
I'VE GOT THE SHAKES!
NOVAK ST
STEWART AVE
BRIAN DE PALMA CAMEO
OPEN
BOYS, I'M SORRY FOR THAT KAFUFFLE BACK AT THE CARPET STORE.
IT'S OKAY, DAD.
THANKS, ROD. I GUESS I'M NOT MUCH OF A RUG WRANGLER.
BEING A SINGLE PARENT MEANS I HAVE TO BE A MOMMY AND A DADDY.
LIKE RUPAUL?
NO, NOT LIKE THAT!
PICKING OUT RUGS AND FURNITURE AND DISHES WAS YOUR MOM'S JOB.
I'M STILL TRYING TO FILL HER SHOES.
NOT THAT I'M WEARING YOUR MOM'S SHOES OR--
WHAA--?!
THAT WOMAN...!
SHE LOOKS LIKE...

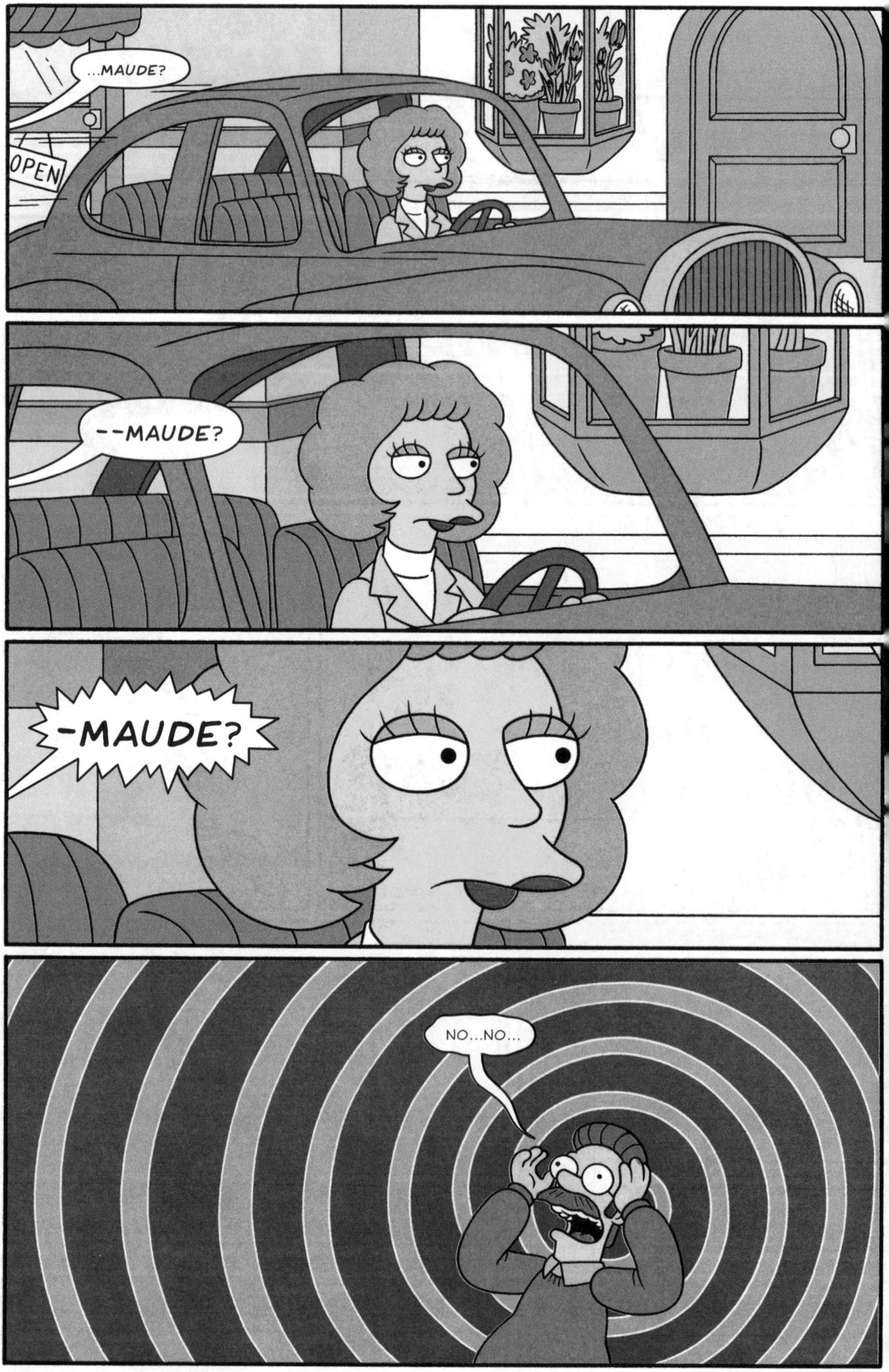
...MAUDE?
OPEN
--MAUDE?
-MAUDE?
NO...NO...

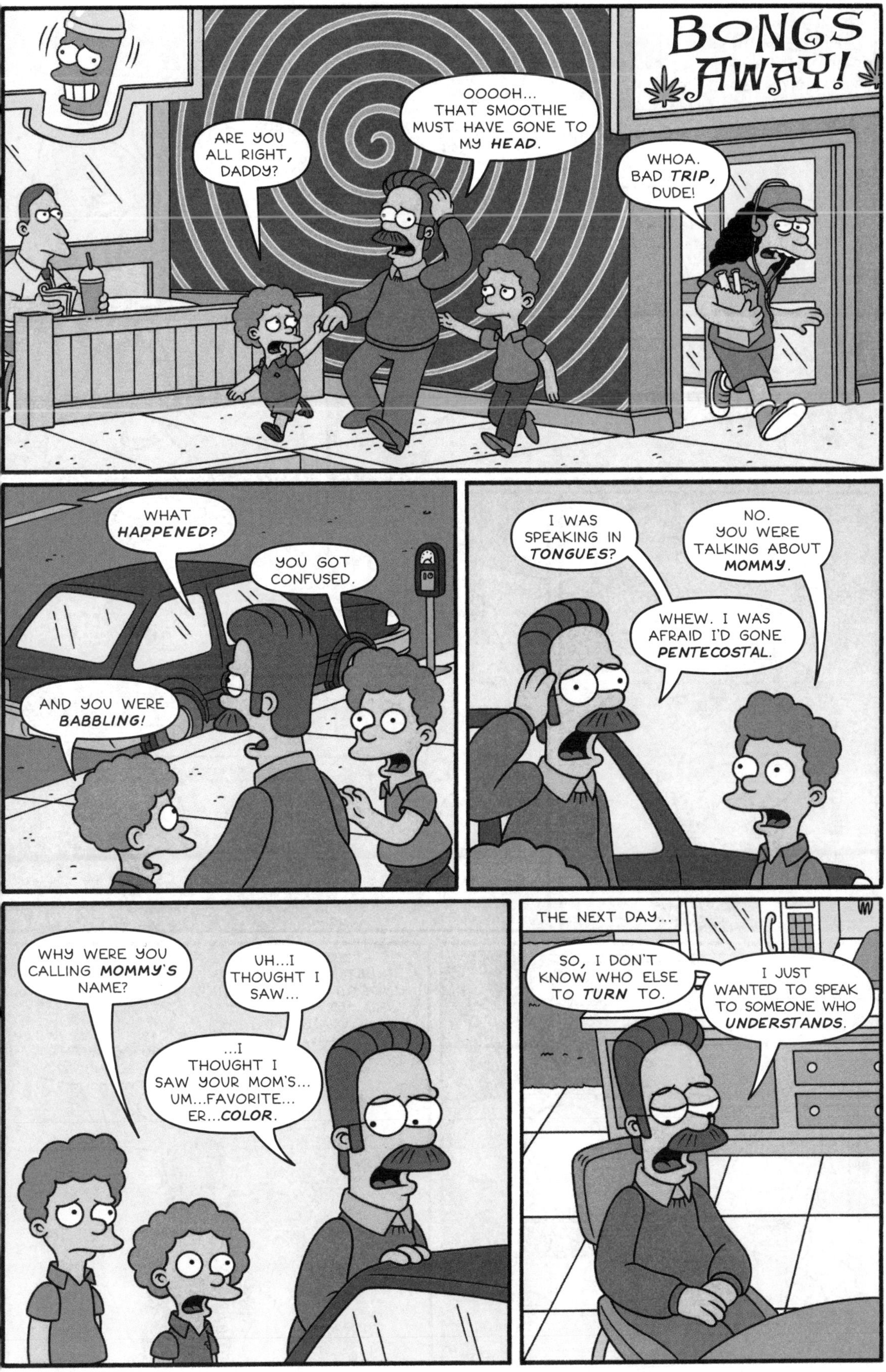

BONGS AWAY!
ARE YOU ALL RIGHT, DADDY?
OOOOH... THAT SMOOTHIE MUST HAVE GONE TO MY **HEAD**.
WHOA. BAD **TRIP**, DUDE!
WHAT **HAPPENED**?
YOU GOT CONFUSED.
AND YOU WERE **BABBLING**!
I WAS SPEAKING IN **TONGUES**?
NO. YOU WERE TALKING ABOUT **MOMMY**.
WHEW. I WAS AFRAID I'D GONE **PENTECOSTAL**.
WHY WERE YOU CALLING **MOMMY'S** NAME?
UH...I THOUGHT I SAW...
...I THOUGHT I SAW YOUR MOM'S... UM...FAVORITE... ER...**COLOR**.
THE NEXT DAY...
SO, I DON'T KNOW WHO ELSE TO **TURN** TO.
I JUST WANTED TO SPEAK TO SOMEONE WHO **UNDERSTANDS**.

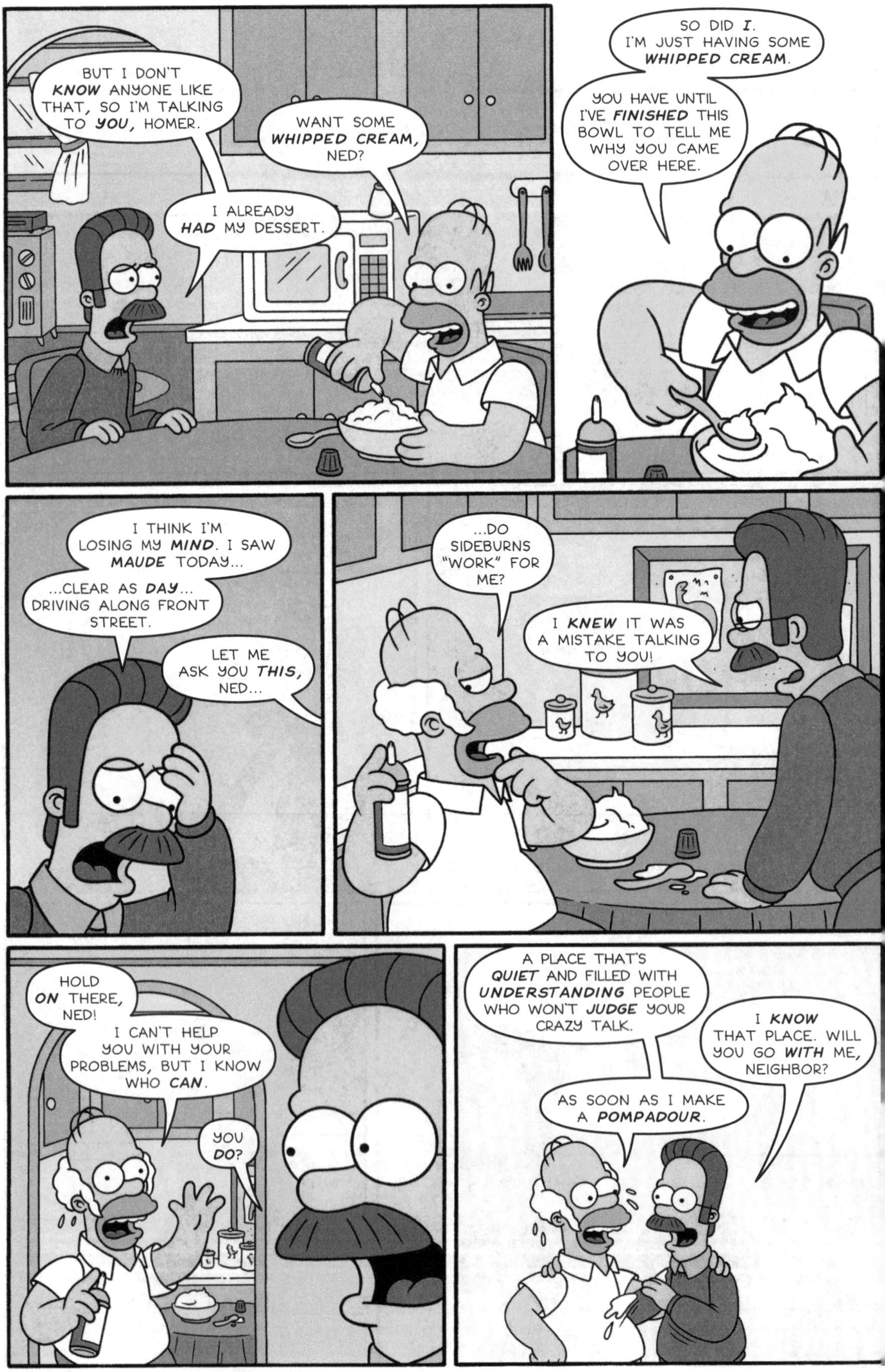
BUT I DON'T KNOW ANYONE LIKE THAT, SO I'M TALKING TO YOU, HOMER.
WANT SOME WHIPPED CREAM, NED?
I ALREADY HAD MY DESSERT.
SO DID I. I'M JUST HAVING SOME WHIPPED CREAM.
YOU HAVE UNTIL I'VE FINISHED THIS BOWL TO TELL ME WHY YOU CAME OVER HERE.
I THINK I'M LOSING MY MIND. I SAW MAUDE TODAY...
...CLEAR AS DAY... DRIVING ALONG FRONT STREET.
LET ME ASK YOU THIS, NED...
...DO SIDEBURNS "WORK" FOR ME?
I KNEW IT WAS A MISTAKE TALKING TO YOU!
HOLD ON THERE, NED!
I CAN'T HELP YOU WITH YOUR PROBLEMS, BUT I KNOW WHO CAN.
YOU DO?
A PLACE THAT'S QUIET AND FILLED WITH UNDERSTANDING PEOPLE WHO WON'T JUDGE YOUR CRAZY TALK.
I KNOW THAT PLACE. WILL YOU GO WITH ME, NEIGHBOR?
AS SOON AS I MAKE A POMPADOUR.

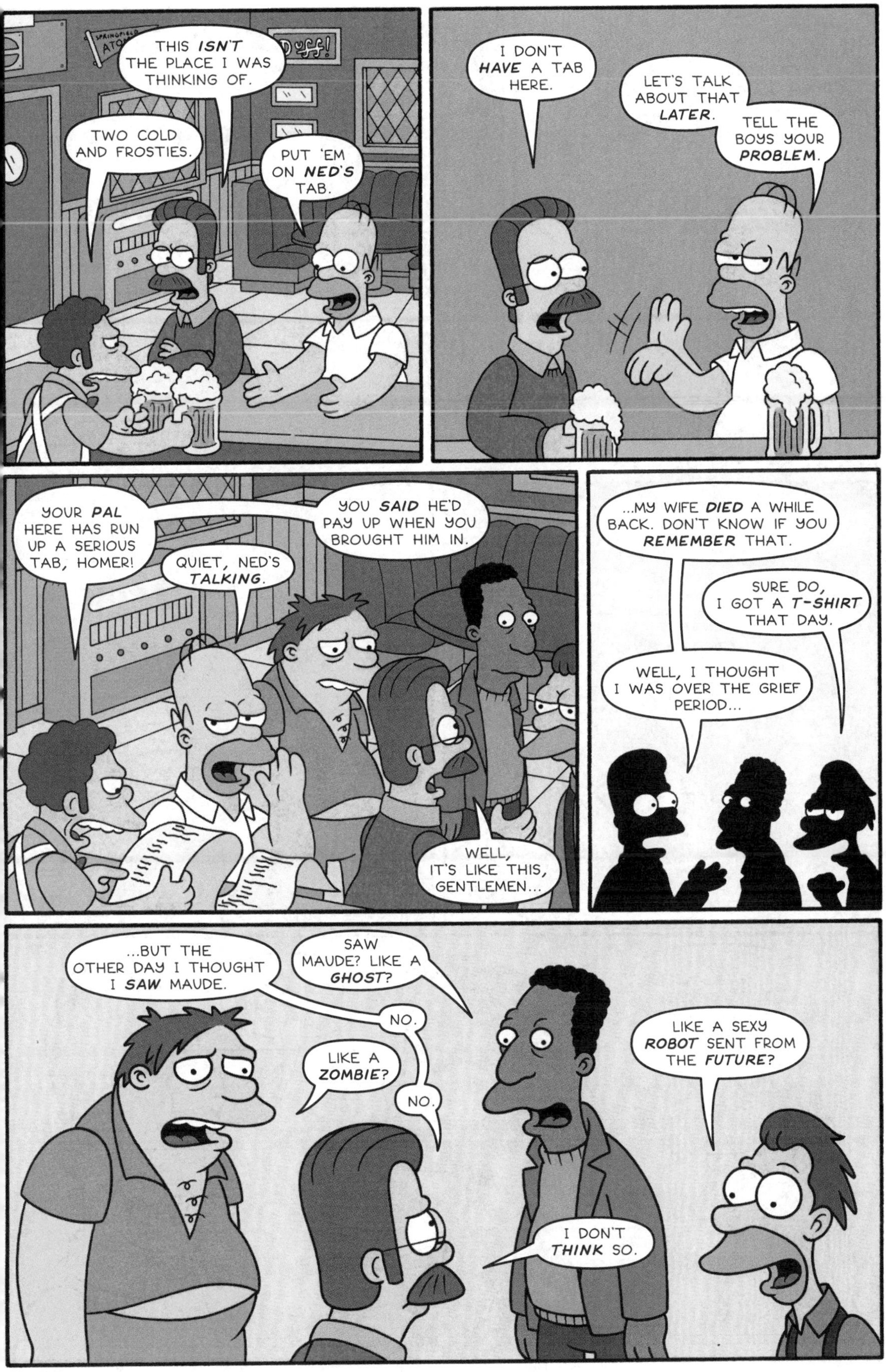

THIS ISN'T THE PLACE I WAS THINKING OF.
TWO COLD AND FROSTIES.
PUT 'EM ON NED'S TAB.
I DON'T HAVE A TAB HERE.
LET'S TALK ABOUT THAT LATER.
TELL THE BOYS YOUR PROBLEM.
YOUR PAL HERE HAS RUN UP A SERIOUS TAB, HOMER!
YOU SAID HE'D PAY UP WHEN YOU BROUGHT HIM IN.
QUIET, NED'S TALKING.
WELL, IT'S LIKE THIS, GENTLEMEN...
...MY WIFE DIED A WHILE BACK. DON'T KNOW IF YOU REMEMBER THAT.
SURE DO, I GOT A T-SHIRT THAT DAY.
WELL, I THOUGHT I WAS OVER THE GRIEF PERIOD...
...BUT THE OTHER DAY I THOUGHT I SAW MAUDE.
SAW MAUDE? LIKE A GHOST?
NO.
LIKE A ZOMBIE?
NO.
LIKE A SEXY ROBOT SENT FROM THE FUTURE?
I DON'T THINK SO.

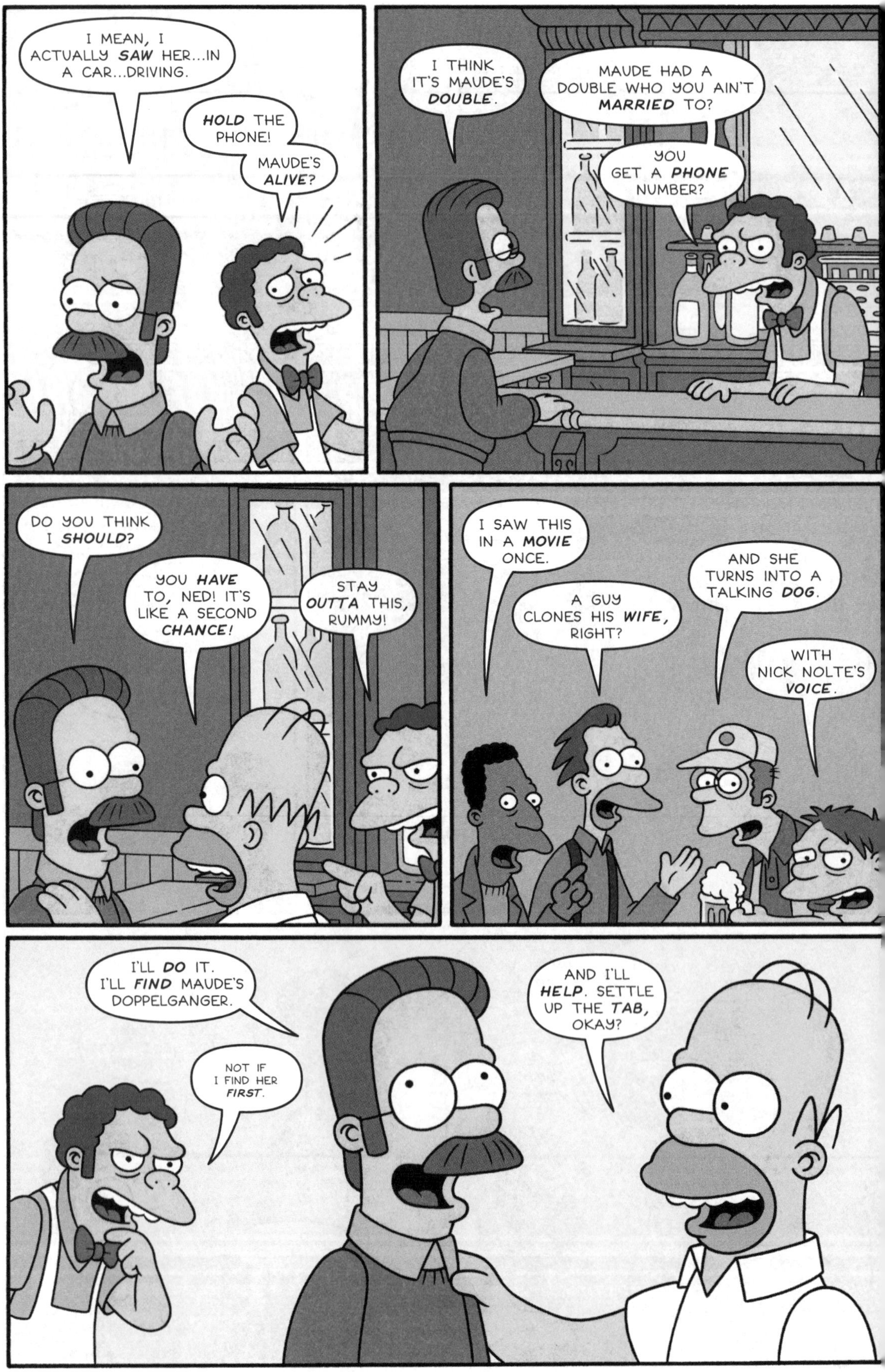

I MEAN, I ACTUALLY SAW HER...IN A CAR...DRIVING.
HOLD THE PHONE!
MAUDE'S ALIVE?
I THINK IT'S MAUDE'S DOUBLE.
MAUDE HAD A DOUBLE WHO YOU AIN'T MARRIED TO?
YOU GET A PHONE NUMBER?
DO YOU THINK I SHOULD?
YOU HAVE TO, NED! IT'S LIKE A SECOND CHANCE!
STAY OUTTA THIS, RUMMY!
I SAW THIS IN A MOVIE ONCE.
A GUY CLONES HIS WIFE, RIGHT?
AND SHE TURNS INTO A TALKING DOG.
WITH NICK NOLTE'S VOICE.
I'LL DO IT. I'LL FIND MAUDE'S DOPPELGANGER.
NOT IF I FIND HER FIRST.
AND I'LL HELP. SETTLE UP THE TAB, OKAY?

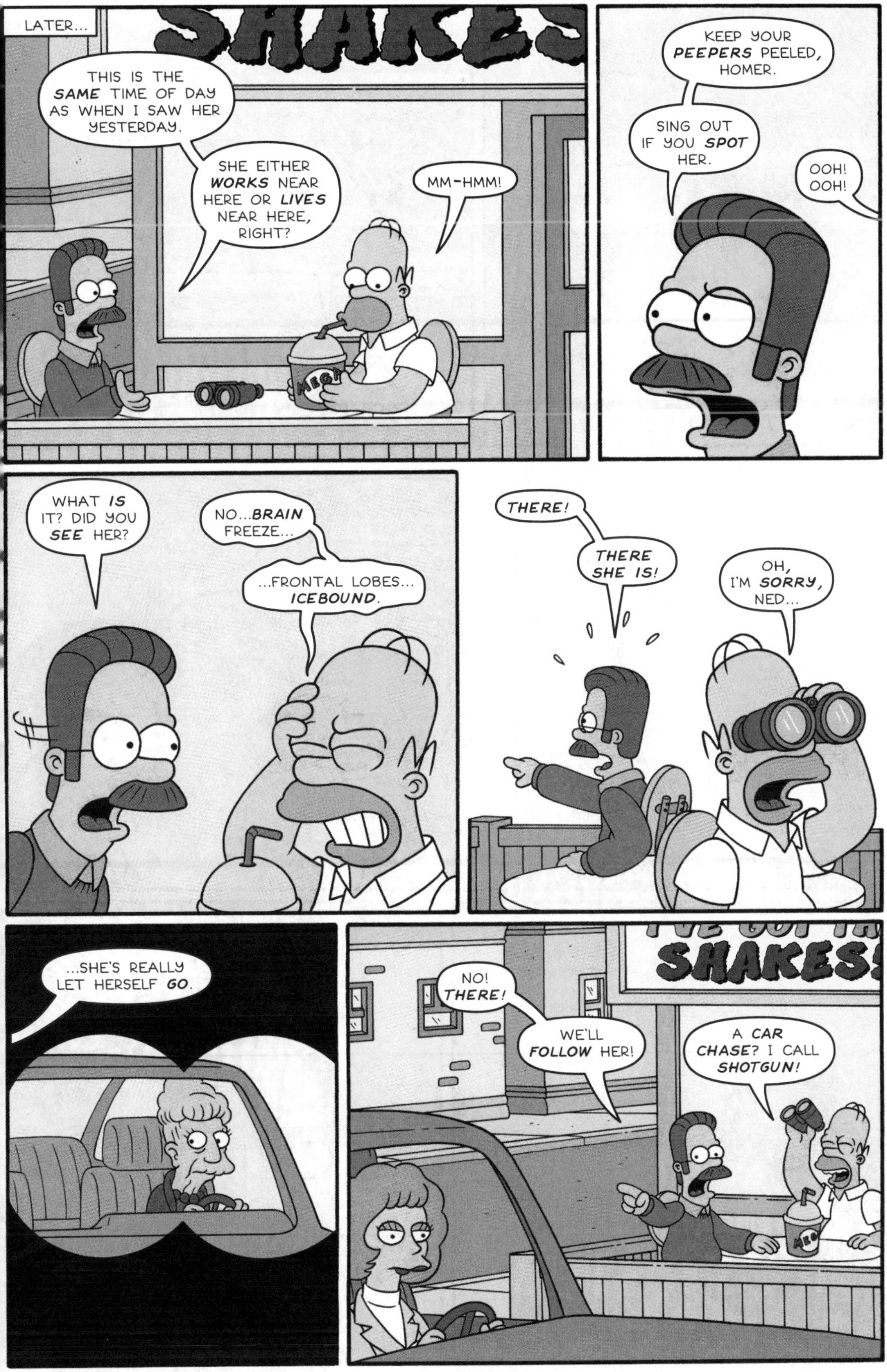
LATER...
SHAKES
THIS IS THE SAME TIME OF DAY AS WHEN I SAW HER YESTERDAY.
SHE EITHER WORKS NEAR HERE OR LIVES NEAR HERE, RIGHT?
MM-HMM!
MEGA
KEEP YOUR PEEPERS PEELED, HOMER.
SING OUT IF YOU SPOT HER.
OOH! OOH!
WHAT IS IT? DID YOU SEE HER?
NO...BRAIN FREEZE...
...FRONTAL LOBES... ICEBOUND.
THERE!
THERE SHE IS!
OH, I'M SORRY, NED...
...SHE'S REALLY LET HERSELF GO.
SHAKES!
NO! THERE!
WE'LL FOLLOW HER!
A CAR CHASE? I CALL SHOTGUN!
MEGA

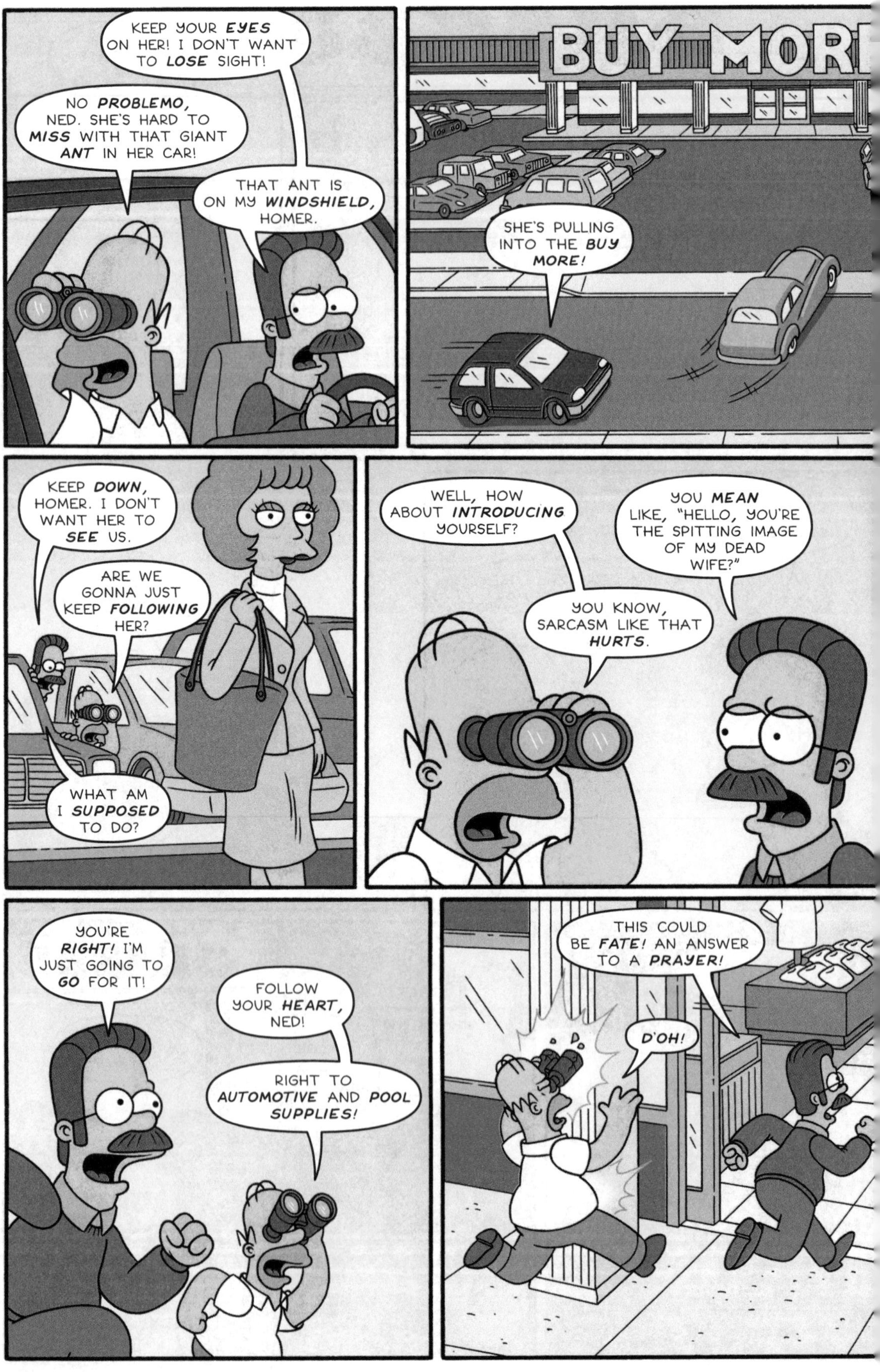
KEEP YOUR EYES ON HER! I DON'T WANT TO LOSE SIGHT!
NO PROBLEMO, NED. SHE'S HARD TO MISS WITH THAT GIANT ANT IN HER CAR!
THAT ANT IS ON MY WINDSHIELD, HOMER.
BUY MORE
SHE'S PULLING INTO THE BUY MORE!
KEEP DOWN, HOMER. I DON'T WANT HER TO SEE US.
ARE WE GONNA JUST KEEP FOLLOWING HER?
WHAT AM I SUPPOSED TO DO?
WELL, HOW ABOUT INTRODUCING YOURSELF?
YOU MEAN LIKE, "HELLO, YOU'RE THE SPITTING IMAGE OF MY DEAD WIFE?"
YOU KNOW, SARCASM LIKE THAT HURTS.
YOU'RE RIGHT! I'M JUST GOING TO GO FOR IT!
FOLLOW YOUR HEART, NED!
RIGHT TO AUTOMOTIVE AND POOL SUPPLIES!
THIS COULD BE FATE! AN ANSWER TO A PRAYER!
D'OH!

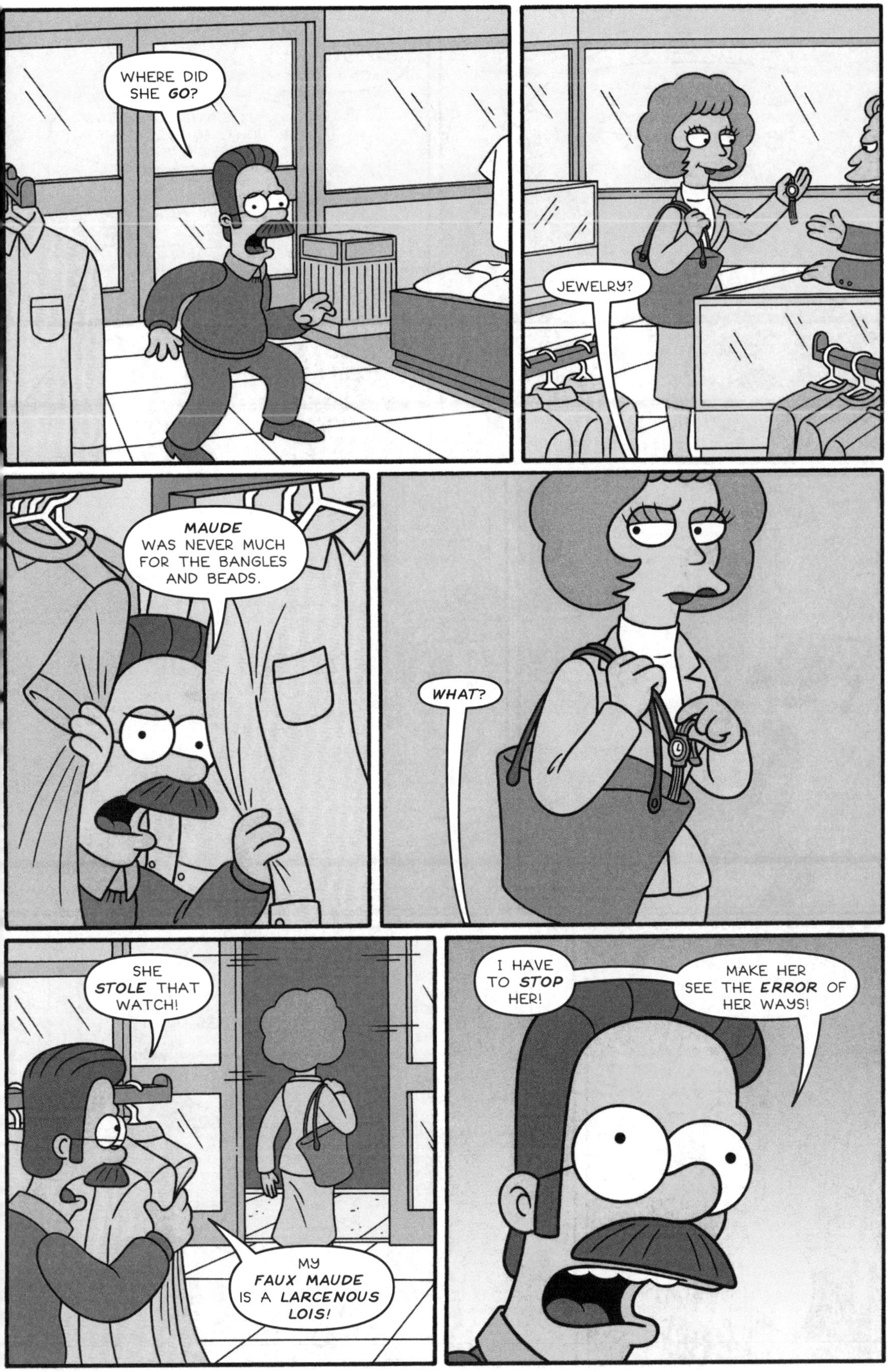
WHERE DID SHE GO?
JEWELRY?
MAUDE WAS NEVER MUCH FOR THE BANGLES AND BEADS.
WHAT?
SHE STOLE THAT WATCH!
MY FAUX MAUDE IS A LARCENOUS LOIS!
I HAVE TO STOP HER!
MAKE HER SEE THE ERROR OF HER WAYS!

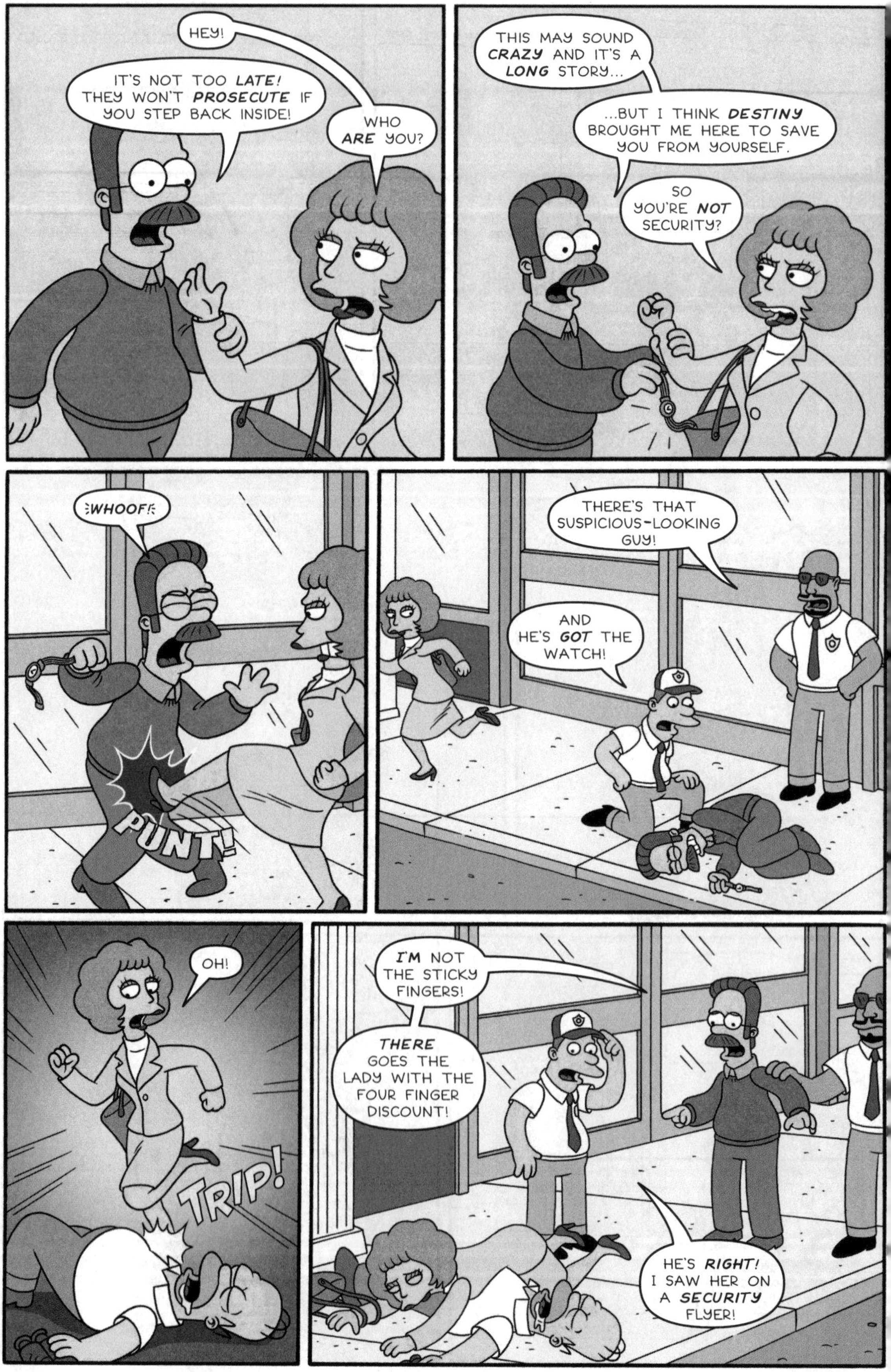
HEY!
IT'S NOT TOO LATE! THEY WON'T PROSECUTE IF YOU STEP BACK INSIDE!
WHO ARE YOU?
THIS MAY SOUND CRAZY AND IT'S A LONG STORY...
...BUT I THINK DESTINY BROUGHT ME HERE TO SAVE YOU FROM YOURSELF.
SO YOU'RE NOT SECURITY?
WHOOF!
PUNT!
THERE'S THAT SUSPICIOUS-LOOKING GUY!
AND HE'S GOT THE WATCH!
OH!
TRIP!
I'M NOT THE STICKY FINGERS!
THERE GOES THE LADY WITH THE FOUR FINGER DISCOUNT!
HE'S RIGHT! I SAW HER ON A SECURITY FLYER!

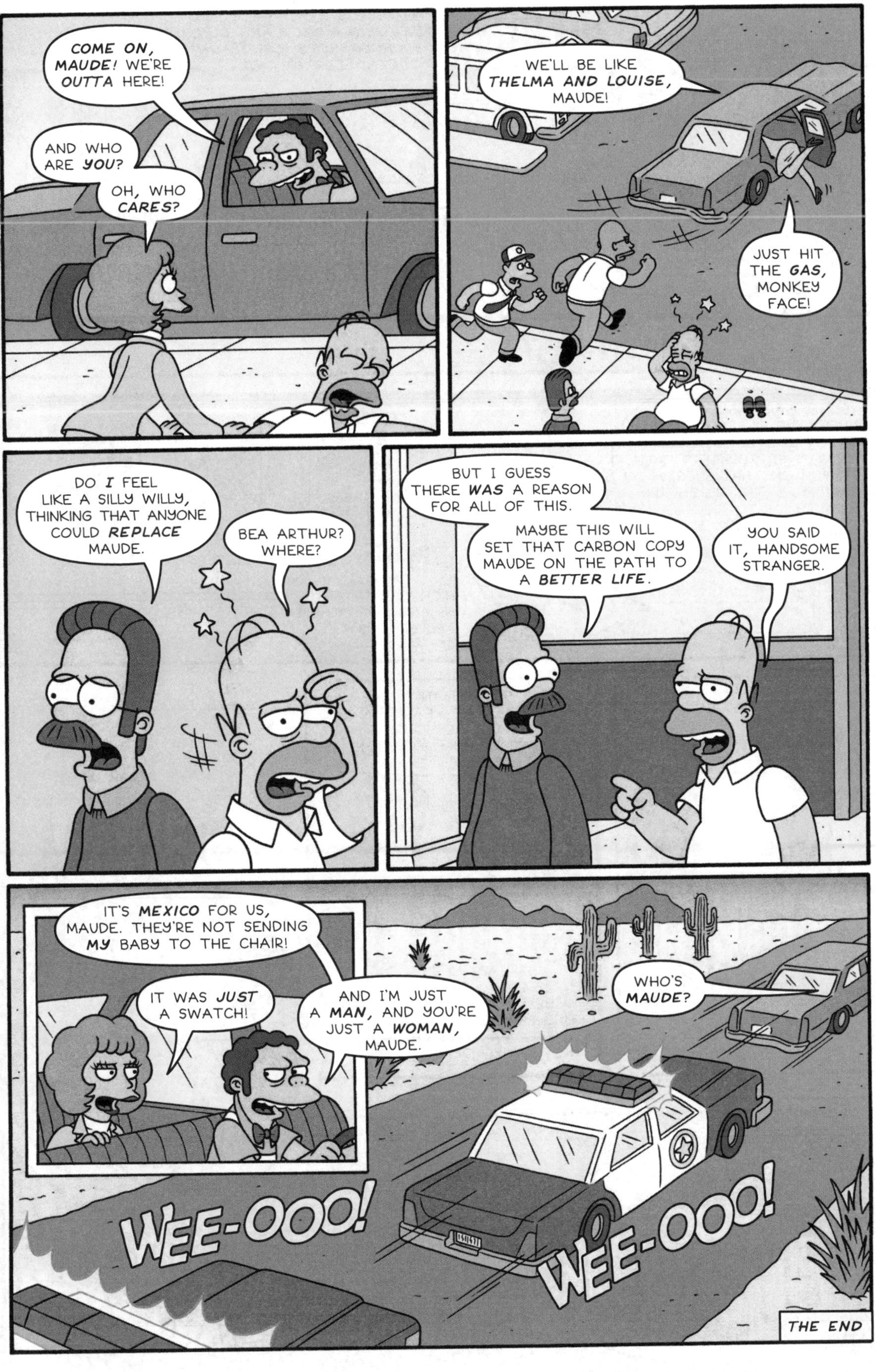

COME ON, MAUDE! WE'RE OUTTA HERE!
AND WHO ARE YOU?
OH, WHO CARES?
WE'LL BE LIKE THELMA AND LOUISE, MAUDE!
JUST HIT THE GAS, MONKEY FACE!
DO I FEEL LIKE A SILLY WILLY, THINKING THAT ANYONE COULD REPLACE MAUDE.
BEA ARTHUR? WHERE?
BUT I GUESS THERE WAS A REASON FOR ALL OF THIS.
MAYBE THIS WILL SET THAT CARBON COPY MAUDE ON THE PATH TO A BETTER LIFE.
YOU SAID IT, HANDSOME STRANGER.
IT'S MEXICO FOR US, MAUDE. THEY'RE NOT SENDING MY BABY TO THE CHAIR!
IT WAS JUST A SWATCH!
AND I'M JUST A MAN, AND YOU'RE JUST A WOMAN, MAUDE.
WHO'S MAUDE?
WEE-OOO!
WEE-OOO!
THE END

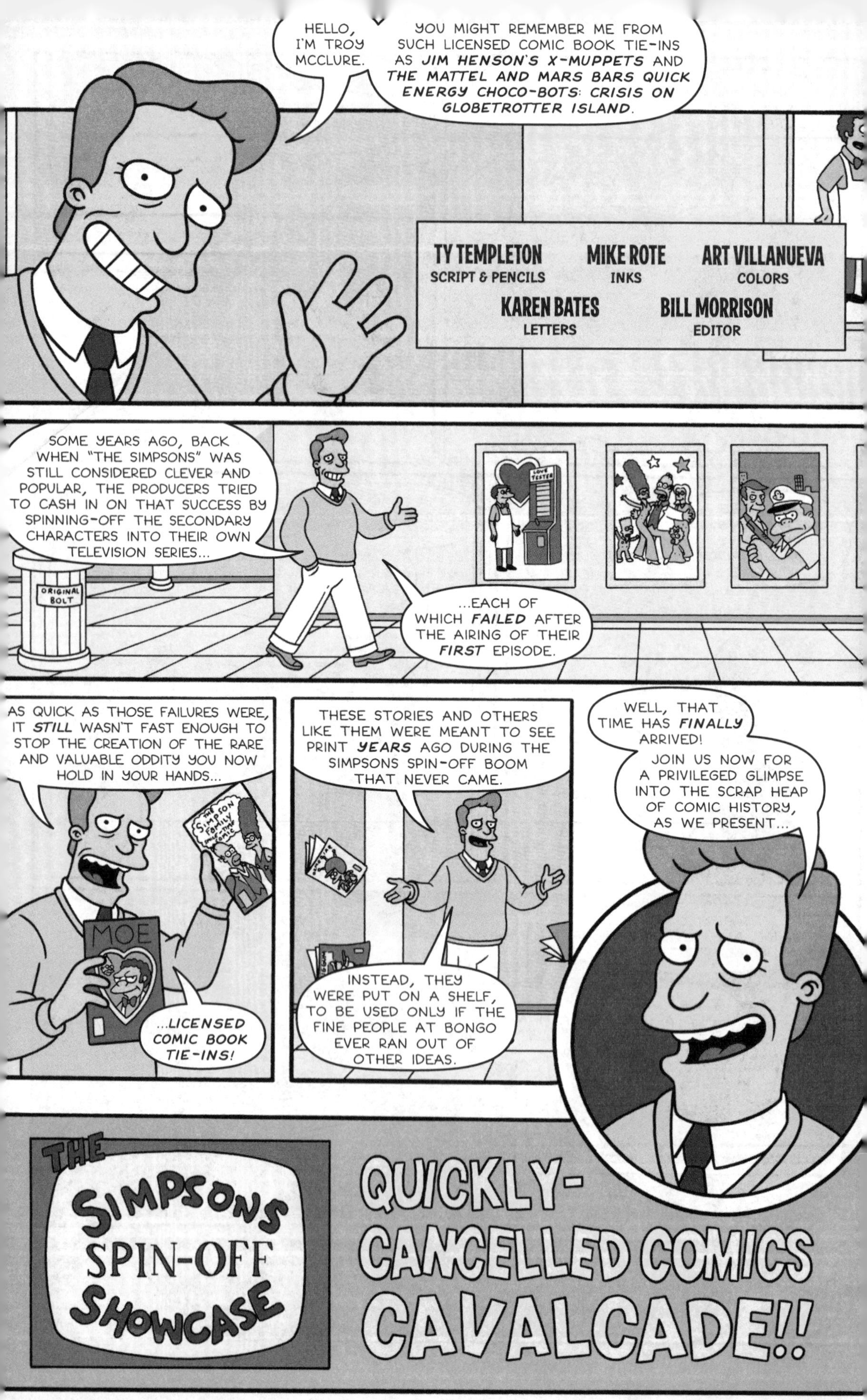
HELLO, I'M TROY MCCLURE.
YOU MIGHT REMEMBER ME FROM SUCH LICENSED COMIC BOOK TIE-INS AS *JIM HENSON'S X-MUPPETS* AND *THE MATTEL AND MARS BARS QUICK ENERGY CHOCO-BOTS: CRISIS ON GLOBETROTTER ISLAND*.
TY TEMPLETON SCRIPT & PENCILS
MIKE ROTE INKS
ART VILLANUEVA COLORS
KAREN BATES LETTERS
BILL MORRISON EDITOR
SOME YEARS AGO, BACK WHEN "THE SIMPSONS" WAS STILL CONSIDERED CLEVER AND POPULAR, THE PRODUCERS TRIED TO CASH IN ON THAT SUCCESS BY SPINNING-OFF THE SECONDARY CHARACTERS INTO THEIR OWN TELEVISION SERIES...
ORIGINAL BOLT
LOVE TESTER
...EACH OF WHICH *FAILED* AFTER THE AIRING OF THEIR *FIRST* EPISODE.
AS QUICK AS THOSE FAILURES WERE, IT *STILL* WASN'T FAST ENOUGH TO STOP THE CREATION OF THE RARE AND VALUABLE ODDITY YOU NOW HOLD IN YOUR HANDS...
THE SIMPSON FAMILY SMILE-TIME COMIC
MOE
...*LICENSED COMIC BOOK TIE-INS!*
THESE STORIES AND OTHERS LIKE THEM WERE MEANT TO SEE PRINT *YEARS* AGO DURING THE SIMPSONS SPIN-OFF BOOM THAT NEVER CAME.
INSTEAD, THEY WERE PUT ON A SHELF, TO BE USED ONLY IF THE FINE PEOPLE AT BONGO EVER RAN OUT OF OTHER IDEAS.
WELL, THAT TIME HAS *FINALLY* ARRIVED!
JOIN US NOW FOR A PRIVILEGED GLIMPSE INTO THE SCRAP HEAP OF COMIC HISTORY, AS WE PRESENT...
THE SIMPSONS SPIN-OFF SHOWCASE
QUICKLY-CANCELLED COMICS CAVALCADE!!

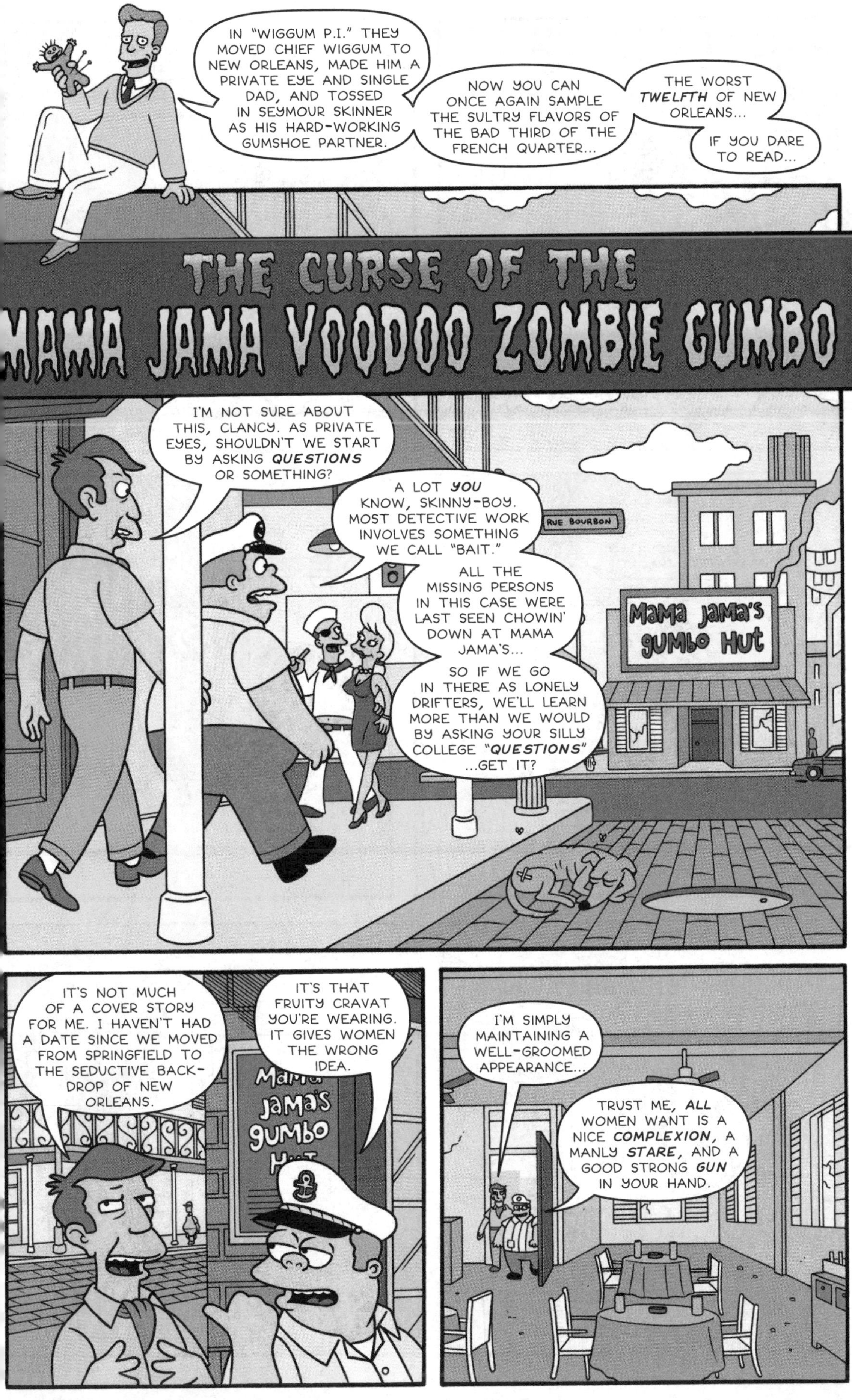
IN "WIGGUM P.I." THEY MOVED CHIEF WIGGUM TO NEW ORLEANS, MADE HIM A PRIVATE EYE AND SINGLE DAD, AND TOSSED IN SEYMOUR SKINNER AS HIS HARD-WORKING GUMSHOE PARTNER.
NOW YOU CAN ONCE AGAIN SAMPLE THE SULTRY FLAVORS OF THE BAD THIRD OF THE FRENCH QUARTER...
THE WORST *TWELFTH* OF NEW ORLEANS...
IF YOU DARE TO READ...
THE CURSE OF THE
MAMA JAMA VOODOO ZOMBIE GUMBO
I'M NOT SURE ABOUT THIS, CLANCY. AS PRIVATE EYES, SHOULDN'T WE START BY ASKING *QUESTIONS* OR SOMETHING?
A LOT *YOU* KNOW, SKINNY-BOY. MOST DETECTIVE WORK INVOLVES SOMETHING WE CALL "BAIT."
RUE BOURBON
ALL THE MISSING PERSONS IN THIS CASE WERE LAST SEEN CHOWIN' DOWN AT MAMA JAMA'S...
SO IF WE GO IN THERE AS LONELY DRIFTERS, WE'LL LEARN MORE THAN WE WOULD BY ASKING YOUR SILLY COLLEGE "*QUESTIONS*" ...GET IT?
MaMa JaMa's gumbo Hut
IT'S NOT MUCH OF A COVER STORY FOR ME. I HAVEN'T HAD A DATE SINCE WE MOVED FROM SPRINGFIELD TO THE SEDUCTIVE BACK-DROP OF NEW ORLEANS.
IT'S THAT FRUITY CRAVAT YOU'RE WEARING. IT GIVES WOMEN THE WRONG IDEA.
I'M SIMPLY MAINTAINING A WELL-GROOMED APPEARANCE...
TRUST ME, *ALL* WOMEN WANT IS A NICE *COMPLEXION*, A MANLY *STARE*, AND A GOOD STRONG *GUN* IN YOUR HAND.

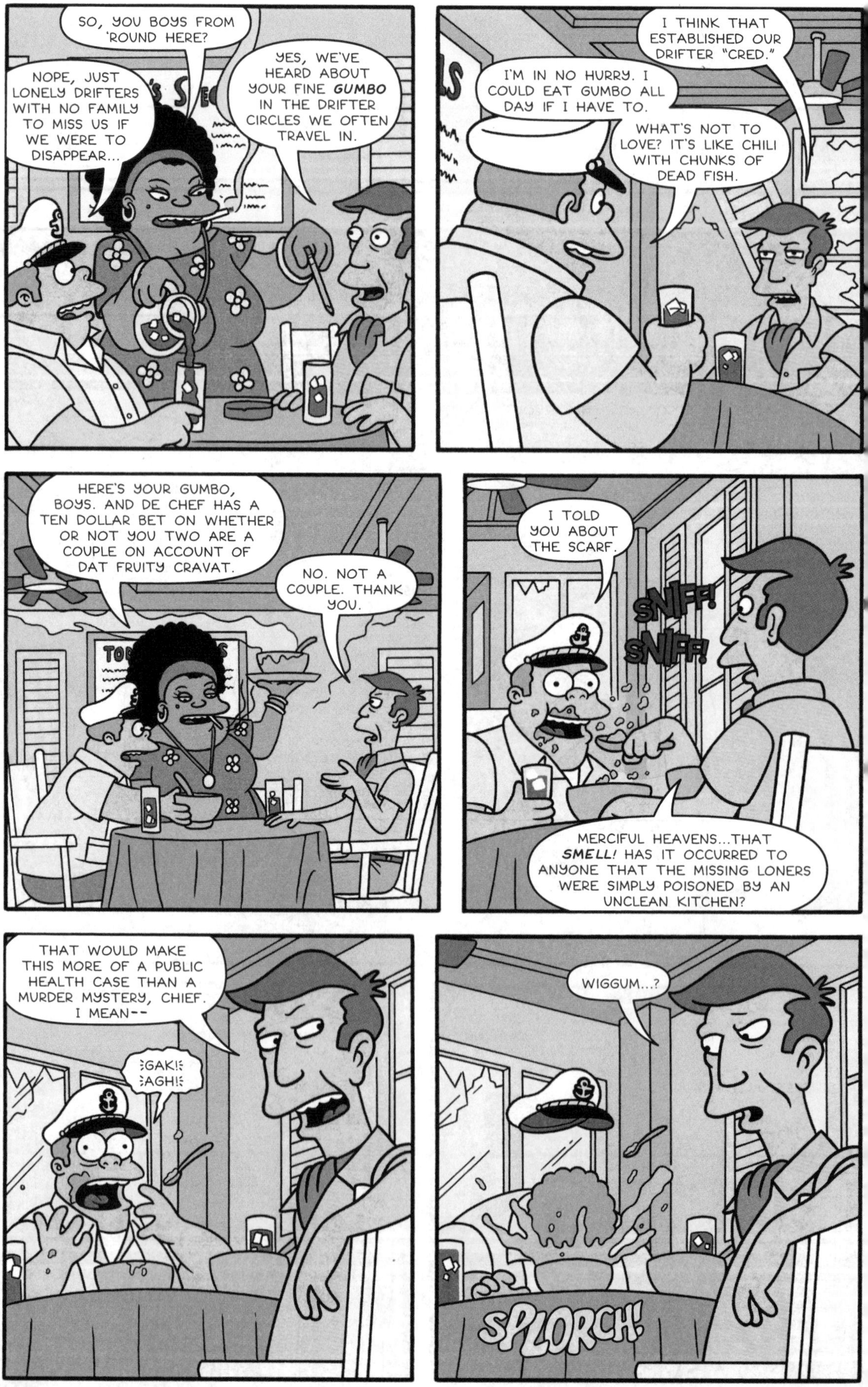
SO, YOU BOYS FROM 'ROUND HERE?
NOPE, JUST LONELY DRIFTERS WITH NO FAMILY TO MISS US IF WE WERE TO DISAPPEAR...
YES, WE'VE HEARD ABOUT YOUR FINE GUMBO IN THE DRIFTER CIRCLES WE OFTEN TRAVEL IN.
I THINK THAT ESTABLISHED OUR DRIFTER "CRED."
I'M IN NO HURRY. I COULD EAT GUMBO ALL DAY IF I HAVE TO.
WHAT'S NOT TO LOVE? IT'S LIKE CHILI WITH CHUNKS OF DEAD FISH.
HERE'S YOUR GUMBO, BOYS. AND DE CHEF HAS A TEN DOLLAR BET ON WHETHER OR NOT YOU TWO ARE A COUPLE ON ACCOUNT OF DAT FRUITY CRAVAT.
NO. NOT A COUPLE. THANK YOU.
I TOLD YOU ABOUT THE SCARF.
SNIFF!
SNIFF!
MERCIFUL HEAVENS...THAT SMELL! HAS IT OCCURRED TO ANYONE THAT THE MISSING LONERS WERE SIMPLY POISONED BY AN UNCLEAN KITCHEN?
THAT WOULD MAKE THIS MORE OF A PUBLIC HEALTH CASE THAN A MURDER MYSTERY, CHIEF. I MEAN--
GAK! AGH!
WIGGUM...?
SPLORCH!

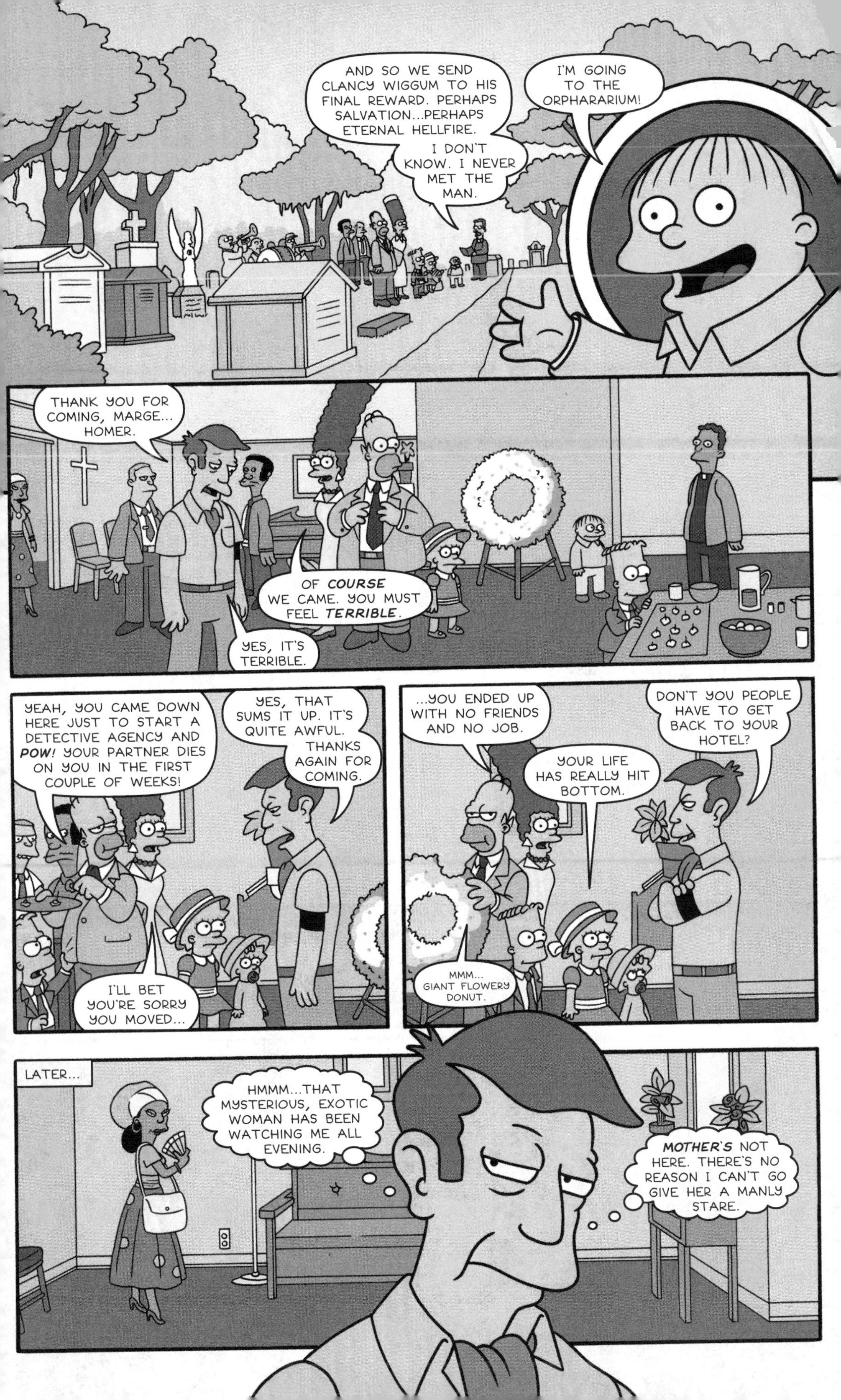
AND SO WE SEND CLANCY WIGGUM TO HIS FINAL REWARD. PERHAPS SALVATION...PERHAPS ETERNAL HELLFIRE.
I DON'T KNOW. I NEVER MET THE MAN.
I'M GOING TO THE ORPHARARIUM!
THANK YOU FOR COMING, MARGE... HOMER.
OF *COURSE* WE CAME. YOU MUST FEEL *TERRIBLE*.
YES, IT'S TERRIBLE.
YEAH, YOU CAME DOWN HERE JUST TO START A DETECTIVE AGENCY AND *POW!* YOUR PARTNER DIES ON YOU IN THE FIRST COUPLE OF WEEKS!
YES, THAT SUMS IT UP. IT'S QUITE AWFUL.
THANKS AGAIN FOR COMING.
I'LL BET YOU'RE SORRY YOU MOVED...
...YOU ENDED UP WITH NO FRIENDS AND NO JOB.
YOUR LIFE HAS REALLY HIT BOTTOM.
DON'T YOU PEOPLE HAVE TO GET BACK TO YOUR HOTEL?
MMM... GIANT FLOWERY DONUT.
LATER...
HMMM...THAT MYSTERIOUS, EXOTIC WOMAN HAS BEEN WATCHING ME ALL EVENING.
MOTHER'S NOT HERE. THERE'S NO REASON I CAN'T GO GIVE HER A MANLY STARE.

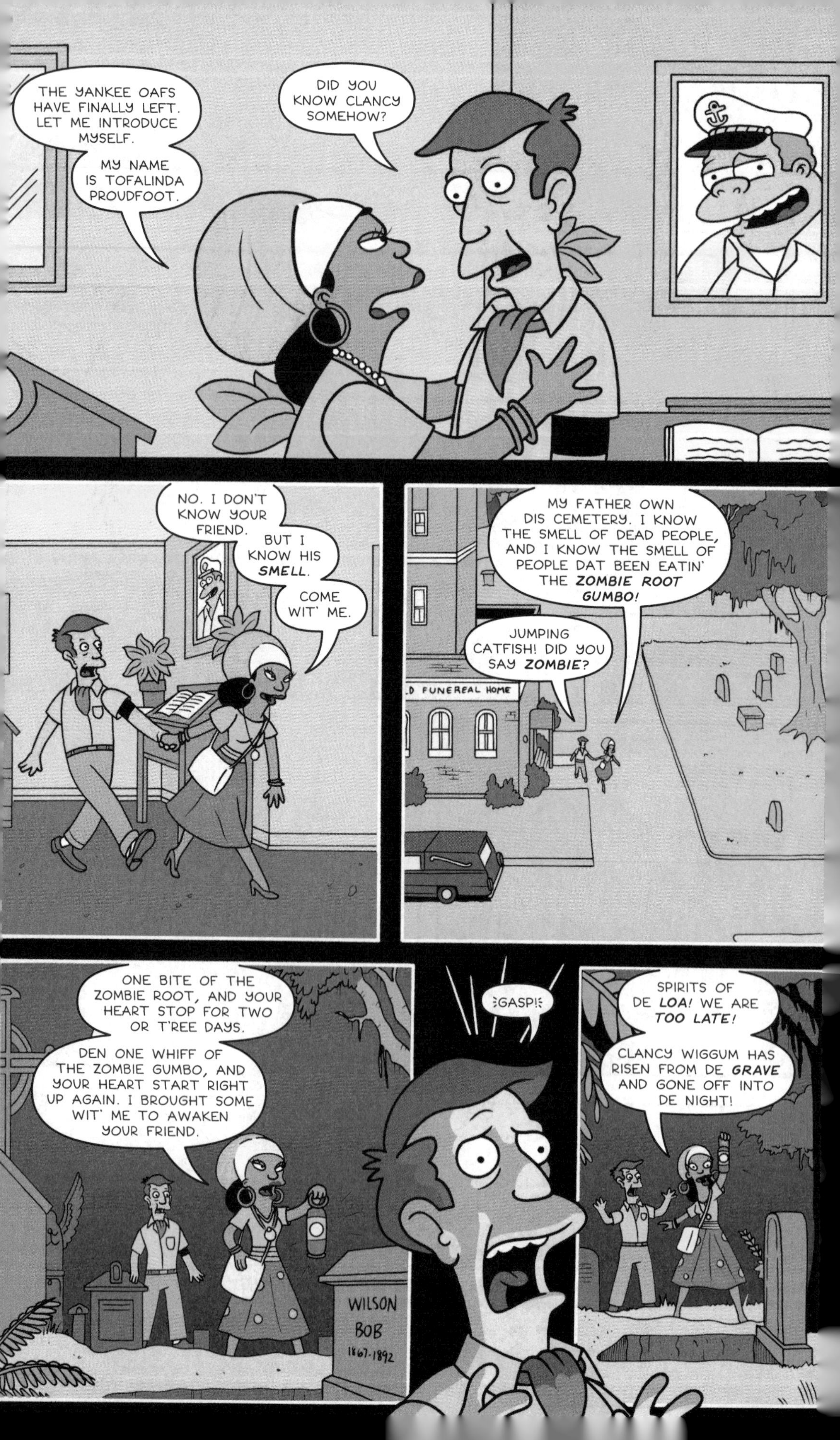

THE YANKEE OAFS HAVE FINALLY LEFT. LET ME INTRODUCE MYSELF.
MY NAME IS TOFALINDA PROUDFOOT.
DID YOU KNOW CLANCY SOMEHOW?
NO. I DON'T KNOW YOUR FRIEND.
BUT I KNOW HIS SMELL.
COME WIT' ME.
MY FATHER OWN DIS CEMETERY. I KNOW THE SMELL OF DEAD PEOPLE, AND I KNOW THE SMELL OF PEOPLE DAT BEEN EATIN' THE ZOMBIE ROOT GUMBO!
JUMPING CATFISH! DID YOU SAY ZOMBIE?
FUNERAL HOME
ONE BITE OF THE ZOMBIE ROOT, AND YOUR HEART STOP FOR TWO OR T'REE DAYS.
DEN ONE WHIFF OF THE ZOMBIE GUMBO, AND YOUR HEART START RIGHT UP AGAIN. I BROUGHT SOME WIT' ME TO AWAKEN YOUR FRIEND.
WILSON BOB 1867-1892
GASP!
SPIRITS OF DE LOA! WE ARE TOO LATE!
CLANCY WIGGUM HAS RISEN FROM DE GRAVE AND GONE OFF INTO DE NIGHT!

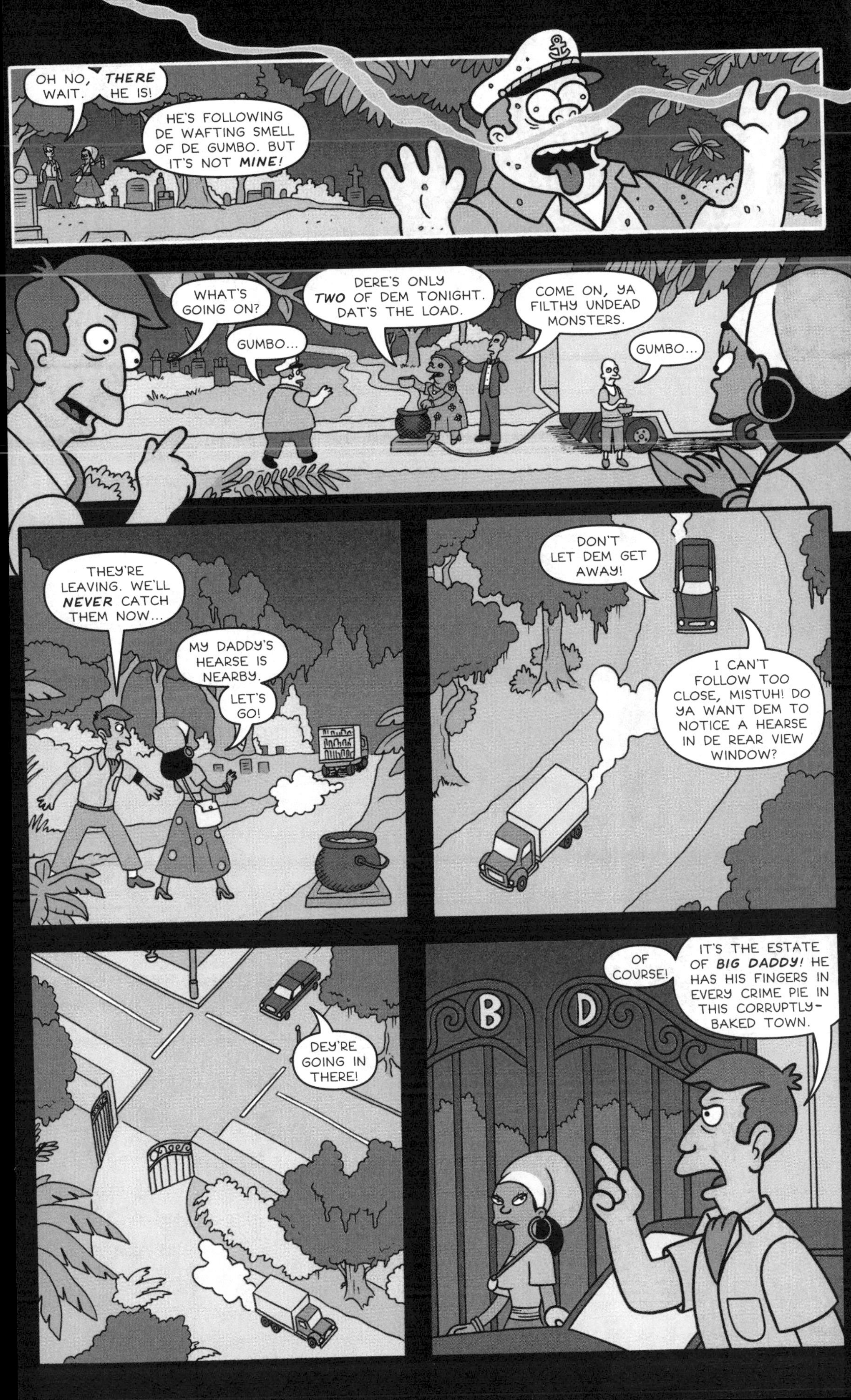

OH NO, WAIT.
THERE HE IS!
HE'S FOLLOWING DE WAFTING SMELL OF DE GUMBO. BUT IT'S NOT MINE!
WHAT'S GOING ON?
GUMBO...
DERE'S ONLY TWO OF DEM TONIGHT. DAT'S THE LOAD.
COME ON, YA FILTHY UNDEAD MONSTERS.
GUMBO...
THEY'RE LEAVING. WE'LL NEVER CATCH THEM NOW...
MY DADDY'S HEARSE IS NEARBY.
LET'S GO!
DON'T LET DEM GET AWAY!
I CAN'T FOLLOW TOO CLOSE, MISTUH! DO YA WANT DEM TO NOTICE A HEARSE IN DE REAR VIEW WINDOW?
DEY'RE GOING IN THERE!
OF COURSE!
IT'S THE ESTATE OF BIG DADDY! HE HAS HIS FINGERS IN EVERY CRIME PIE IN THIS CORRUPTLY-BAKED TOWN.
B
D

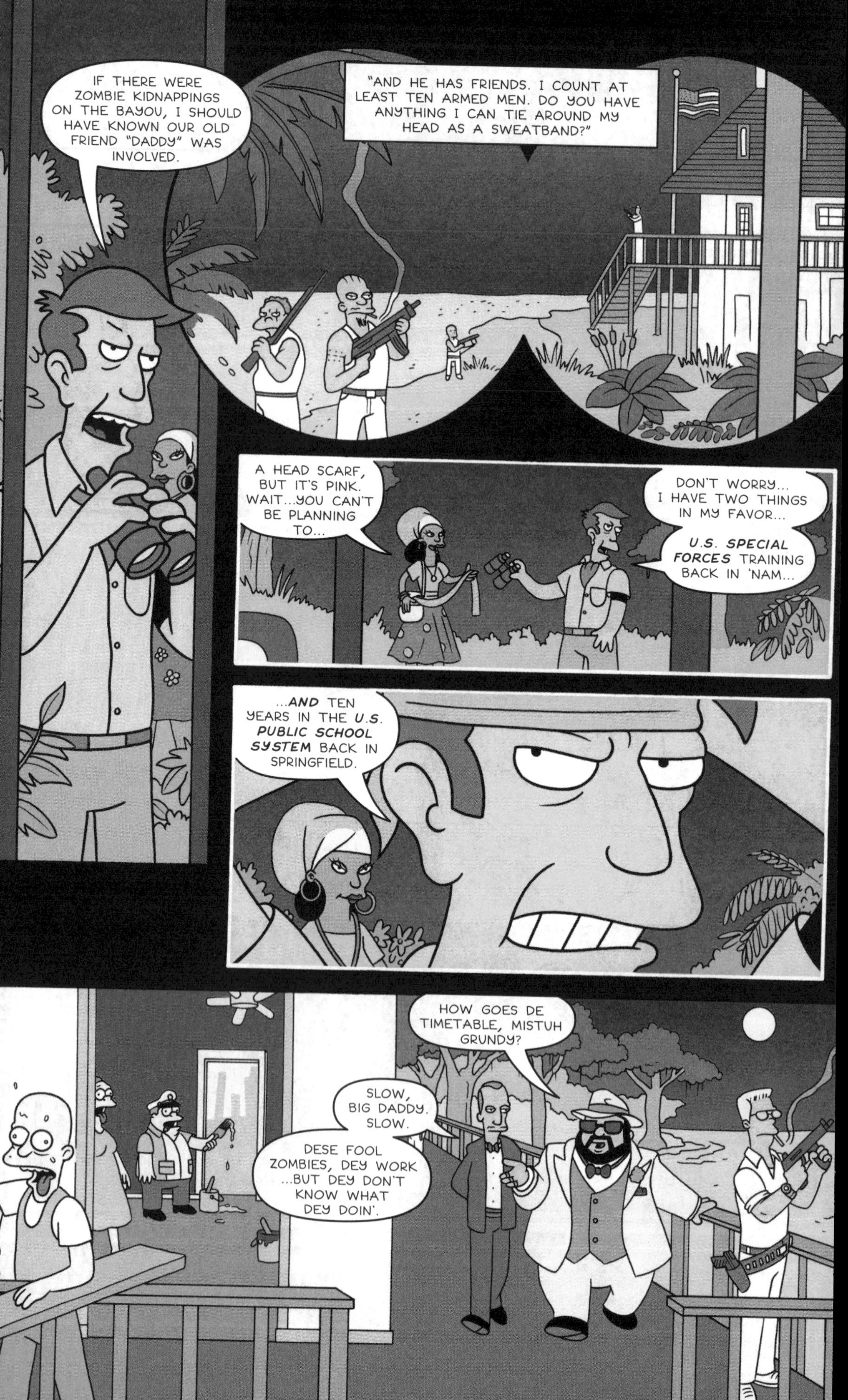
IF THERE WERE ZOMBIE KIDNAPPINGS ON THE BAYOU, I SHOULD HAVE KNOWN OUR OLD FRIEND "DADDY" WAS INVOLVED.
"AND HE HAS FRIENDS. I COUNT AT LEAST TEN ARMED MEN. DO YOU HAVE ANYTHING I CAN TIE AROUND MY HEAD AS A SWEATBAND?"
A HEAD SCARF, BUT IT'S PINK. WAIT...YOU CAN'T BE PLANNING TO...
DON'T WORRY... I HAVE TWO THINGS IN MY FAVOR...
U.S. SPECIAL FORCES TRAINING BACK IN 'NAM...
...AND TEN YEARS IN THE U.S. PUBLIC SCHOOL SYSTEM BACK IN SPRINGFIELD.
HOW GOES DE TIMETABLE, MISTUH GRUNDY?
SLOW, BIG DADDY. SLOW.
DESE FOOL ZOMBIES, DEY WORK ...BUT DEY DON'T KNOW WHAT DEY DOIN'.

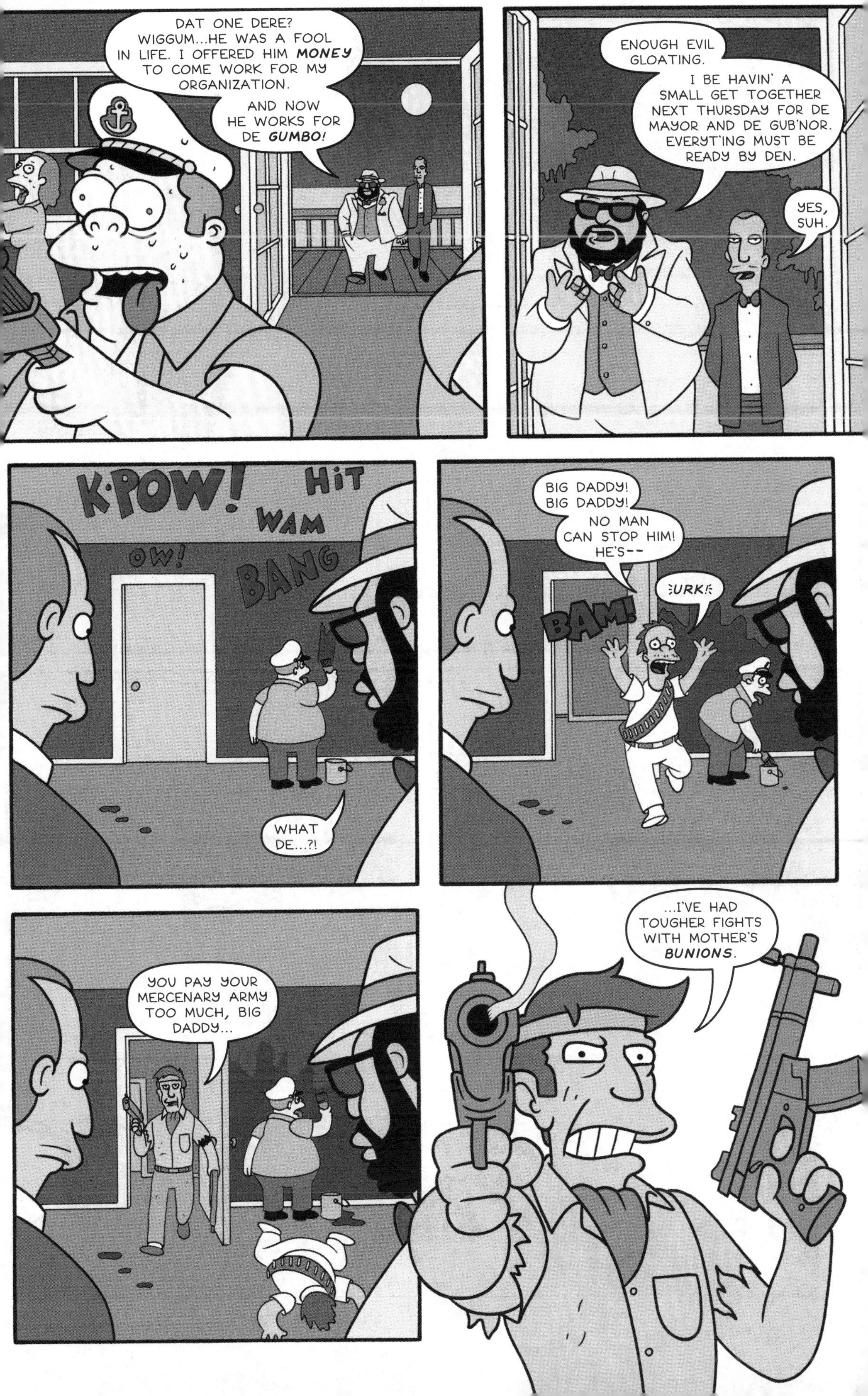
DAT ONE DERE? WIGGUM...HE WAS A FOOL IN LIFE. I OFFERED HIM MONEY TO COME WORK FOR MY ORGANIZATION.
AND NOW HE WORKS FOR DE GUMBO!
ENOUGH EVIL GLOATING.
I BE HAVIN' A SMALL GET TOGETHER NEXT THURSDAY FOR DE MAYOR AND DE GUB'NOR. EVERYT'ING MUST BE READY BY DEN.
YES, SUH.
K-POW!
HIT
WAM
OW!
BANG
WHAT DE...?!
BIG DADDY! BIG DADDY!
NO MAN CAN STOP HIM! HE'S--
BAM!
URK!
YOU PAY YOUR MERCENARY ARMY TOO MUCH, BIG DADDY...
...I'VE HAD TOUGHER FIGHTS WITH MOTHER'S BUNIONS.

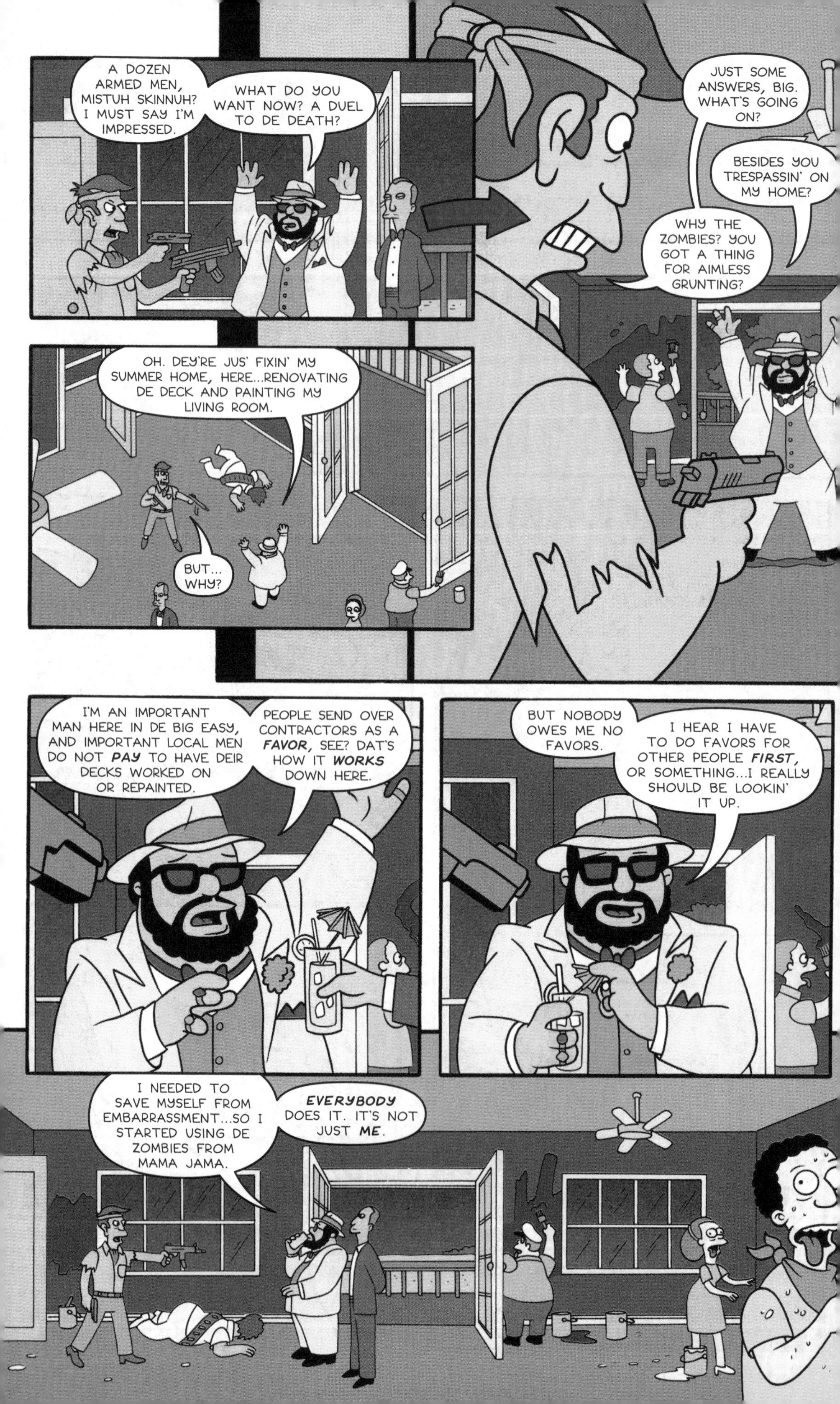
A DOZEN ARMED MEN, MISTUH SKINNUH? I MUST SAY I'M IMPRESSED.
WHAT DO YOU WANT NOW? A DUEL TO DE DEATH?
JUST SOME ANSWERS, BIG. WHAT'S GOING ON?
BESIDES YOU TRESPASSIN' ON MY HOME?
WHY THE ZOMBIES? YOU GOT A THING FOR AIMLESS GRUNTING?
OH. DEY'RE JUS' FIXIN' MY SUMMER HOME, HERE...RENOVATING DE DECK AND PAINTING MY LIVING ROOM.
BUT... WHY?
I'M AN IMPORTANT MAN HERE IN DE BIG EASY, AND IMPORTANT LOCAL MEN DO NOT PAY TO HAVE DEIR DECKS WORKED ON OR REPAINTED.
PEOPLE SEND OVER CONTRACTORS AS A FAVOR, SEE? DAT'S HOW IT WORKS DOWN HERE.
BUT NOBODY OWES ME NO FAVORS.
I HEAR I HAVE TO DO FAVORS FOR OTHER PEOPLE FIRST, OR SOMETHING...I REALLY SHOULD BE LOOKIN' IT UP.
I NEEDED TO SAVE MYSELF FROM EMBARRASSMENT...SO I STARTED USING DE ZOMBIES FROM MAMA JAMA.
EVERYBODY DOES IT. IT'S NOT JUST ME.

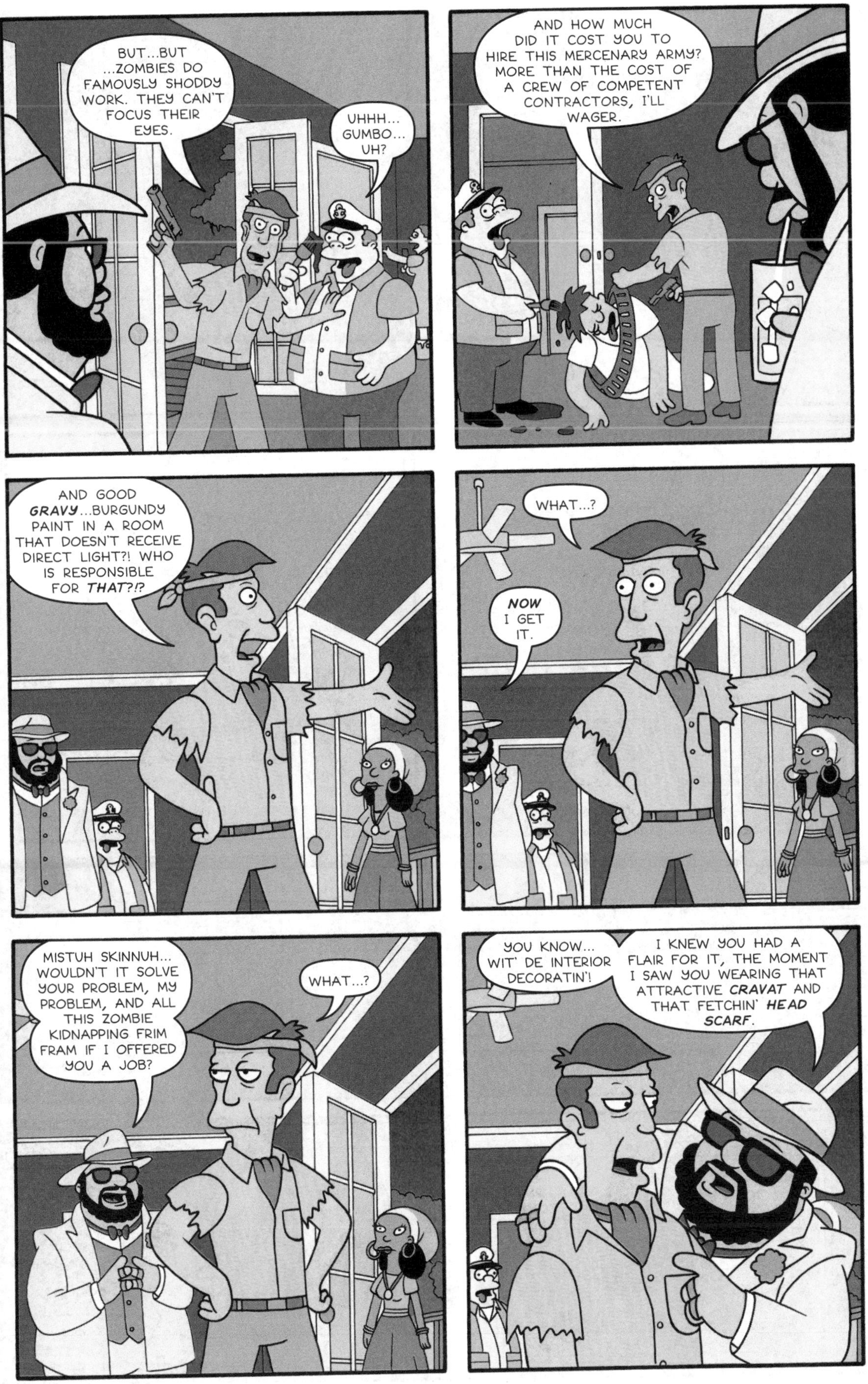
BUT...BUT ...ZOMBIES DO FAMOUSLY SHODDY WORK. THEY CAN'T FOCUS THEIR EYES.
UHHH... GUMBO... UH?
AND HOW MUCH DID IT COST YOU TO HIRE THIS MERCENARY ARMY? MORE THAN THE COST OF A CREW OF COMPETENT CONTRACTORS, I'LL WAGER.
AND GOOD **GRAVY**...BURGUNDY PAINT IN A ROOM THAT DOESN'T RECEIVE DIRECT LIGHT?! WHO IS RESPONSIBLE FOR **THAT**?!?
WHAT...?
NOW I GET IT.
MISTUH SKINNUH... WOULDN'T IT SOLVE YOUR PROBLEM, MY PROBLEM, AND ALL THIS ZOMBIE KIDNAPPING FRIM FRAM IF I OFFERED YOU A JOB?
WHAT...?
YOU KNOW... WIT' DE INTERIOR DECORATIN'!
I KNEW YOU HAD A FLAIR FOR IT, THE MOMENT I SAW YOU WEARING THAT ATTRACTIVE **CRAVAT** AND THAT FETCHIN' **HEAD SCARF**.

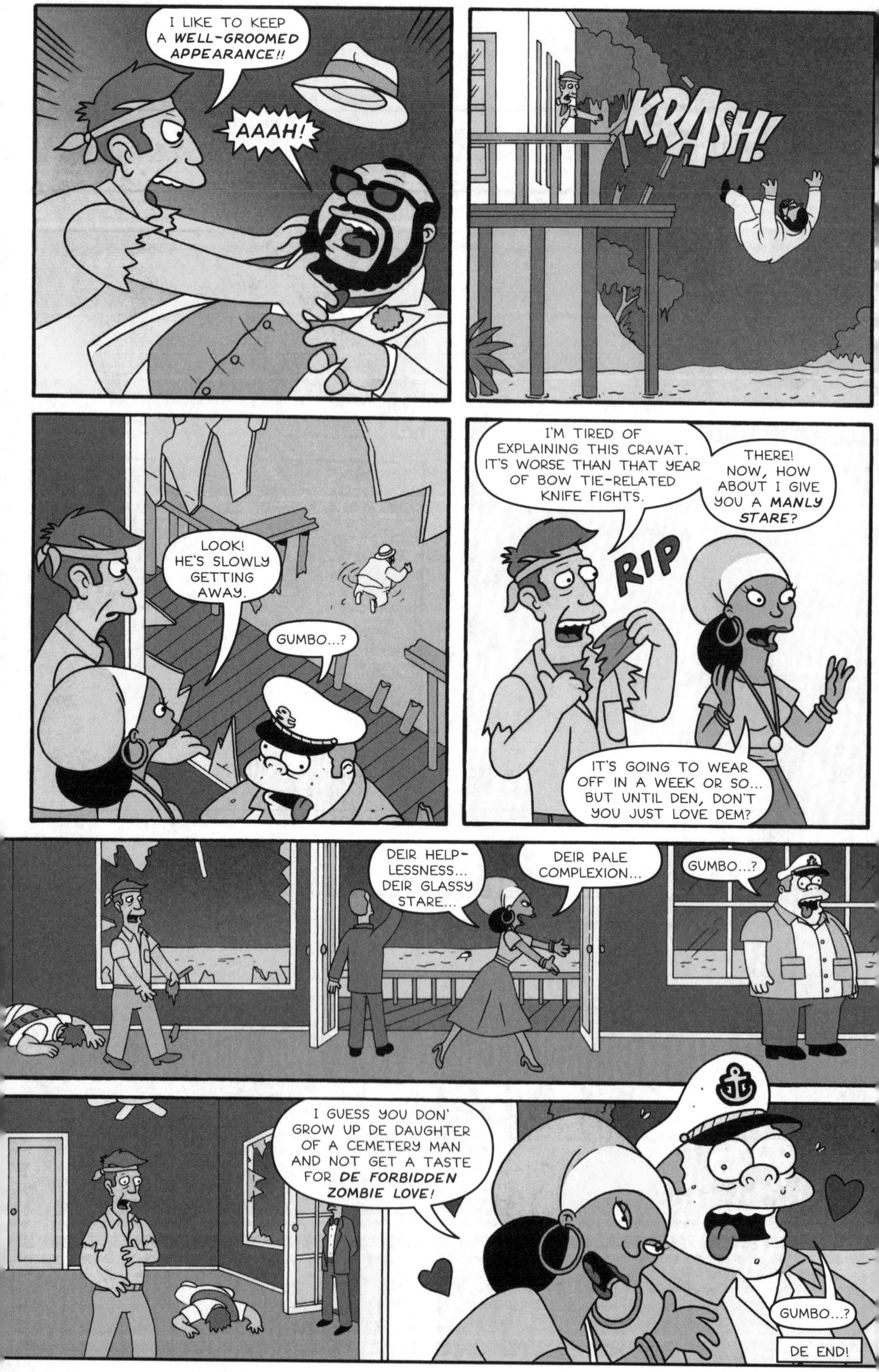

I LIKE TO KEEP A WELL-GROOMED APPEARANCE!!
AAAH!
KRASH!
LOOK! HE'S SLOWLY GETTING AWAY.
GUMBO...?
I'M TIRED OF EXPLAINING THIS CRAVAT. IT'S WORSE THAN THAT YEAR OF BOW TIE-RELATED KNIFE FIGHTS.
RIP
THERE! NOW, HOW ABOUT I GIVE YOU A MANLY STARE?
IT'S GOING TO WEAR OFF IN A WEEK OR SO... BUT UNTIL DEN, DON'T YOU JUST LOVE DEM?
DEIR HELP-LESSNESS... DEIR GLASSY STARE...
DEIR PALE COMPLEXION...
GUMBO...?
I GUESS YOU DON' GROW UP DE DAUGHTER OF A CEMETERY MAN AND NOT GET A TASTE FOR DE FORBIDDEN ZOMBIE LOVE!
GUMBO...?
DE END!

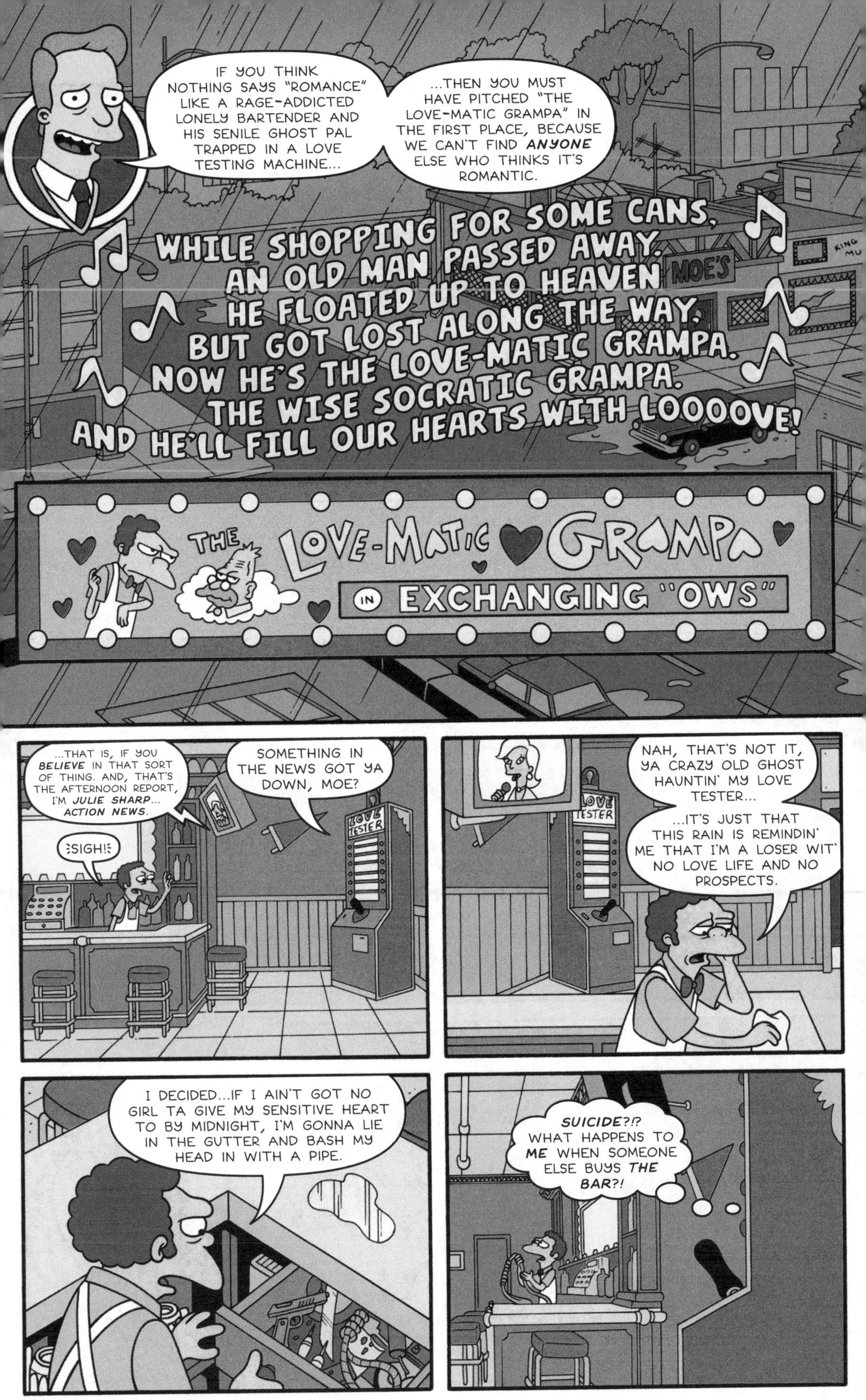
IF YOU THINK NOTHING SAYS "ROMANCE" LIKE A RAGE-ADDICTED LONELY BARTENDER AND HIS SENILE GHOST PAL TRAPPED IN A LOVE TESTING MACHINE...
...THEN YOU MUST HAVE PITCHED "THE LOVE-MATIC GRAMPA" IN THE FIRST PLACE, BECAUSE WE CAN'T FIND ***ANYONE*** ELSE WHO THINKS IT'S ROMANTIC.
WHILE SHOPPING FOR SOME CANS, AN OLD MAN PASSED AWAY. HE FLOATED UP TO HEAVEN BUT GOT LOST ALONG THE WAY. NOW HE'S THE LOVE-MATIC GRAMPA. THE WISE SOCRATIC GRAMPA. AND HE'LL FILL OUR HEARTS WITH LOOOOVE!
MOE'S
THE LOVE-MATIC GRAMPA
IN EXCHANGING "OWS"
...THAT IS, IF YOU ***BELIEVE*** IN THAT SORT OF THING. AND, THAT'S THE AFTERNOON REPORT, I'M ***JULIE SHARP***... ***ACTION NEWS***.
SIGH!
SOMETHING IN THE NEWS GOT YA DOWN, MOE?
LOVE TESTER
NAH, THAT'S NOT IT, YA CRAZY OLD GHOST HAUNTIN' MY LOVE TESTER...
...IT'S JUST THAT THIS RAIN IS REMINDIN' ME THAT I'M A LOSER WIT' NO LOVE LIFE AND NO PROSPECTS.
I DECIDED...IF I AIN'T GOT NO GIRL TA GIVE MY SENSITIVE HEART TO BY MIDNIGHT, I'M GONNA LIE IN THE GUTTER AND BASH MY HEAD IN WITH A PIPE.
SUICIDE?!? WHAT HAPPENS TO ***ME*** WHEN SOMEONE ELSE BUYS ***THE BAR?!***

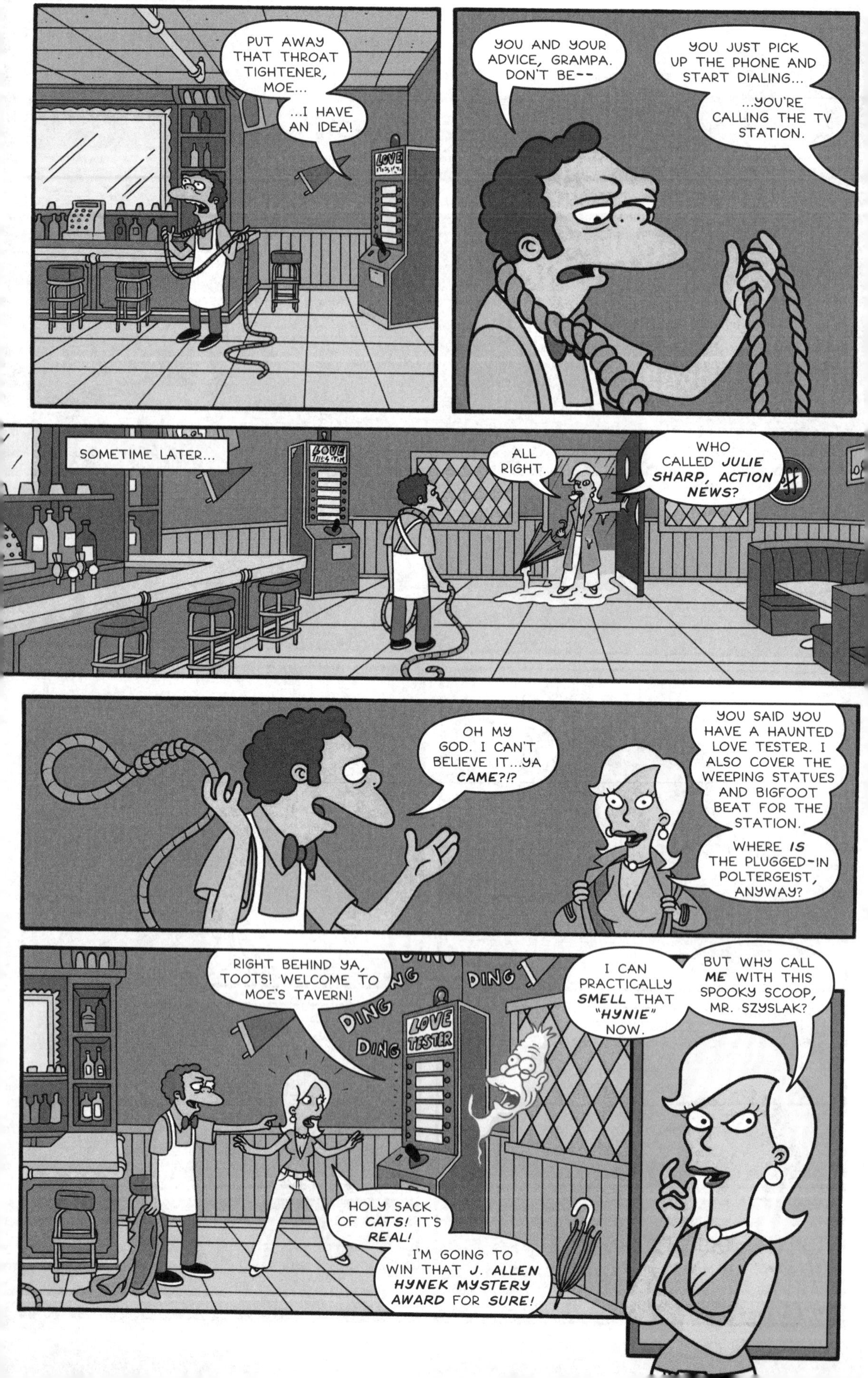
PUT AWAY THAT THROAT TIGHTENER, MOE...
...I HAVE AN IDEA!
LOVE TESTER
YOU AND YOUR ADVICE, GRAMPA. DON'T BE--
YOU JUST PICK UP THE PHONE AND START DIALING...
...YOU'RE CALLING THE TV STATION.
SOMETIME LATER...
ALL RIGHT.
WHO CALLED **JULIE SHARP, ACTION NEWS**?
OH MY GOD. I CAN'T BELIEVE IT...YA ***CAME***?!?
YOU SAID YOU HAVE A HAUNTED LOVE TESTER. I ALSO COVER THE WEEPING STATUES AND BIGFOOT BEAT FOR THE STATION.
WHERE ***IS*** THE PLUGGED-IN POLTERGEIST, ANYWAY?
RIGHT BEHIND YA, TOOTS! WELCOME TO MOE'S TAVERN!
DING DING DING DING DING
LOVE TESTER
I CAN PRACTICALLY **SMELL** THAT ***"HYNIE"*** NOW.
BUT WHY CALL **ME** WITH THIS SPOOKY SCOOP, MR. SZYSLAK?
HOLY SACK OF ***CATS!*** IT'S ***REAL!***
I'M GOING TO WIN THAT ***J. ALLEN HYNEK MYSTERY AWARD*** FOR ***SURE!***

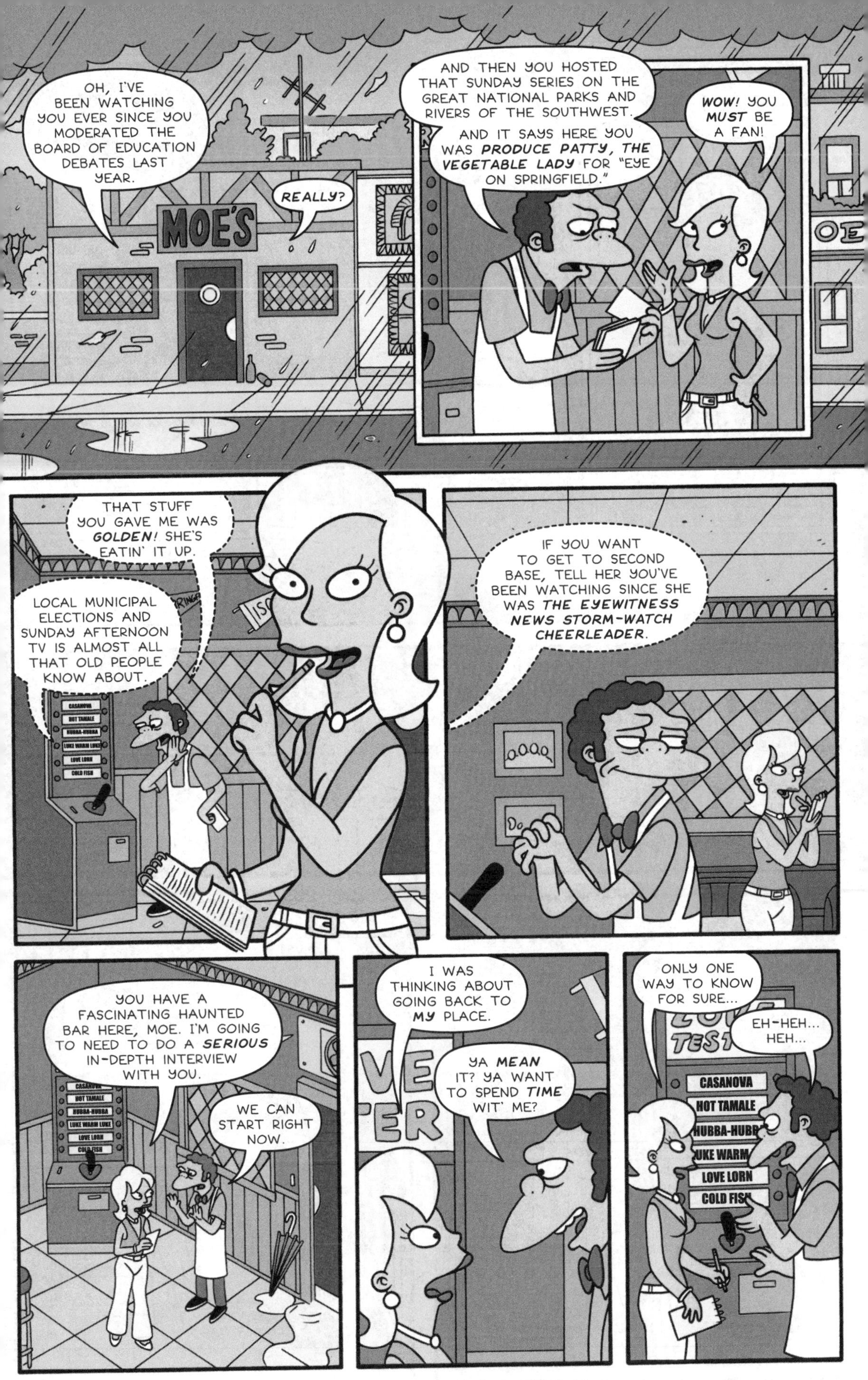

OH, I'VE BEEN WATCHING YOU EVER SINCE YOU MODERATED THE BOARD OF EDUCATION DEBATES LAST YEAR.
REALLY?
MOE'S
AND THEN YOU HOSTED THAT SUNDAY SERIES ON THE GREAT NATIONAL PARKS AND RIVERS OF THE SOUTHWEST.
AND IT SAYS HERE YOU WAS PRODUCE PATTY, THE VEGETABLE LADY FOR "EYE ON SPRINGFIELD."
WOW! YOU MUST BE A FAN!
THAT STUFF YOU GAVE ME WAS GOLDEN! SHE'S EATIN' IT UP.
LOCAL MUNICIPAL ELECTIONS AND SUNDAY AFTERNOON TV IS ALMOST ALL THAT OLD PEOPLE KNOW ABOUT.
CASANOVA
HOT TAMALE
HUBBA-HUBBA
LUKE WARM LUKE
LOVE LORN
COLD FISH
IF YOU WANT TO GET TO SECOND BASE, TELL HER YOU'VE BEEN WATCHING SINCE SHE WAS THE EYEWITNESS NEWS STORM-WATCH CHEERLEADER.
YOU HAVE A FASCINATING HAUNTED BAR HERE, MOE. I'M GOING TO NEED TO DO A SERIOUS IN-DEPTH INTERVIEW WITH YOU.
WE CAN START RIGHT NOW.
I WAS THINKING ABOUT GOING BACK TO MY PLACE.
YA MEAN IT? YA WANT TO SPEND TIME WIT' ME?
ONLY ONE WAY TO KNOW FOR SURE...
EH-HEH... HEH...
CASANOVA
HOT TAMALE
LOVE LORN
COLD FISH

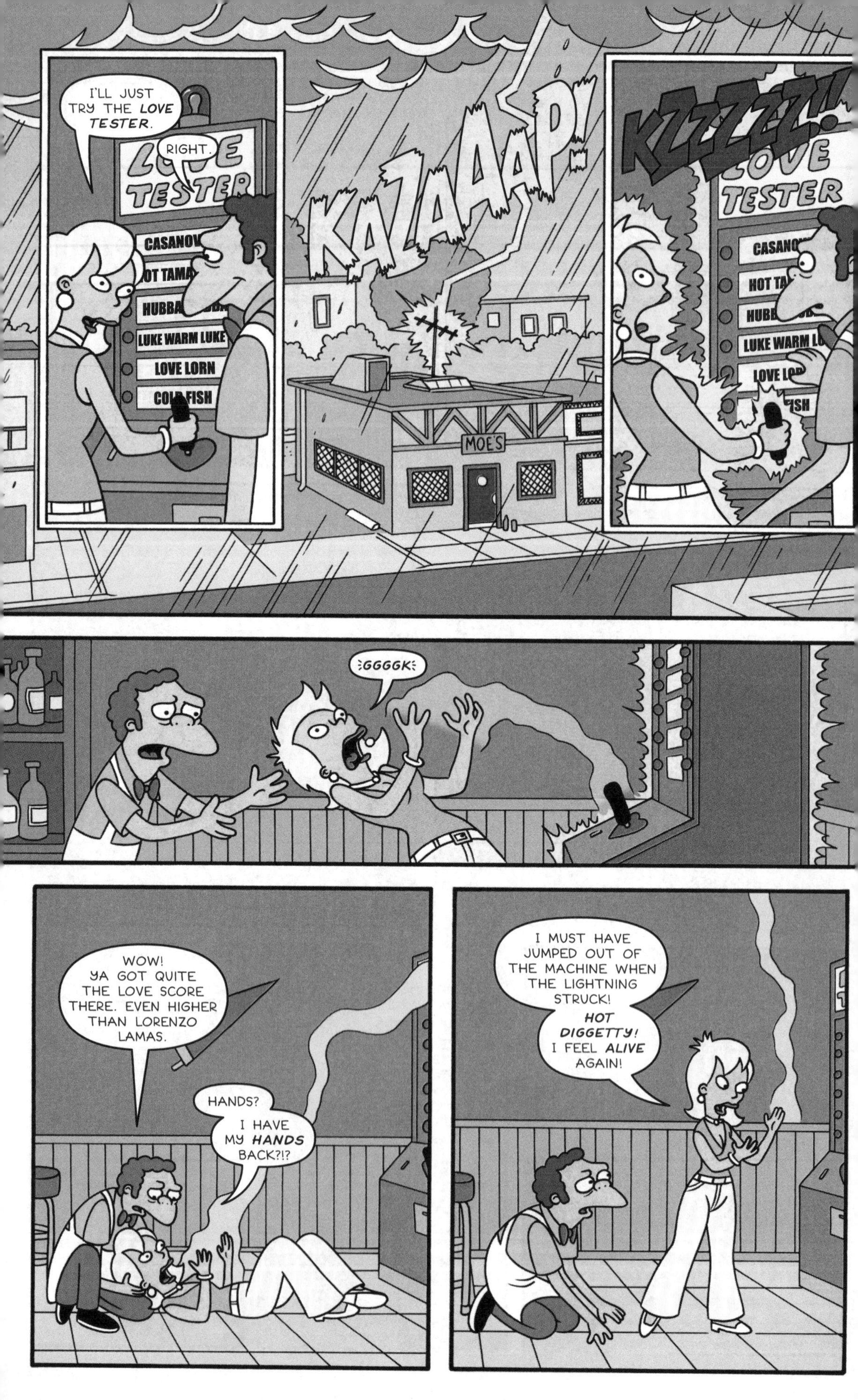

I'LL JUST TRY THE LOVE TESTER.
RIGHT.
LOVE TESTER
CASANOV
HOT TAMA
HUBBA
LUKE WARM LUKE
LOVE LORN
COLD FISH
KAZAAAP!
MOE'S
KZZZZZ!!
LOVE TESTER
GGGGK
WOW! YA GOT QUITE THE LOVE SCORE THERE. EVEN HIGHER THAN LORENZO LAMAS.
HANDS?
I HAVE MY HANDS BACK?!?
I MUST HAVE JUMPED OUT OF THE MACHINE WHEN THE LIGHTNING STRUCK!
HOT DIGGETTY! I FEEL ALIVE AGAIN!

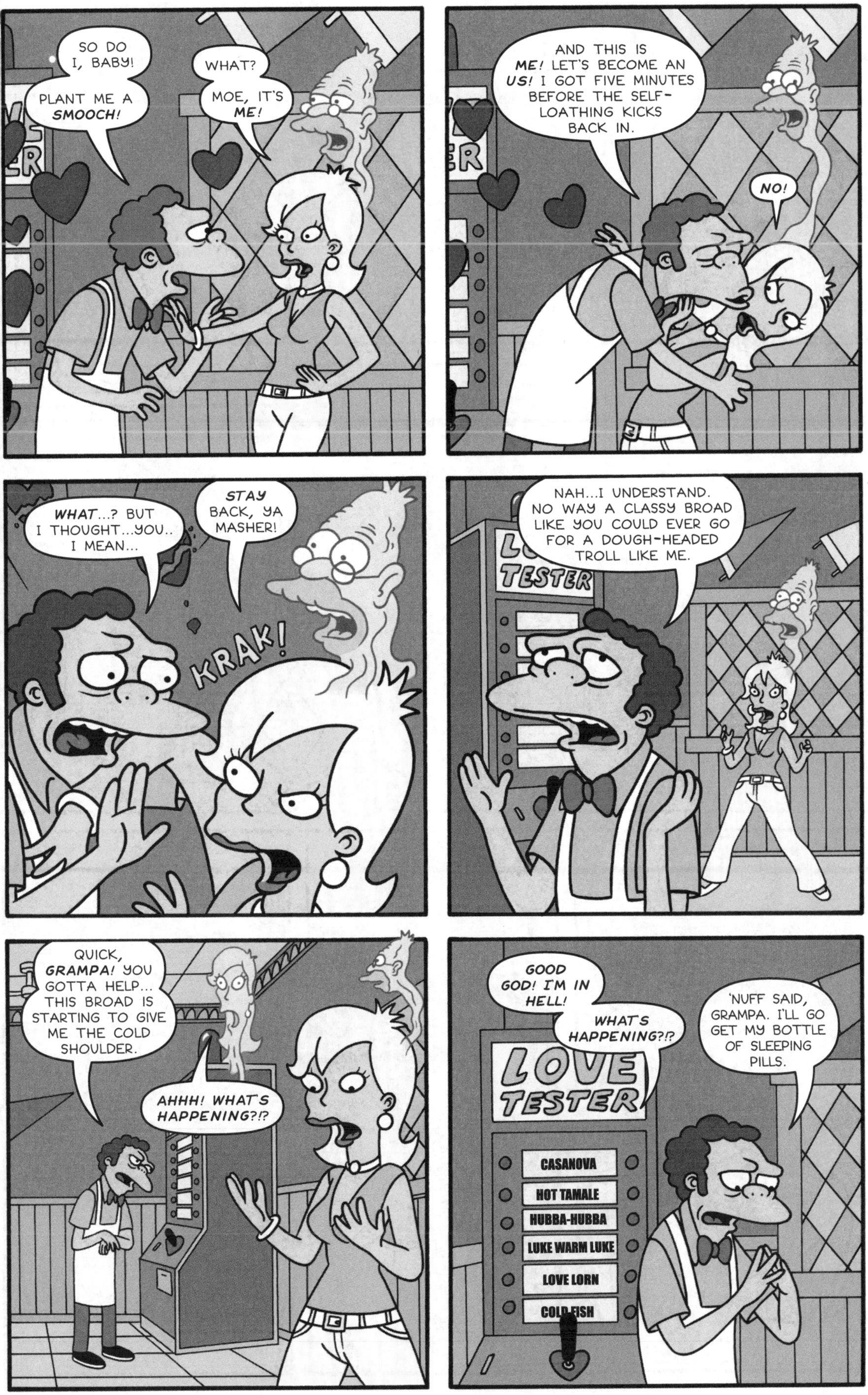
SO DO I, BABY!
PLANT ME A SMOOCH!
WHAT?
MOE, IT'S ME!
AND THIS IS ME! LET'S BECOME AN US! I GOT FIVE MINUTES BEFORE THE SELF-LOATHING KICKS BACK IN.
NO!
WHAT...? BUT I THOUGHT...YOU.. I MEAN...
STAY BACK, YA MASHER!
KRAK!
NAH...I UNDERSTAND. NO WAY A CLASSY BROAD LIKE YOU COULD EVER GO FOR A DOUGH-HEADED TROLL LIKE ME.
LOVE TESTER
QUICK, GRAMPA! YOU GOTTA HELP... THIS BROAD IS STARTING TO GIVE ME THE COLD SHOULDER.
AHHH! WHAT'S HAPPENING?!?
GOOD GOD! I'M IN HELL!
WHAT'S HAPPENING?!?
'NUFF SAID, GRAMPA. I'LL GO GET MY BOTTLE OF SLEEPING PILLS.
LOVE TESTER
CASANOVA
HOT TAMALE
HUBBA-HUBBA
LUKE WARM LUKE
LOVE LORN
COLD FISH

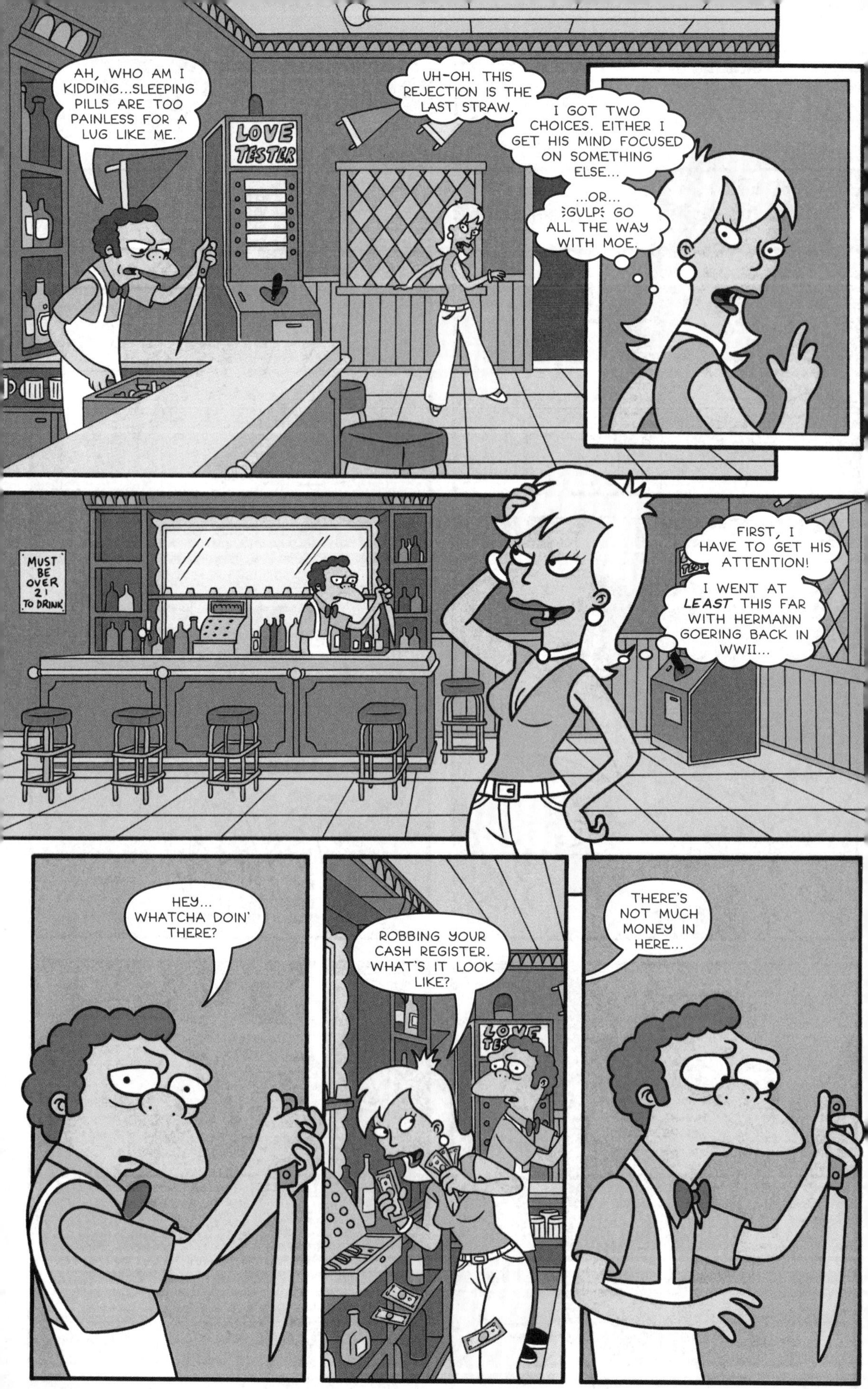
AH, WHO AM I KIDDING...SLEEPING PILLS ARE TOO PAINLESS FOR A LUG LIKE ME.
LOVE TESTER
UH-OH. THIS REJECTION IS THE LAST STRAW.
I GOT TWO CHOICES. EITHER I GET HIS MIND FOCUSED ON SOMETHING ELSE...
...OR... GULP GO ALL THE WAY WITH MOE.
MUST BE OVER 21 TO DRINK
FIRST, I HAVE TO GET HIS ATTENTION!
I WENT AT LEAST THIS FAR WITH HERMANN GOERING BACK IN WWII...
HEY... WHATCHA DOIN' THERE?
ROBBING YOUR CASH REGISTER. WHAT'S IT LOOK LIKE?
THERE'S NOT MUCH MONEY IN HERE...

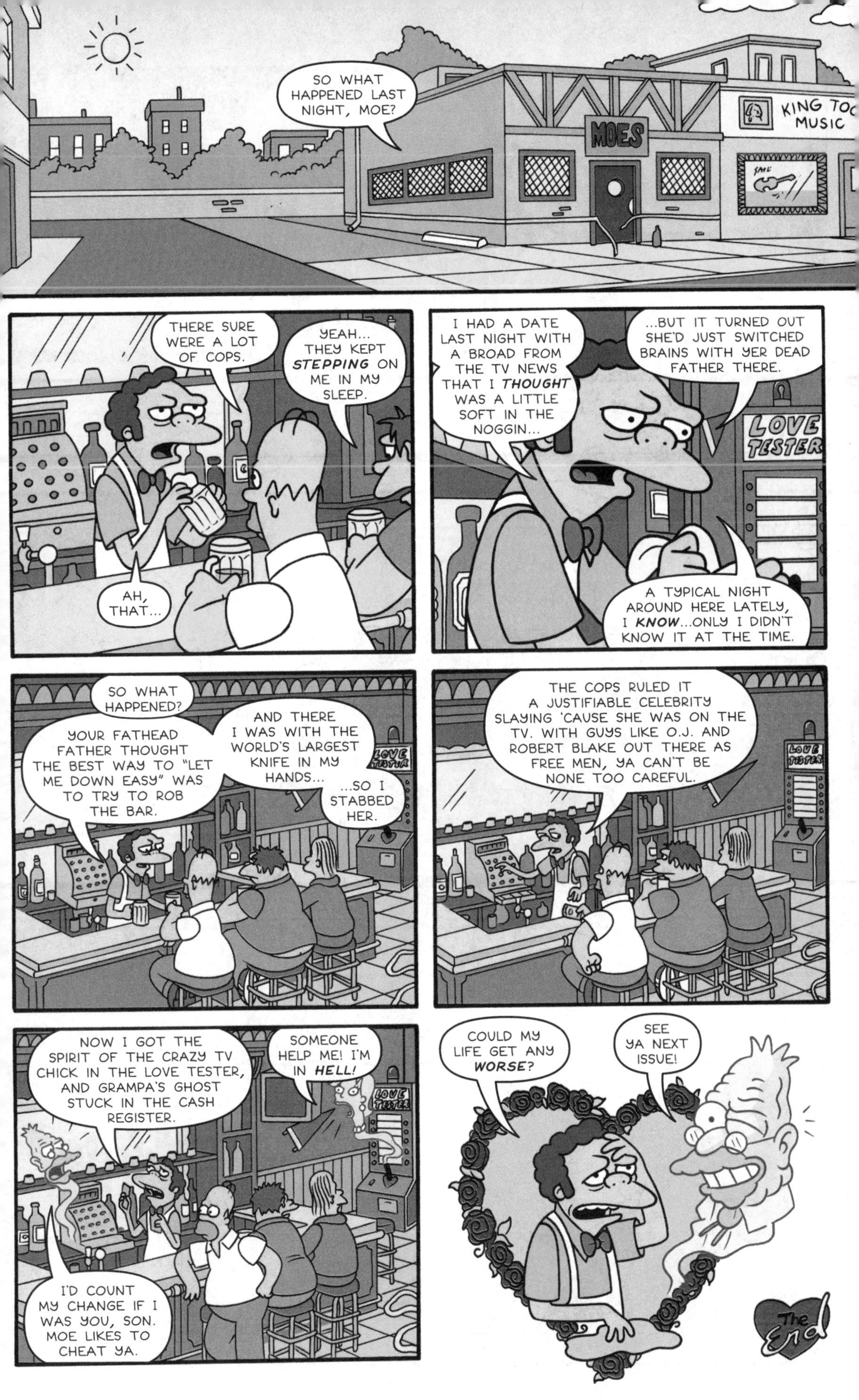
SO WHAT HAPPENED LAST NIGHT, MOE?
MOES
KING TO MUSIC
THERE SURE WERE A LOT OF COPS.
YEAH... THEY KEPT STEPPING ON ME IN MY SLEEP.
AH, THAT...
I HAD A DATE LAST NIGHT WITH A BROAD FROM THE TV NEWS THAT I THOUGHT WAS A LITTLE SOFT IN THE NOGGIN...
...BUT IT TURNED OUT SHE'D JUST SWITCHED BRAINS WITH YER DEAD FATHER THERE.
LOVE TESTER
A TYPICAL NIGHT AROUND HERE LATELY, I KNOW...ONLY I DIDN'T KNOW IT AT THE TIME.
SO WHAT HAPPENED?
YOUR FATHEAD FATHER THOUGHT THE BEST WAY TO "LET ME DOWN EASY" WAS TO TRY TO ROB THE BAR.
AND THERE I WAS WITH THE WORLD'S LARGEST KNIFE IN MY HANDS...
...SO I STABBED HER.
THE COPS RULED IT A JUSTIFIABLE CELEBRITY SLAYING 'CAUSE SHE WAS ON THE TV. WITH GUYS LIKE O.J. AND ROBERT BLAKE OUT THERE AS FREE MEN, YA CAN'T BE NONE TOO CAREFUL.
NOW I GOT THE SPIRIT OF THE CRAZY TV CHICK IN THE LOVE TESTER, AND GRAMPA'S GHOST STUCK IN THE CASH REGISTER.
SOMEONE HELP ME! I'M IN HELL!
I'D COUNT MY CHANGE IF I WAS YOU, SON. MOE LIKES TO CHEAT YA.
COULD MY LIFE GET ANY WORSE?
SEE YA NEXT ISSUE!
The End

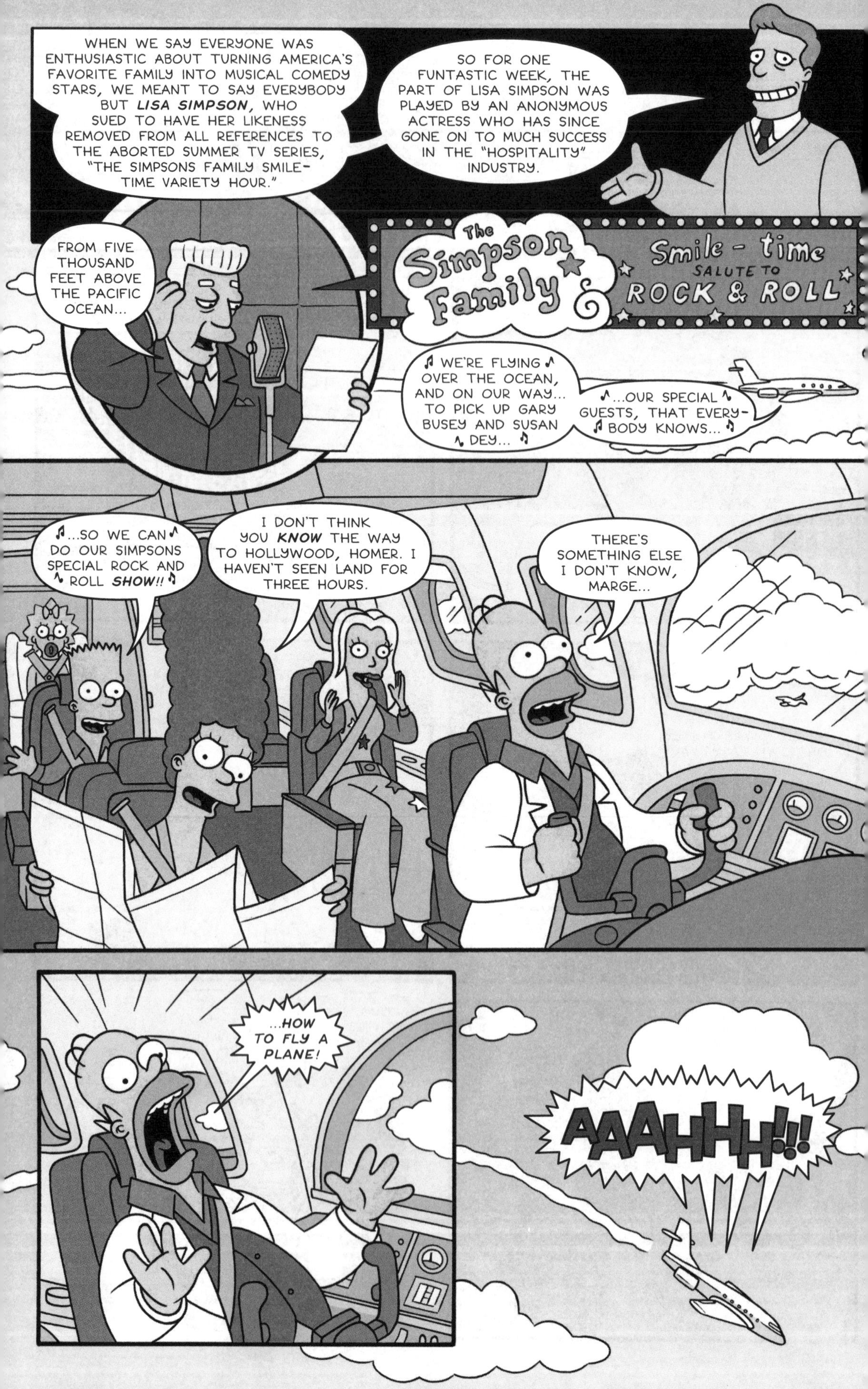

WHEN WE SAY EVERYONE WAS ENTHUSIASTIC ABOUT TURNING AMERICA'S FAVORITE FAMILY INTO MUSICAL COMEDY STARS, WE MEANT TO SAY EVERYBODY BUT **LISA SIMPSON**, WHO SUED TO HAVE HER LIKENESS REMOVED FROM ALL REFERENCES TO THE ABORTED SUMMER TV SERIES, "THE SIMPSONS FAMILY SMILE-TIME VARIETY HOUR."
SO FOR ONE FUNTASTIC WEEK, THE PART OF LISA SIMPSON WAS PLAYED BY AN ANONYMOUS ACTRESS WHO HAS SINCE GONE ON TO MUCH SUCCESS IN THE "HOSPITALITY" INDUSTRY.
FROM FIVE THOUSAND FEET ABOVE THE PACIFIC OCEAN...
The Simpson Family Smile-time SALUTE TO ROCK & ROLL
♪ WE'RE FLYING OVER THE OCEAN, AND ON OUR WAY... TO PICK UP GARY BUSEY AND SUSAN DEY... ♪
♪ ...OUR SPECIAL GUESTS, THAT EVERYBODY KNOWS... ♪
♪ ...SO WE CAN DO OUR SIMPSONS SPECIAL ROCK AND ROLL **SHOW!!** ♪
I DON'T THINK YOU **KNOW** THE WAY TO HOLLYWOOD, HOMER. I HAVEN'T SEEN LAND FOR THREE HOURS.
THERE'S SOMETHING ELSE I DON'T KNOW, MARGE...
...HOW TO FLY A PLANE!
AAAHHH!!!

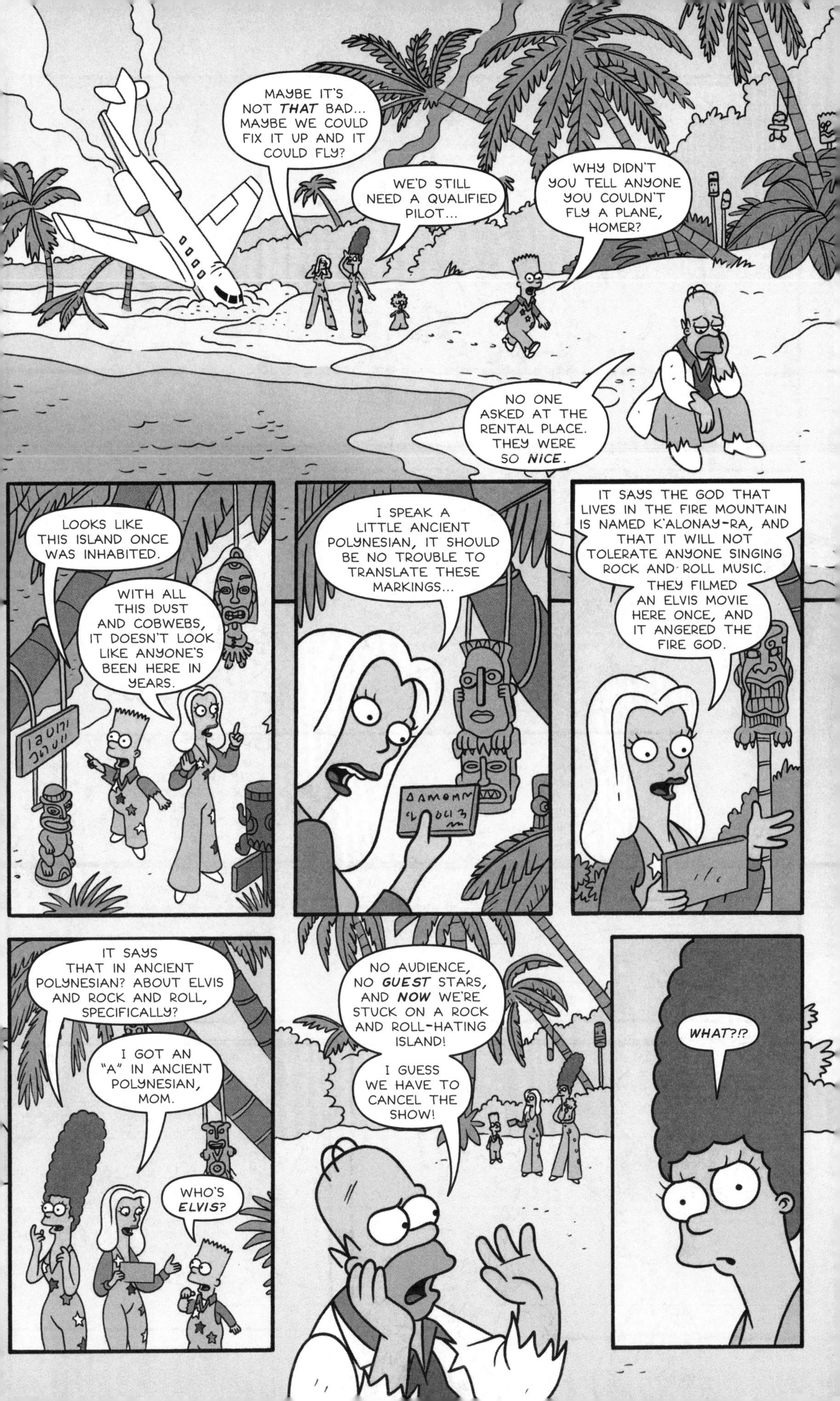

MAYBE IT'S NOT *THAT* BAD... MAYBE WE COULD FIX IT UP AND IT COULD FLY?
WE'D STILL NEED A QUALIFIED PILOT...
WHY DIDN'T YOU TELL ANYONE YOU COULDN'T FLY A PLANE, HOMER?
NO ONE ASKED AT THE RENTAL PLACE. THEY WERE SO *NICE*.
LOOKS LIKE THIS ISLAND ONCE WAS INHABITED.
WITH ALL THIS DUST AND COBWEBS, IT DOESN'T LOOK LIKE ANYONE'S BEEN HERE IN YEARS.
I SPEAK A LITTLE ANCIENT POLYNESIAN, IT SHOULD BE NO TROUBLE TO TRANSLATE THESE MARKINGS...
IT SAYS THE GOD THAT LIVES IN THE FIRE MOUNTAIN IS NAMED K'ALONAY-RA, AND THAT IT WILL NOT TOLERATE ANYONE SINGING ROCK AND ROLL MUSIC.
THEY FILMED AN ELVIS MOVIE HERE ONCE, AND IT ANGERED THE FIRE GOD.
IT SAYS THAT IN ANCIENT POLYNESIAN? ABOUT ELVIS AND ROCK AND ROLL, SPECIFICALLY?
I GOT AN "A" IN ANCIENT POLYNESIAN, MOM.
WHO'S *ELVIS*?
NO AUDIENCE, NO *GUEST* STARS, AND *NOW* WE'RE STUCK ON A ROCK AND ROLL-HATING ISLAND!
I GUESS WE HAVE TO CANCEL THE SHOW!
WHAT?!?

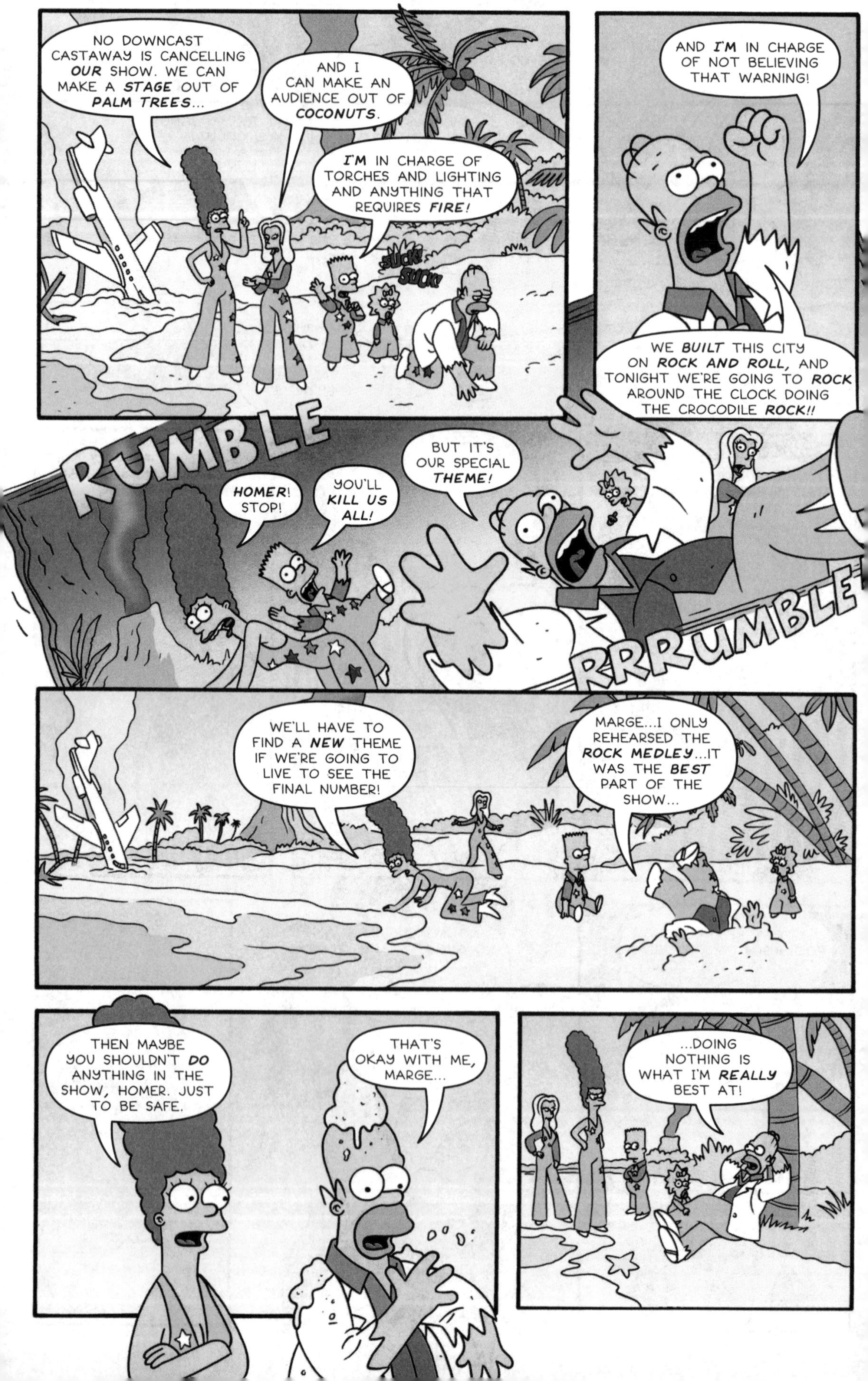
NO DOWNCAST CASTAWAY IS CANCELLING OUR SHOW. WE CAN MAKE A STAGE OUT OF PALM TREES...
AND I CAN MAKE AN AUDIENCE OUT OF COCONUTS.
I'M IN CHARGE OF TORCHES AND LIGHTING AND ANYTHING THAT REQUIRES FIRE!
SUCK! SUCK!
AND I'M IN CHARGE OF NOT BELIEVING THAT WARNING!
WE BUILT THIS CITY ON ROCK AND ROLL, AND TONIGHT WE'RE GOING TO ROCK AROUND THE CLOCK DOING THE CROCODILE ROCK!!
RUMBLE
HOMER! STOP!
YOU'LL KILL US ALL!
BUT IT'S OUR SPECIAL THEME!
RRRUMBLE
WE'LL HAVE TO FIND A NEW THEME IF WE'RE GOING TO LIVE TO SEE THE FINAL NUMBER!
MARGE...I ONLY REHEARSED THE ROCK MEDLEY...IT WAS THE BEST PART OF THE SHOW...
THEN MAYBE YOU SHOULDN'T DO ANYTHING IN THE SHOW, HOMER. JUST TO BE SAFE.
THAT'S OKAY WITH ME, MARGE...
...DOING NOTHING IS WHAT I'M REALLY BEST AT!

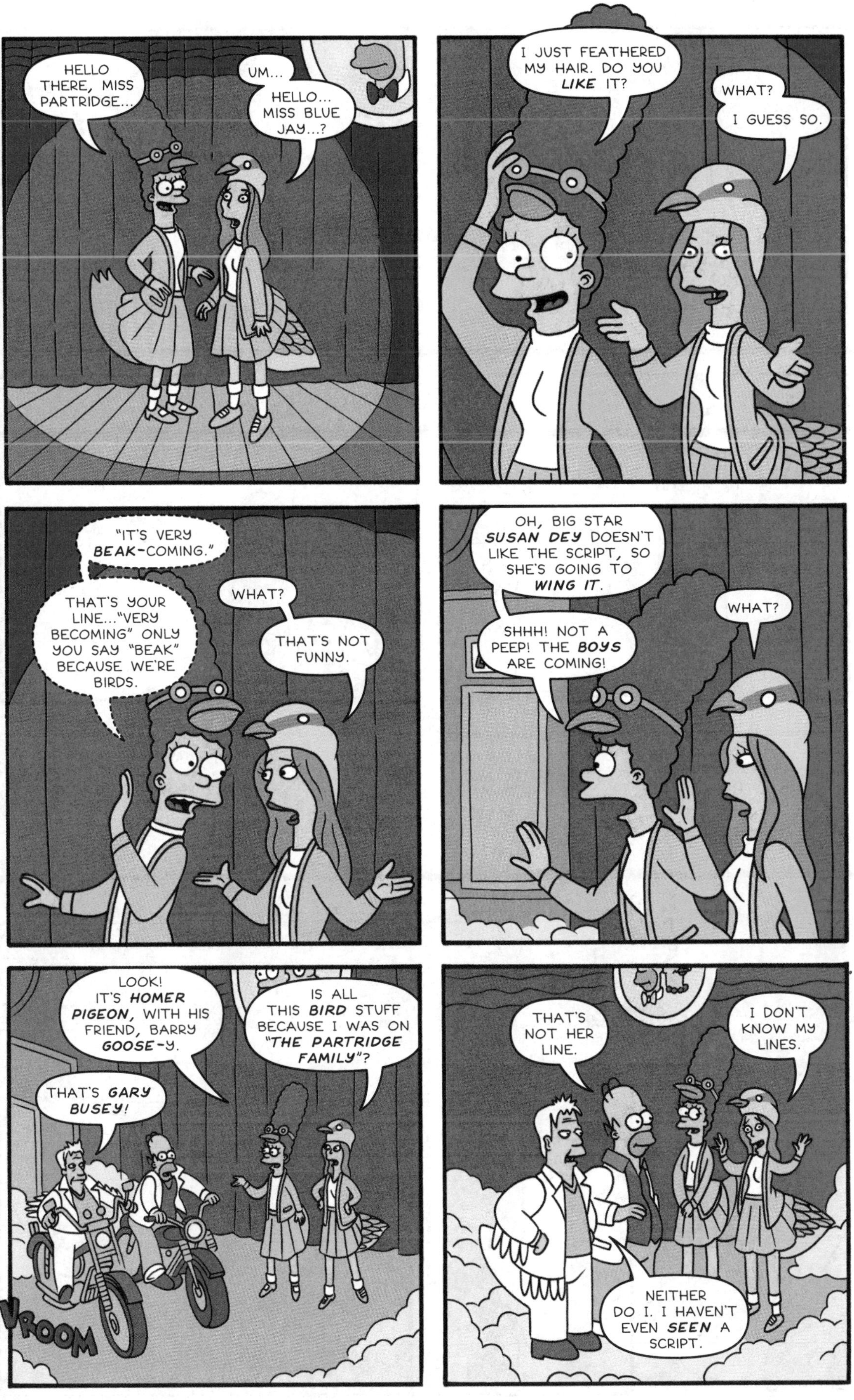
HELLO THERE, MISS PARTRIDGE...
UM...
HELLO... MISS BLUE JAY...?
I JUST FEATHERED MY HAIR. DO YOU LIKE IT?
WHAT?
I GUESS SO.
"IT'S VERY BEAK-COMING."
THAT'S YOUR LINE..."VERY BECOMING" ONLY YOU SAY "BEAK" BECAUSE WE'RE BIRDS.
WHAT?
THAT'S NOT FUNNY.
OH, BIG STAR SUSAN DEY DOESN'T LIKE THE SCRIPT, SO SHE'S GOING TO WING IT.
SHHH! NOT A PEEP! THE BOYS ARE COMING!
WHAT?
LOOK! IT'S HOMER PIGEON, WITH HIS FRIEND, BARRY GOOSE-Y.
THAT'S GARY BUSEY!
IS ALL THIS BIRD STUFF BECAUSE I WAS ON "THE PARTRIDGE FAMILY"?
VROOM
THAT'S NOT HER LINE.
I DON'T KNOW MY LINES.
NEITHER DO I. I HAVEN'T EVEN SEEN A SCRIPT.

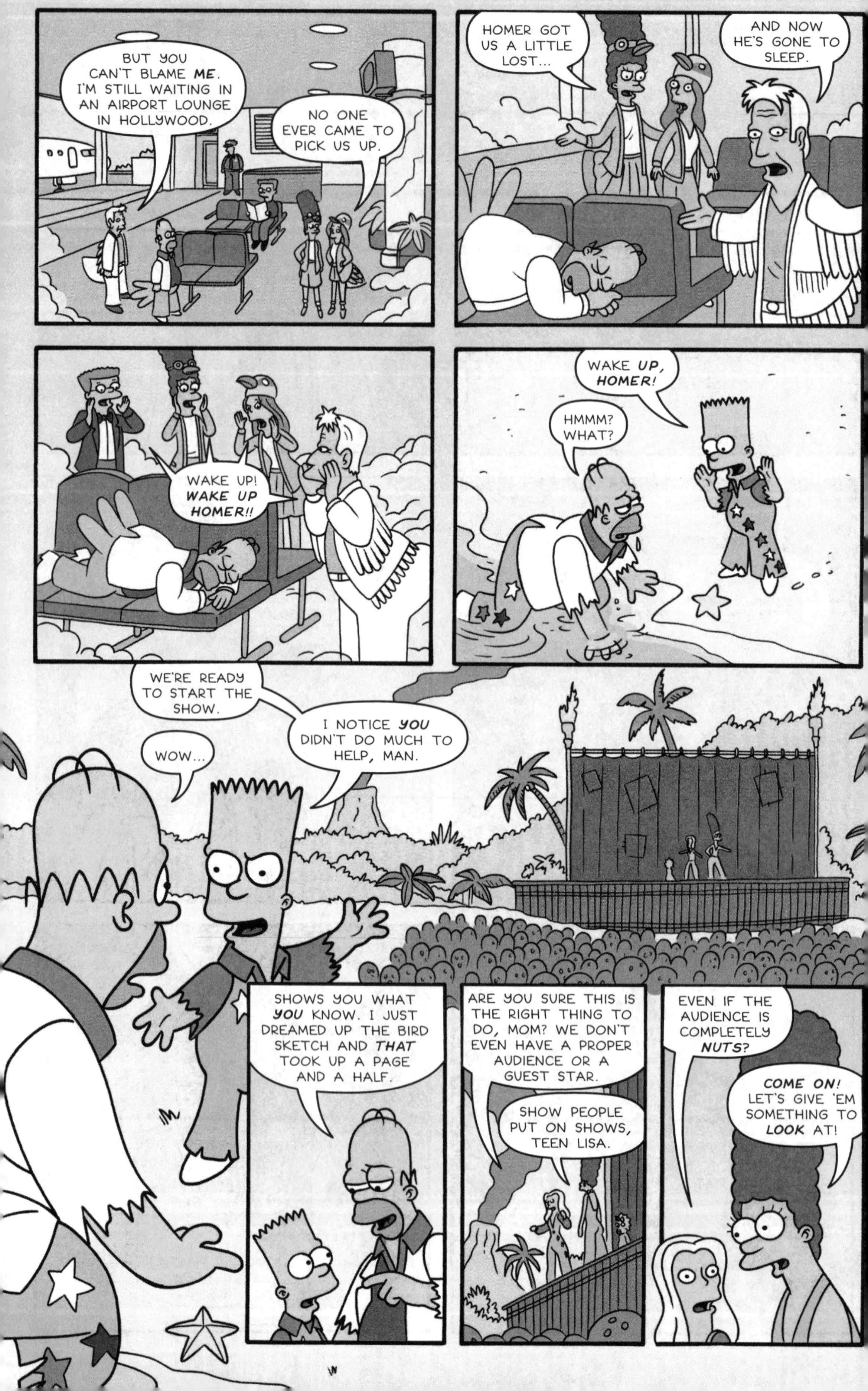
BUT YOU CAN'T BLAME ME. I'M STILL WAITING IN AN AIRPORT LOUNGE IN HOLLYWOOD.
NO ONE EVER CAME TO PICK US UP.
HOMER GOT US A LITTLE LOST...
AND NOW HE'S GONE TO SLEEP.
WAKE UP! WAKE UP HOMER!!
WAKE UP, HOMER!
HMMM? WHAT?
WE'RE READY TO START THE SHOW.
I NOTICE YOU DIDN'T DO MUCH TO HELP, MAN.
WOW...
SHOWS YOU WHAT YOU KNOW. I JUST DREAMED UP THE BIRD SKETCH AND THAT TOOK UP A PAGE AND A HALF.
ARE YOU SURE THIS IS THE RIGHT THING TO DO, MOM? WE DON'T EVEN HAVE A PROPER AUDIENCE OR A GUEST STAR.
SHOW PEOPLE PUT ON SHOWS, TEEN LISA.
EVEN IF THE AUDIENCE IS COMPLETELY NUTS?
COME ON! LET'S GIVE 'EM SOMETHING TO LOOK AT!

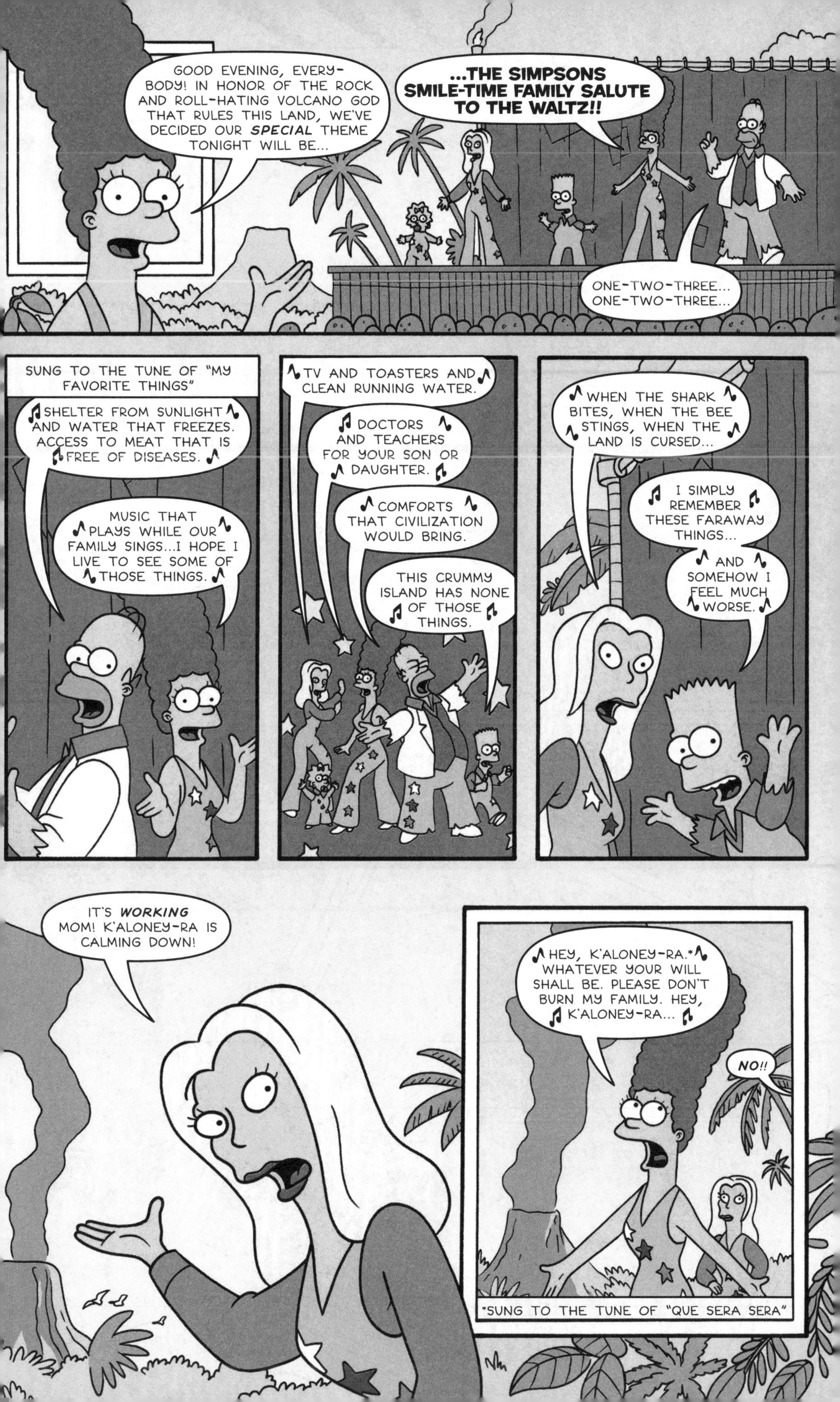
GOOD EVENING, EVERYBODY! IN HONOR OF THE ROCK AND ROLL-HATING VOLCANO GOD THAT RULES THIS LAND, WE'VE DECIDED OUR *SPECIAL* THEME TONIGHT WILL BE...
...THE SIMPSONS SMILE-TIME FAMILY SALUTE TO THE WALTZ!!
ONE-TWO-THREE... ONE-TWO-THREE...
SUNG TO THE TUNE OF "MY FAVORITE THINGS"
♪SHELTER FROM SUNLIGHT♪ AND WATER THAT FREEZES. ACCESS TO MEAT THAT IS ♪FREE OF DISEASES.♪
♪MUSIC THAT ♪PLAYS WHILE OUR FAMILY SINGS...I HOPE I LIVE TO SEE SOME OF ♪THOSE THINGS.♪
♪TV AND TOASTERS AND♪ CLEAN RUNNING WATER.
♪DOCTORS♪ AND TEACHERS FOR YOUR SON OR ♪DAUGHTER.♪
♪COMFORTS♪ THAT CIVILIZATION WOULD BRING.
THIS CRUMMY ISLAND HAS NONE ♪OF THOSE♪ THINGS.
♪WHEN THE SHARK♪ BITES, WHEN THE BEE ♪STINGS, WHEN THE♪ LAND IS CURSED...
♪I SIMPLY♪ REMEMBER THESE FARAWAY THINGS...
♪AND♪ SOMEHOW I FEEL MUCH ♪WORSE.♪
IT'S *WORKING* MOM! K'ALONEY-RA IS CALMING DOWN!
♪HEY, K'ALONEY-RA.*♪ WHATEVER YOUR WILL SHALL BE. PLEASE DON'T BURN MY FAMILY. HEY, ♪K'ALONEY-RA...♪
NO!!
*SUNG TO THE TUNE OF "QUE SERA SERA"

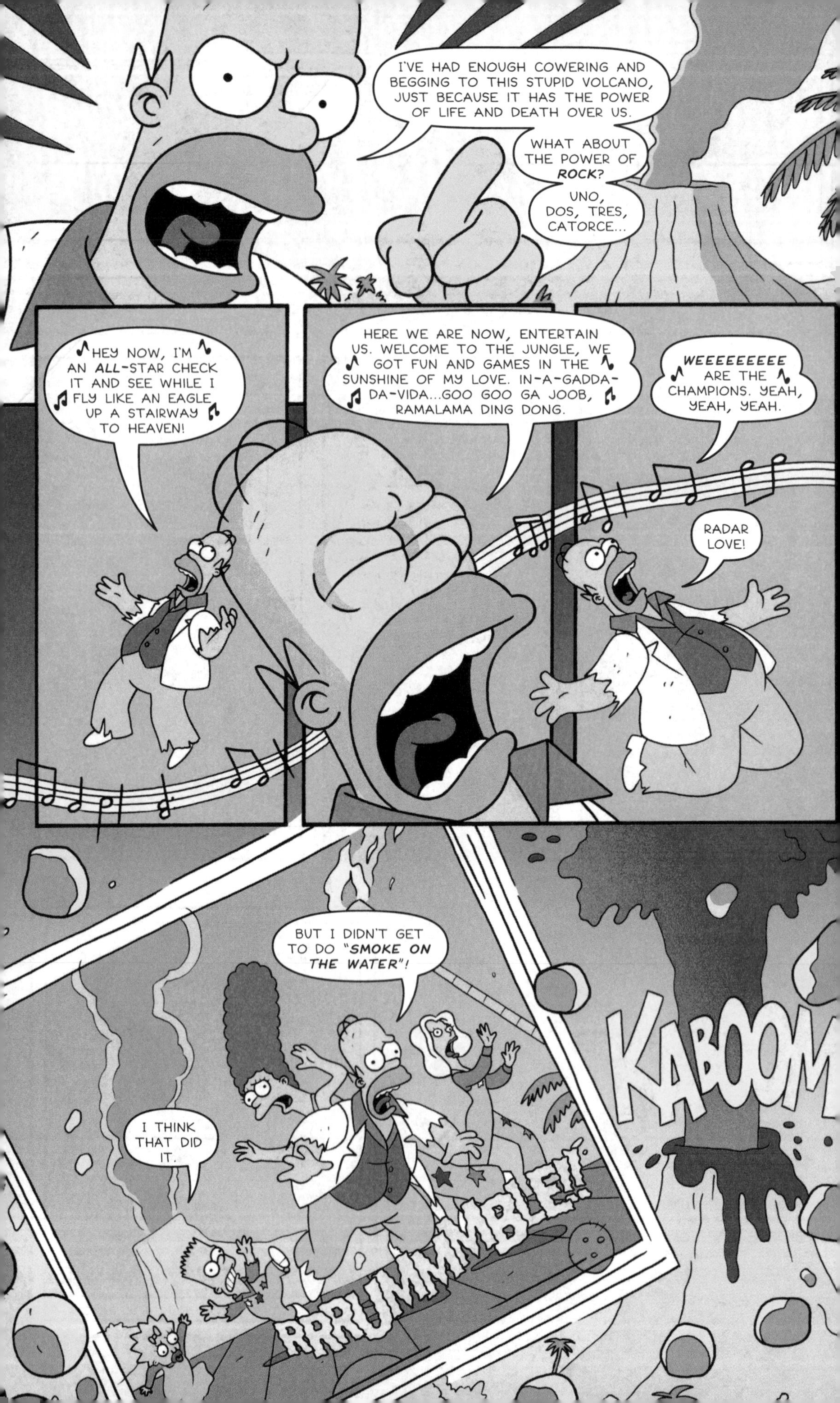

I'VE HAD ENOUGH COWERING AND BEGGING TO THIS STUPID VOLCANO, JUST BECAUSE IT HAS THE POWER OF LIFE AND DEATH OVER US.
WHAT ABOUT THE POWER OF ROCK?
UNO, DOS, TRES, CATORCE...
HEY NOW, I'M AN ALL-STAR CHECK IT AND SEE WHILE I FLY LIKE AN EAGLE UP A STAIRWAY TO HEAVEN!
HERE WE ARE NOW, ENTERTAIN US. WELCOME TO THE JUNGLE, WE GOT FUN AND GAMES IN THE SUNSHINE OF MY LOVE. IN-A-GADDA-DA-VIDA...GOO GOO GA JOOB, RAMALAMA DING DONG.
WEEEEEEEEE ARE THE CHAMPIONS. YEAH, YEAH, YEAH.
RADAR LOVE!
BUT I DIDN'T GET TO DO "SMOKE ON THE WATER"!
KABOOM
I THINK THAT DID IT.
RRRUMMMBLE!!

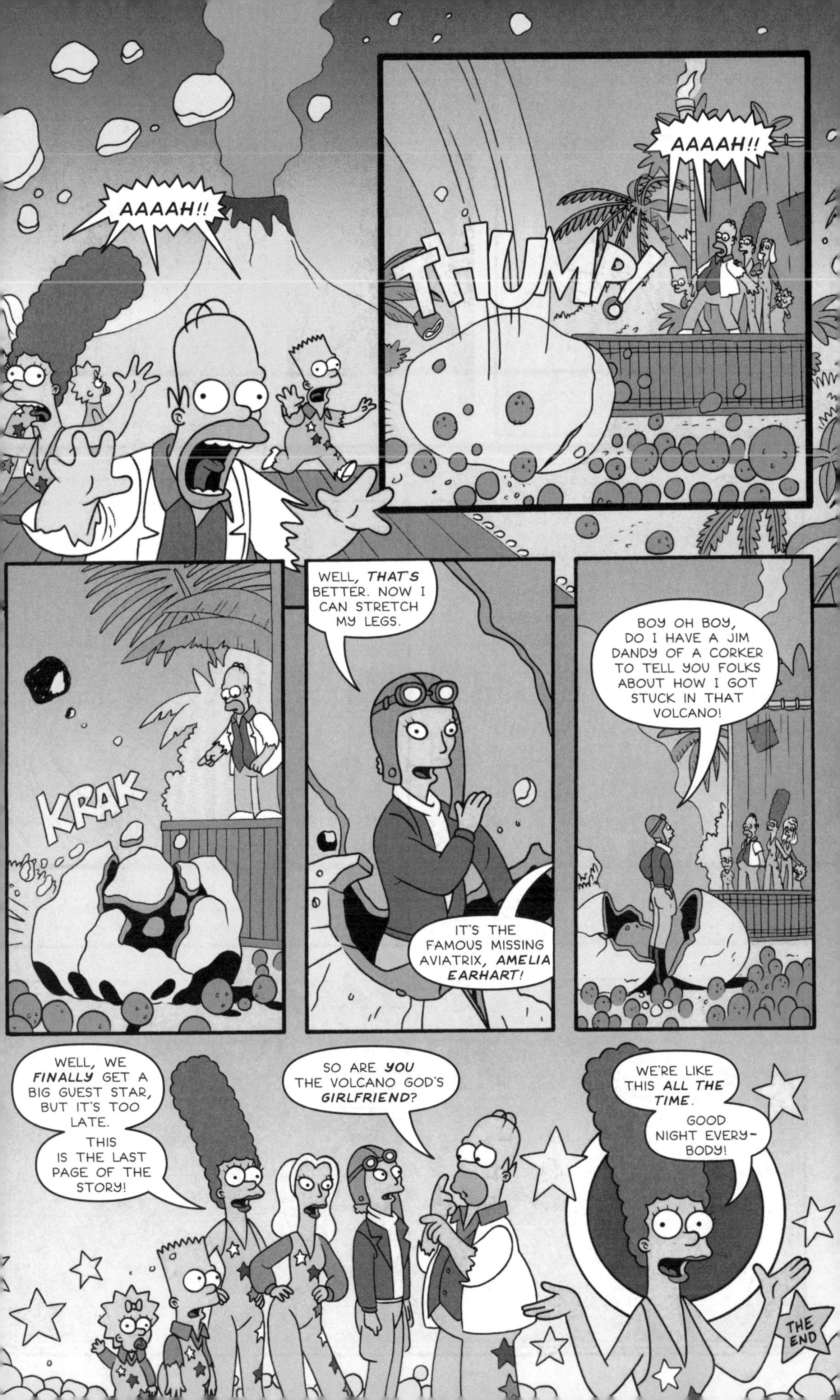
AAAAH!!
AAAAH!!
THUMP!
KRAK
WELL, THAT'S BETTER. NOW I CAN STRETCH MY LEGS.
IT'S THE FAMOUS MISSING AVIATRIX, AMELIA EARHART!
BOY OH BOY, DO I HAVE A JIM DANDY OF A CORKER TO TELL YOU FOLKS ABOUT HOW I GOT STUCK IN THAT VOLCANO!
WELL, WE FINALLY GET A BIG GUEST STAR, BUT IT'S TOO LATE.
THIS IS THE LAST PAGE OF THE STORY!
SO ARE YOU THE VOLCANO GOD'S GIRLFRIEND?
WE'RE LIKE THIS ALL THE TIME.
GOOD NIGHT EVERY-BODY!
THE END

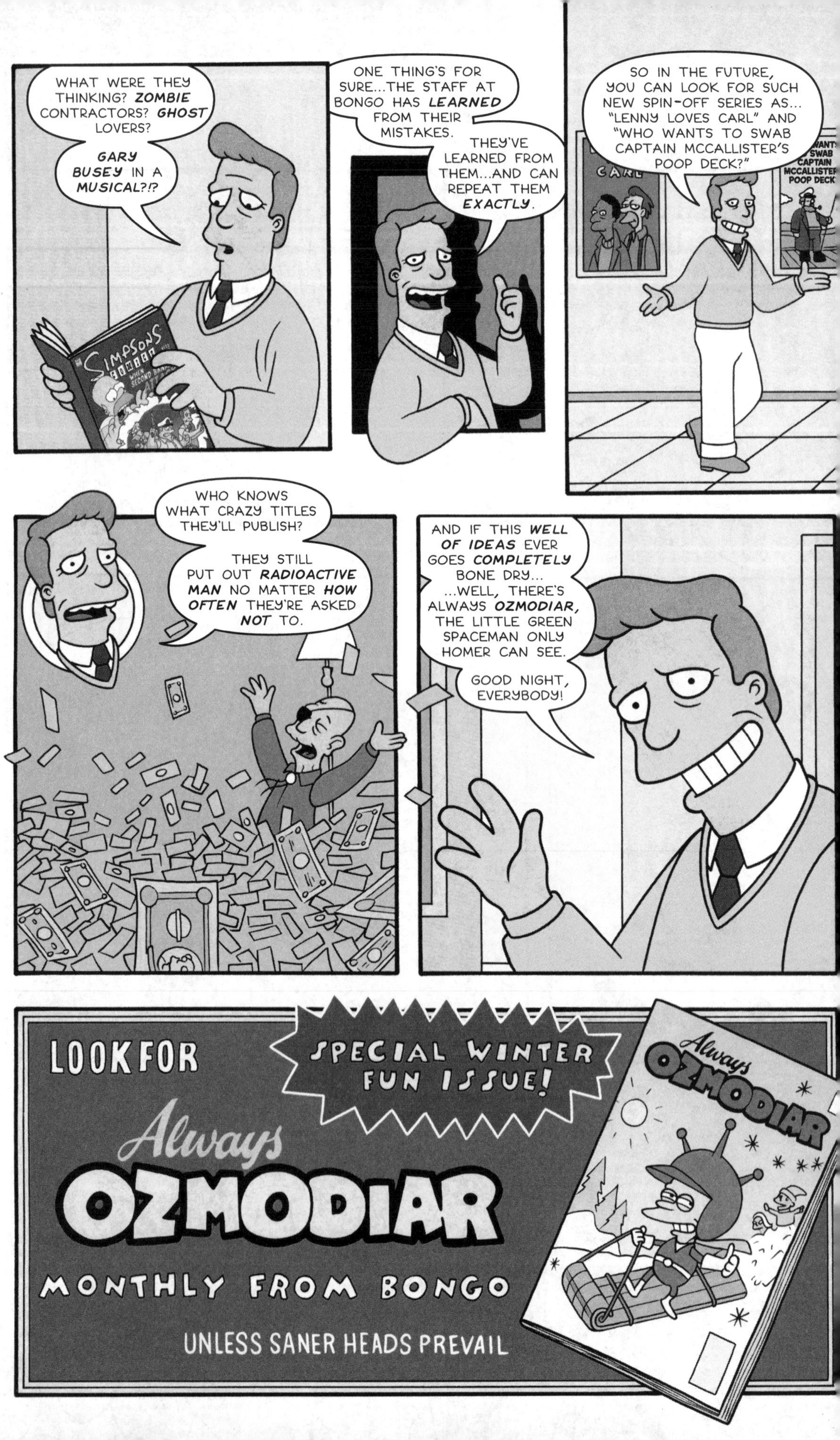
WHAT WERE THEY THINKING? **ZOMBIE** CONTRACTORS? **GHOST** LOVERS?
GARY BUSEY IN A **MUSICAL?!?**
ONE THING'S FOR SURE...THE STAFF AT BONGO HAS **LEARNED** FROM THEIR MISTAKES.
THEY'VE LEARNED FROM THEM...AND CAN REPEAT THEM **EXACTLY**.
SO IN THE FUTURE, YOU CAN LOOK FOR SUCH NEW SPIN-OFF SERIES AS... "LENNY LOVES CARL" AND "WHO WANTS TO SWAB CAPTAIN MCCALLISTER'S POOP DECK?"
WHO KNOWS WHAT CRAZY TITLES THEY'LL PUBLISH?
THEY STILL PUT OUT **RADIOACTIVE MAN** NO MATTER **HOW OFTEN** THEY'RE ASKED **NOT** TO.
AND IF THIS **WELL OF IDEAS** EVER GOES **COMPLETELY** BONE DRY... ...WELL, THERE'S ALWAYS **OZMODIAR,** THE LITTLE GREEN SPACEMAN ONLY HOMER CAN SEE.
GOOD NIGHT, EVERYBODY!
LOOK FOR
SPECIAL WINTER FUN ISSUE!
Always OZMODIAR
MONTHLY FROM BONGO
UNLESS SANER HEADS PREVAIL
Always OZMODIAR